The Psychology of Chinese Gambling

Chi Chuen Chan • William Wai Lim Li
Amy Sau Lam Chiu

The Psychology of Chinese Gambling

A Cultural and Historical Perspective

Springer

Chi Chuen Chan
Upper Iowa University - Hong Kong Center
Hong Kong

William Wai Lim Li
Upper Iowa University - Hong Kong Center
Hong Kong

Amy Sau Lam Chiu
Upper Iowa University - Hong Kong Center
Hong Kong

ISBN 978-981-13-3485-6 ISBN 978-981-13-3486-3 (eBook)
https://doi.org/10.1007/978-981-13-3486-3

Library of Congress Control Number: 2018964564

This Springer imprint is published by the registered company Springer Nature Singapore Pte Ltd.
The registered company address is: 152 Beach Road, #21-01/04 Gateway East, Singapore 189721, Singapore

This book is dedicated to the loving memory of my father.

陳智川
2018 香港

Preface

The Dream of My Father

The dream of becoming a rich person is often the motivation of most ethnic Chinese. In Chinese communities, parents often teach children, early in their childhood years, to put good efforts in studies so that they can work as doctors, lawyers, and engineers when they grow up. These professions are among the highest-paid careers in China. Children are also trained to save money so that they can accumulate wealth as they start working at adulthood. With the money they save, they can then invest in company stocks and real estate and make more money in the process. For ethnic Chinese, getting riches through legitimate means such as engaging in useful studies and investment is the foundation of success. Yet, for those who are less fortunate and could not pursue a socially prominent career, non-orthodox channels such as gambling may appear to be another pathway for success. Hence, gambling, as this book will demonstrate, is a favorite pastime of Chinese individuals, especially across the lower socioeconomic classes.

This book is about Chinese gambling. We will start by browsing through the history of gambling in ancient China in Chap. 1. In particular, we will focus on the development of ancient Chinese games and what these games meant to Chinese individuals. Next, we will discuss the motivation and personality of Chinese gamblers. Emphasis will be on the similarities and possible differences between Chinese and Western gamblers. The last two chapters propose a treatment model and a conclusion to our analysis of Chinese gambling.

This book is dedicated to my teachers and mentors who have helped and supported me in my journey in the psychology of gambling. Among them, I am particularly grateful for Dr. Keis Ohtsuka of Victoria University, who supervised my doctoral thesis. Also, I have to thank Professor Alum Jackson of the University of Melbourne, Professor Alex Blaszczynski of the University of Sydney and the late Professor Bill Eadington of the University of Nevada, who graciously guided my doctoral research and gave valuable advice on my project. I also thank Mr. Louis Lee (Chap. 1) and Ms. Jamie Ting Chee Ku (Chaps. 2, 3, 4, 5, 6 and 7), who have done a brilliant work editing my manuscripts. Lastly, I dedicate this book to the memory of my father, who passed away during the research and writing processes of this book. My father was never an academic person; he lived and worked a humble job all his life. I grew up in a poor government housing project in Hong Kong. My father saved every penny on his monthly paycheck to send me to excellent colleges in America. The former president of the United States, Mr. Barrack Obama, once wrote in his best seller, *The Audacity of Hope* (2006), "…every man is trying either to live up to his father's expectations or make up for his father's mistakes… (p. 5)." I understand my father's expectations and dreams for me which, of course not just being rich, is the pursuit of excellence in knowledge and career. His hopes are always the motivations for my studies and work. In my 25 years of services as a psychologist, a teacher, and a researcher in psychology, I trust I am fulfilling his dream – everyday.

Hong Kong Chi Chuen Chan

Contents

About the Authors

Dr. Chi Chuen Chan, Trained in the United States and Australia, he is a professional psychologist with over 20 years of clinical practices in Hong Kong and Macao. His more prominent services include serving as a clinical psychologist in the Hong Kong Government for 6 years. As the clinical psychologist in correctional services, Dr. Chan was successful in developing treatment programs for prisoners and staff working in prisons. His PhD in psychology was obtained from Victoria University in Australia. In addition to his training in psychology, Dr. Chan has a Master of Arts in Religion degree from Yale University and was appointed as a Yale Research Fellow in the summer of 1995. His mentor was the late Professor Rowan Greer.

Dr. Chan's current research is in the area of gambling disorders and treatment. Funded by the Mother Mary Social Studies Centre in Macao, Dr. Chan (with his students) has authored two Chinese books in gambling psychology [賭博心理學 (*Psychology of Gambling*) and 十二步匿名戒賭互助小組工作手冊 (*A Twelve Steps Self-Help Manual for Problem Gamblers*)]. His latest book is *Problem Gambling in Hong Kong and Macao: Etiology, Prevalence and Treatment* (published by Springer in 2016). In the last decade, he has authored 21 journal articles and conference proceedings in gambling research. And his research team has presented 47 papers in international conferences. Dr. Chan's research interests are the personality and the psychological treatment of problem gamblers in Hong Kong and Macao. At present, he is a research fellow with the Mother Mary Social Studies

Centre in Macao and the managing editor of the *Asian Journal of Gambling Issues and Public Health*. Professionally, Dr. Chan currently serves as a consulting psychologist with the Union Concordia Medical Group, a major medical services provider in Hong Kong and Macao, and is on the adjunct faculty of the Upper Iowa University, Hong Kong Center.

Chi Chuen is very happy to receive comments and enquiries on his research. His e-mail is chuenchan@yahoo.com.

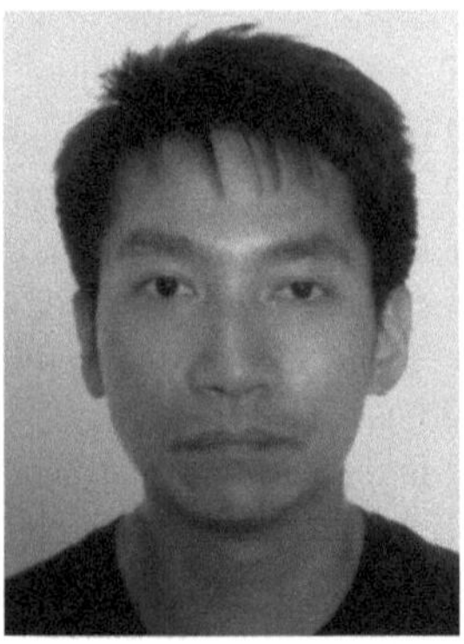

William Wai Lim Li is a professional physiotherapist with over 17 years of clinical practice in Hong Kong. At present, he is serving as a physiotherapist in mental health setting. His main responsibilities include providing physiotherapy and counseling for psychiatric patients. William has a master's degree in geriatric rehabilitation from the Hong Kong Polytechnic University (2005). His second master's degree is on mental health from the Chinese University Hong Kong (2016). He also has a bachelor's degree in psychology and a professional diploma in counseling and health psychology. Professionally, he is a registered certified gambling counselor, serving for a Hong Kong chapter of Gamblers' Anonymous (GA) on a weekly basis. His email address is wailimli@yahoo.com.

Amy Sau Lam Chiu has long been interested in psychology since high school. Her passion in this area has been a driving force for her studies in the Upper Iowa University (Hong Kong Center), where she obtained her bachelor's degree in 2013. Her mentor is Dr. Chi Chuen Chan. In her research studies in problem gambling, she has presented three conference papers and published two journal articles. Further to her studies in psychology, Amy has achieved professional qualification in family mediation and family therapy. Professionally, Amy is a treasury accountant with a major business group in Hong Kong.

Also from the First Author

Chan, C. C., Li, W. L. & Leung, C. I. (2016). *Problem gambling in Hong Kong and Macao: etiology, prevalence and treatment.* Singapore: Springer. ISBN 978-981-10-1066-8.

陳智川、李威廉、梁頌業 (2014). 賭博心理學. 澳門高志慈社會研究中心. ISBN 978-99937-644-9-6. Available free online: http://caritas.org.mo/zh-hant/publication/other-publications

吳淑珠、胡海峰、黃妙芬、楊穎、石一玲、陳智川 (2015). 十二步匿名戒賭互助小組工作手冊. 澳門高志慈社會研究中心.

Chapter 1
A Cultural History of Chinese Gambling I (From Ancient Period to Yuan Dynasty)

1.1 Chinese Gambling History

China is a land of diverse cultures and peoples. Kiang Fan in his book *The Gambling Chinese* (好賭的中國人) has argued that gambling in China began as Chinese civilization began. While contemporary academics from the United States and Australia define gambling as "risking something of value on the unknown outcome of some future event…, the ultimate hope of gambling is to realize a value greater than that risked" (Aasved 2003, p. 3), the Chinese conception of gambling carries a behavioral connotation much more than wagering. The Chinese words for gambling are" 賭"and "博." These two words "gambling in the Chinese way means wagering in a risky fashion." The ancient word for gambling in Chinese is "簙." This word means playing a chess game together with others. On this particular word, *Shuowen Jiezi* (說文解字), the earliest Chinese dictionary compiled by Xu Shen (許慎, 58–147) in the Han Dynasty, has this description – "Gambling is a table game: it is a game with six sticks and twelve chesses (簙,局戲也。六箸十二棋也)."

Before going into the gambling history in China, a brief discussion of Chinese history is in order. Since ancient times, it has been home for a variety of tribes and clans who ruled specific locations for lengthy periods. Emperor Qin Shi Huang (秦始皇, 259 B.C.–210 B.C.) achieved the first unification of ancient China in 221 B.C. The establishment of dynasties and kingdom brought peace and prosperity to the land and her people. Table 1.1 illustrates a history of dynasties or ruling families in power over China's 4000 years of history. In each of these dynasties, the ruling emperor never believed in true democracy. He was the source of all power based on the mandate he received from heaven. Further, there were no limits on his jurisdiction as the idea of a constitution with limits on power is a later foreign, mostly European, heritage. As such, he would be responsible for all rules, including those on gambling, for the country. The only checks and balances on his authority were his moral values and adherence to the Confucian beliefs that stress family relationships and interpersonal protocol known as *Li* (禮) or etiquette, which we will discuss

C. C. Chan et al., *The Psychology of Chinese Gambling*,
https://doi.org/10.1007/978-981-13-3486-3_1

Table 1.1 Ancient dynasties and modern political rulers of China

Ancient period			
The era of Three Sovereigns and Five Emperors			
Xia 2100 B.C.–1600 B.C.			
Shang 1700 B.C.–1100 B. C.			
Zhou 1100 B.C.–256 B.C.	Western Zhou 1100 B.C.–771 B.C.		
	Eastern Zhou 770 B.C.–256 B.C.	Era of Spring and Autumn 770 B.C.–476 B.C.	
		Warring States Period 476 B.C.–221 B.C.	
Periods of empires (era of feudalism)			
Qin 221 B.C.–207 B.C.			
West Chu (206 B.C.–202 B.C.)			
Han 202 B. C.–A.D. 220	Western Han 202 B.C.–A.D. 9		
	Xin 9–23		
	Hyun Han 23–25		
	Eastern Han Dynasty 25–220		
Three Kingdoms 220–280			
Jin 265–420	Western Jin 265–316		
	Eastern Jin 317–420	Five Barbarians and Sixteen Kingdoms 304–439	
Northern and Southern Dynasties 420–589			
Sui 581–619			
Tang 618–907			
(Wu Zhou 690–705)			
Five Dynasties and Ten Kingdoms 907–979		Liao 916–1125	Western Xia 1038–1227
Song 960–1279	Northern Song 960–1127	(Western Liao 1124–1218)	
	Southern Song 1127–1279	Jin 1115–1234	
Great Mongolia 1206–1271			
Yuan 1271–1368 (Northern Yuan 1368–1388)			
Ming 1368–1644 (Southern Ming 1644–1662)			
Qing 1636–1912			
Modern period			
Republic of China 1912–1949			
People's Republic of China (Mainland China) 1949–now		Republic of China (Taiwan) 1949–now	

in detail later in this chapter. The rule of kingship and feudalism lasted until Mr. Sun Yat-sen (孫逸仙, 1866–1925), who overthrew the government of Qing and put an end to feudalism in 1911. However, the beginning of the modern period did not immediately bring peace and prosperity to China. The warlord era and later the Japanese invasion in 1937 and the Civil War between the Nationalist Party and the Communist Party (1927–1937; 1946–1949) created enormous hardships for the majority of the Chinese people. Political instability continued when Mao Zedong (毛澤東, 1893–1976) became the first President of People's Republic of China established in 1949 as he instigated a series of political campaigns (1950–1966) and the Cultural Revolution (文化大革命1966–1976) in China. Not until the enforcement of "Four Modernizations (四個現代化)," the economic reforms proposed by President Deng Xiaoping (鄧小平, 1904–1997) since the 1980s have Chinese people begun living in a relatively stable political environment.

1.1.1 Beginning of Chinese Gambling

The earliest Chinese game is Liubo (六博) (Fig. 1.1). It was reportedly invented by Wu Cao (烏曹), a minister of the Emperor Xia Jie (夏桀, 1728 B.C.–1675 B.C.) during Xia Dynasty (2100 B.C.–1600 B.C.), the earliest dynasty in Chinese history (Guo and Xiao 1995). Liubo is a kind of board game played by two or four persons. In the beginning of each game set, the players have six chess to play with. The players have to employ specific strategies to beat the opponent, although there is a chance element in the game as the player has to roll a dice that has 18 sides, each signaling a specific number (see Fig. 1.2). The basic strategy is to take or kill the opponent's chess. It's been found that Mawangdui Han Tombs (漢代馬王堆古墓) contain Liubo with dice made of jade and precious stones. The gaming instruments were skillfully constructed and served more as cultural artifacts. The famous Chinese philosopher Han Fei Tze (韓非子, 281 B.C.–233 B.C.) once wrote: "In order to win the game, it is important to kill the opponent's chess (博者貴梟,勝者必殺梟)." Han pictured the game as a competition and rivalry between opponents. And the winning of the game involves an element of hurting and destroying the opponent. No wagering was involved in the early version of the game – it was started as a mind game for the elite class. As the inventor of Liubo, Wu Cao was worshiped as a god by people running gambling stalls during Qing (清朝) Dynasty (Fan and Zheng 2010).

Fig. 1.1 Liubo. (The figures were drawn by Olga, a professional artist. The copyright of these figures belongs to the authors)

Fig. 1.2 Eighteen-sided dice. (The figures were drawn by Olga, a professional artist. The copyright of these figures belongs to the authors)

Historical records indicated that Liubo was popular among upper class society or nobles in the late Shang (商) Dynasty (Shi 2005). According to the *Record of the Grand Historian* (史記) written by Sima Qian (司馬遷, 145 B.D.–90 B.D.), a great historian and scholar in Western Han (西漢), Wu Yi (武乙), the emperor of late Shang, played Liubo with a "god," an imaginary opponent that represents a spiritual force. The emperor won the games and insulted the "god." This interesting story nonetheless indicated the popularity of Liubo among the elite class at that period.

Modern scholars have doubts on the assertion that Wu Cao invented Liubo. It has long been a Chinese traditional belief that good emperors would promote all policies beneficial to the people while atrocious emperors carried out policies that are harmful to them. As Xia Jie was notorious for his cruel policies, it is thus not surprising that Chinese people would attribute the invention of the gambling devices and tools (which are integral components of gambling, a social vice) to the associates of Xia Jie. In the earliest days of the game, Liubo was considered an elegant entertainment of the aristocrat class. The game was even employed as a form of political propaganda for Emperor Wu Yi – betting with a god and overcoming it symbolized the supernatural and the heavenly mandate of the emperor. Notwithstanding its popularity among the elite class, the game of Liubo was not popular among the common people.

1.1.2 Gambling During Era of Spring and Autumn (春秋時代) and Warring States Period (戰國時代)

The nature of gambling was concerned mainly with leisure and entertainment in Xia and Shang. As gambling became more popular among the common people, the wagering component was slowly added into games during the Era from Spring and Autumn (700 B.C.–476 B. C.) Gambling among commoners in this period was characterized by two main features:

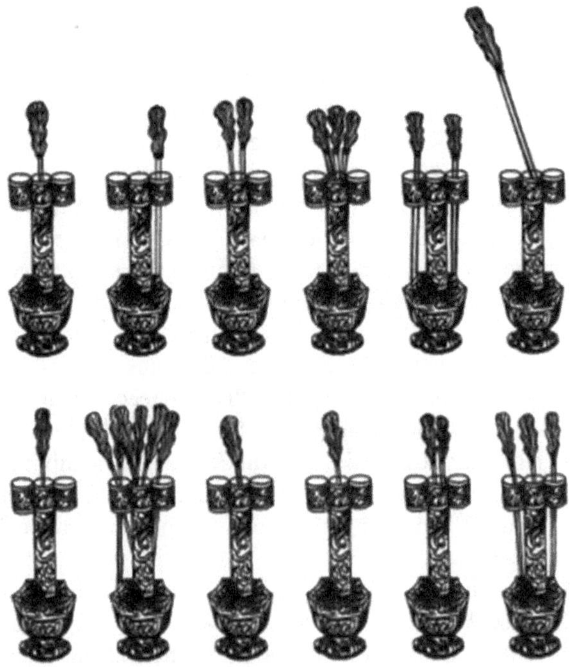

Fig. 1.3 Pitch-pot game. (The figure was drawn by Olga, a professional artist. The copyright of this figure belongs to the authors)

1. The monetary component: In every game, the losing party, by virtue of the rules, was obliged to lose the bets, mostly money, to the winner.
2. The diversified nature of the games: Types of gambling were diversified in this period. In addition to the popularity of Liubo, chess (奕棋), kickball (蹴鞠), pitch-pot game (投壺, Fig. 1.3), cockfighting (鬥雞), and dog fighting (鬥狗) were widely enjoyed by common people.
   Compared with the elite class, the gambling patterns of commoners differed mainly on the monetary returns of the games. During this period, some experienced gamblers relied on gambling for a living. And many gambling-related conflicts were reported. Gambling events causing violence or even death were recorded (Guo and Xiao 1995).

1.1.2.1 Philosophers' Perspectives Toward Gambling

Philosophers and sages were active during eras of Spring and Autumn and Warring States Period in Chinese history. These sages often traveled from state to state persuading the rulers of their political theories and strategies to manage a country. Good examples of these sages were Confucius (孔子, 551 B.C.–479 B.C.) and Mencius (孟子, 372 B.C.–289 B.C.). The following is a summary of their teachings:

- Confucius and Mencius: The two philosophers are the founders of Confucianism (儒家). The sayings of Confucius are recorded in *Confucian Analects* (論語). Confucianism preaches the practice of virtues of life. The following is a list of virtues that a man should have: benevolence (仁), righteousness (義), etiquette (禮), wisdom (智), filial piety (孝), fraternity (悌), loyalty (忠), and credibility (信). For him, these virtues are essential elements for human dignity and elegance, which can be trained or cultivated through the arts, namely, music, archery, painting, calligraphy, chess, and mathematics. Etiquette lays a foundation for relationships in the family and society. Confucius believed that the training of *Li* among the common people is important as it can help people develop a strong sense of morality. In politics, Confucianism teaches obedience and loyalty to the emperor. For instance, Confucius once said that "a benevolent individual is invincible; a brave person has no need to fear; a person who has wisdom has no need to be puzzled (仁者無敵,勇者無懼,智者不惑)."
- However, Confucius's attitude toward gambling is ambiguous. Confucius believed: "People who gamble are better than those who have nothing to do." Thus, it is probable that many people have rationalized gambling as a kind of "play."
- Mencius was another famous scholar in Confucianism during mid-Warring States Period (476 B. C.–221 B.C.). He taught that individuals were born with four good qualities: compassion, independence, the judgment of what is right or wrong, and a good sense of propriety. Unlike his master, Confucius, Mencius had a clear position toward gambling by considering it "one of the five sinful behaviors." He proposed that people who were addicted to gambling were prone to ignore their families and did not care for their parents. As filial piety is the major duty and responsibility of a person, Mencius opposed gambling in terms of conduct and moral value.
- Li Kui (李悝, 455 B.C.–395 B.C.), Shang Yang (商鞅, 390 B.C.–338 B.C.), and Han Fei: These philosophers were advocates of Legalism (法家), a system of thought that emphasizes the role of law and justice in the management and social system of the country. This approach carries a totally different perspective from Confucianism, which puts an emphasis on human relationships rather than an external system. Legalism, however, advocates political and economic reforms instead of maintaining the traditional and Confucian culture. For the legalist, the law is both the rules and the moral basis of the country. Thus, a well-defined system should govern the many aspects of taxation, civil services, and criminal proceedings. Legalism supports the centralization of monarchical power and succinct rewards and punishments through a legal and penal code. A famous logion of Legalism captures well the basic ideal of legalism: Even if the son of the emperor committed an offense, he should be guilty like a commoner (天子犯法與庶民同罪). In the area of foreign policies, while Confucianism favors a more benign government that emphasized humility and family relationships, Legalism is more aggressive in military development of the state.

In the area of gambling policies, Legalism strongly prohibited gambling. For the legalist, there was a clear line between what is right and wrong, and gambling, with its emphasis on beating the opponent and winning money, was a definite social vice. During the Warring States Period, several legalist philosophers proposed laws to ban gambling. Commoners who violated laws would be heavily fined. Further, nobles or members of the elite class who were guilty of gambling would be punished severely. There are records of crown princes being stripped of their titles because of their gambling (Lau 1998).

1.1.3 *Gambling During Qin (秦) and Han Dynasties (西漢、 東漢)*

Emperor Qin Shi Huang ended the 250-year Warring States Period as he conquered all other states and established a united empire – Qin Dynasty. He was an infamous dictator as he ruled the country with strict rules and policies. A follower of legalism, he relatively suppressed (it is believed) gambling activities during his rule. Individuals arrested for illegal gambling were punished by marking a tattoo on the face or beating with wooden staves (Luo and Xu 1994).

The laws did not take into account human freedom and dignity. Qin Dynasty only lasted for 15 years before it was overthrown by West Chu (西楚). Nevertheless, anti-gambling laws were enforced during Qin, and heavy punishments on underground gambling were effective in controlling gambling among common people (Ge 1995).

A series of wars between West Chu and Han (楚漢相爭) lasted for 5 years after Qin's death. At that period, one of the new popular games was football betting. The game was invented by the Great General Han Xin (韓信, 231 B.C.–196 B.C.), one of the most outstanding founding ministers of Western Han. He designed the game primarily for the soldiers who left from their hometowns for wars. Han understood the pains and the difficulties of these young soldiers. Participating in football betting, whether by actually playing the game or placing a small wager and enjoying the game on the sidelines, provided the warriors a source of emotional escape. This is the first record of a major state-sponsored gambling activity that brought social benefits and enjoyment for the common people.

1.1.3.1 Ambivalence Between Promoting and Prohibiting Gambling in Han

Emperors during Han followed the anti-gambling laws of the Qin Dynasty. Paradoxically, a number of emperors in Han loved gambling. Emperor Han Jing (漢景帝, 188 B.C.–141 B.C.) (ruled China during 157 B.C.–141 B.C.) is one good example. Legend has it that before he became the emperor, he once gambled Liubo with another prince of the feudal vassal. They had a serious conflict during gambling. Jing lifted the chessboard and crushed the prince to death. This triggered a civil war between Han and the relevant vassal state when Jing succeeded his father Emperor Han Wen (漢文帝, 202 B.C.–157 B.C.) (ruled China during 180 B.C.–157 B.C.) as the emperor several years later (Y. Y. Chan 2014). This is a famous historical event known as "Civil War of the Seven Vassal States" (七王之亂), which was supposedly initiated by a conflict in gambling. These two legends might well be fictional stories. However, they demonstrate how the historians and scholars pictured gambling as a source of social conflicts and war. The moral is plain and simple: gambling is a social vice and a good moral person should not gamble – an assumption that underlies the traditional beliefs of four major sins of Chinese men: visiting prostitutes (嫖), gambling (賭), drinking (飲), and smoking (吹).

During the rule of Emperor Han Wu (漢武帝, 156 B.C.–87 B.C.) (ruled China during 141 B.C.–87 B.C.) of the Western Han Dynasty, Dong Zhongshu (董仲舒, 179 B.C.–104 B.C.), the chancellor of the state, formally adopted Confucianism as the guiding political ideology of the state. From that time onward, almost all emperors in Chinese history advocated Confucianism, which preached moral values and family relationships as the basis of political stability. For Dong and his successors, strict legal laws and severe punishment should not be the priority in government policies. Instead, people should be taught the principles of *Li* and family virtues and values. In the area of gambling, Dong opposed severe punishment to ban all gambling. Consequently, gambling among the common people flourished during this time. Some Chinese historians generally believed even Emperor Han Wu loved gambling (Guo and Xiao 1995; Ge 1995).

Emperor Han Xuan (漢宣帝, 91 B.C.–48 B.C.) (ruled China during 74 B.C.–48 B.C.), great grandson of Han Wu, gambled even more seriously than his ancestors. According to *History of the Former Han Dynasty* (前漢書) composed by Ban Gu (班固, A.D. 32–A.D. 92) in A.D. 92, an outstanding historian in Eastern Han, Han Xuan started to gamble when he was young. Han Xuan once owed a huge debt to a civilian named Chen Sui (陳遂). At the time Han Xuan became the emperor, he returned the debt to Chen Sui by appointing him the prefecture chief in Taiyuan (太原), the provincial capital of current province Shanxi (山西). This historical event demonstrates the widespread nature of gambling in the Han Dynasty (Tu 2006).

Gambling among the commoners had become more popular, secularized, and diversified. Some gamblers even took gambling as their professions. A great number of people were addicted to gambling (Shi 2005).

We have examined briefly the development of gambling from the Xia Dynasty (2000 B.C.) to the Han Dynasty (A.D. 220). The following is a list of our analysis:

1. Gaming precedes gambling.
   The earliest reported games required cognitive skills and strategies. The wagering of money was not a major element in the game. Instead, the players invested mental efforts in the gaming process. As noble pastimes, the games were often played by members of the elite class during festivals and dinners. Thus, the gaming instruments were considered a part of the cultural artifacts and treasures. Contemporary

theories of gambling argue that gambling, especially disordered gambling, represents the outcome of a complex interplay of multiple factors – a paradigm that resembles the public health triad of host, environment, and agent (Griffiths et al. 2009). In this vein of thought, the earliest gambling in China was mainly geared to the particular needs of the aristocratic ruling class at that time.

A similar scenario can be found in the historical development of horse racing in Hong Kong. Chan et al. (2016) argue that horse racing started in Hong Kong in the late nineteenth century and in the first few years of operation, there was no wagering on the winning horses. Horse racing was mostly enjoyed by the European elite class who worked in Hong Kong. It was only in the early twentieth century when the game became more popular among the Hong Kong people that horse racing evolved into a gambling activity.

2. There are strong discrepancies between public policies and the gambling behavior of the ruling class.

   While most emperors in Han Dynasty passed laws which strictly prohibited gambling, a number of emperors actively participated in gambling. They gambled heavily with royal members and ministers. A detailed reading of the historical records indicates that some of them (e.g., Emperor Han Xuan) were probable disordered gamblers. Gambling was a popular pastime for commoners as well as the elite class.

3. There was a significant shift in the motivation for gambling in the Han Dynasty among commoners.

   The motivation for gambling changed from a cultural pastime to a channel of becoming rich. As more people gambled, there were more reported cases of disordered gamblers and professional gamblers simply because they wanted to take a shortcut to earn money in gambling. In practice, gambling changed from a cultural pastime to a channel for becoming rich.

4. Games experienced a gradual change during 400 years of Han Dynasties. Toward the end of Eastern Han, Liubo gradually faded out. A new game called Chupu (樗蒲, Fig. 1.4) became more popular. The main element of Liubo was entertainment, while the gambling ingredient was dominant in Chupu. In Western Jin (A.D. 265–A.D.316), Liubo was completely phased out of the gambling history of China.

Chupu is one of the oldest dice games in Chinese history. The game was very popular among commoners in the period of Wei, Jin, Northern and Southern Dynasties (魏晉南北朝, A.D. 420–A.D. 589), and the Late Tang Dynasty (唐朝, A.D. 618–A.D. 907). To date, there is little substantive evidence on the origins of Chupu. Among the available literature, Zhang Hua (張華, A.D. 232–A.D. 300) in the Jin Dynasty (晉朝, A.D. 265–A.D. 420) once wrote a book called *Bowu Zhi*《博物誌》, in which he argued that Chupu was invented by the Chinese philosopher, Laozi (老子). Ma Rong (馬融, A.D. 79–A.D. 166) in the East Han Dynasty put a similar account forward. Ma argued, in a paper named "Chupu Fu"《樗蒲賦》, that "Laozi traveled around the capital city. He was a moral person. As the country was invaded by foreign powers, he invented Chupu for the people as their entertainment so that

Fig. 1.4 Chupu. (The figure was drawn by Olga, a professional artist. The copyright of this figure belongs to the authors)

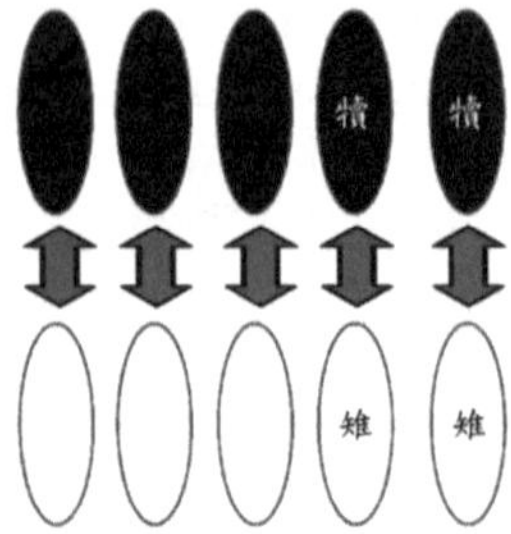

Figure 4: Combination of Teeth Results **Combination**	**Nickname**	**Points**	**Class**
B B B Ca Ca	盧	16	王采
B B B Ca Ch	塞	11	氓采
B B Ca Ca W	秃	4	氓采
B B B Ch Ch	雉	14	王采
B B Ca Ch W	梟	2	氓采
B Ca Ca W W	梟	2	氓采
B B Ch Ch W	撅	3	氓采
B Ca Ch W W	撅	3	氓采
Ca Ca W W W	犢	10	王采
B Ch Ch W W	塔	5	氓采
Ca Ch W W W	開	12	氓采
Ch Ch W W W	白	8	王采

Remark: Black (B), Ca (Calf), Ch (Chick), W (White)

they might not worry about the wars" (「昔玄通先生遊於京都,道德既備,號此樗蒲。伯陽入戎,以斯消憂。」《樗蒲賦》, 東漢馬融) (Chen and He 2006).

The suggestion that Chupu was originally a foreign game has been presented by historians. In the book *The Ancient Chinese Gambling Cultures*《中國古代賭博習俗》, Luo and Xu (1994) suggested that Chupu was first invented in the Western Regions (西域) (meaning Persia and Iran at that time) and later, with the increased trade and economic activities during the period of Qin and Han Dynasty, introduced to China by foreigners. This assertion might be convincing as the Chinese pronunciation of "Chupu" is similar to that of an Indian game "Chaupar." In the earlier version of the game, Chupu was restricted to the elite class.

The exact rules of the game were lost to history by the Late Tang Dynasty. Guo and Xiao (1996), in their book *The History of Chinese Gambling*, stated that the movement of the chess is governed by the tossing results of five small wooden sticks. Consequently, Chupu was also called "Five Wood" (五木). A more detailed explanation about the game was published by Li Ao (李翱, A.D. 772–A.D. 841) in the Tang Dynasty. Li in his "Wumu Jing" 《五木經》 or Book of Five Woods described a full Chupu game to include the following components: (1) the Chupu board for moving chesses (枰); (2) the "cup" (栝) for holding the dice; (3) wooden teeth (博齒), i.e., the dice; (4) counting sticks (箸); (5) the chess (馬); and (6) the chips (籌). The key of the Chupu game is the "five teeth," which are almond-shaped wooden sticks. These sticks function like dice. One side of the stick is painted black while the other side is painted white. Two of the five wooden teeth are marked with a word "犢 (calf) on the black side and "雉"(chick) on the white side. Each combination was given its own name, for example, "3 black and 2 calf" was named "Donkey" (盧); "3 black and 2 chick" was named "Chick" (雉). In each round, the player throws out the five wooden teeth altogether. Points will be given according to the number of "black" and "calf" the player gets, for example, "3 blacks and 2 calf" will get the highest point 16. In the "Wumu Jing" 《五木經》, Li categorizes the teeth combinations into two main groups: "*Wangcai*" (王采) and "*Mangcai*" (氓采). There were a total of ten combinations of the sticks: four in "*Wangcai*" (盧,白,雉,牛) and six in "*Mangcai*" (開,塞,塔,禿,撅,梟). Li Zhao (李肇) wrote the *Supplementary to the History of Tang Dynasty* 《唐國史補》, which described the game in more detail. In the book, he added two more combinations of sticks, bringing the total combinations to 12.

Recent archaeological discovery has thrown more light on the popularity of the game. In 1973, archaeologists unearthed a painting from Weijun tombs (魏晉古墓), in Jiayuguan (嘉峪關), a rural village in China. The painting pictures two people kneeling in front of a chessboard and playing Chupu. One person (in a white gown) lifts up his hands and throws the dice onto the chessboard, while the other party (in a red gown) is looking intently at the dice for the result. Similar findings were unearthed from China's Gansu Province (甘肅省) in 2001. These paintings indicate that Chupu was a popular game during the Period of Northern and Southern Dynasties (Pictures 1.1, 1.2, and 1.3) (Huang 2015).

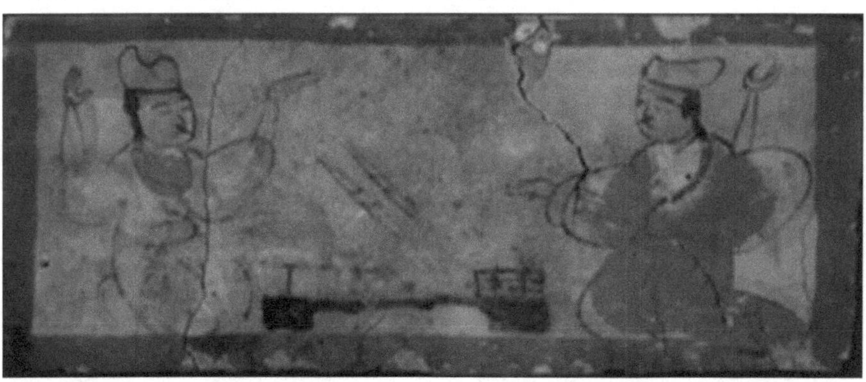

Picture 1.1 Chupu Brick from Jiayuguan Xinchengxiang Weijin Tomb Room #7 (嘉峪關新城鄉7號魏晉墓室). (Source: Huang 2015)

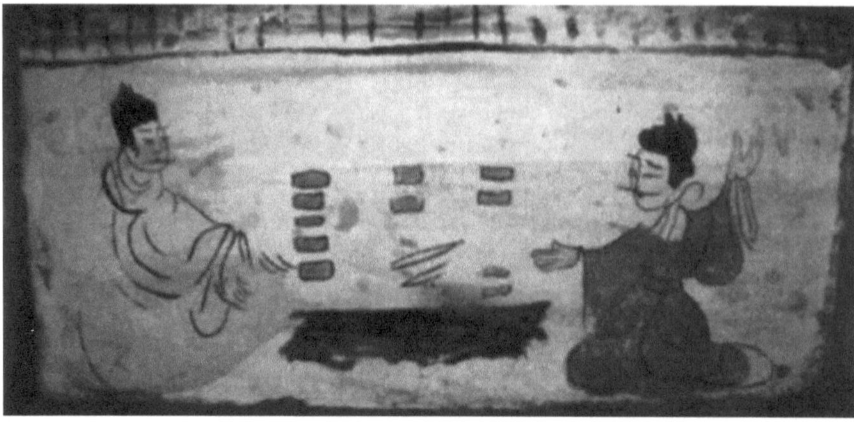

Picture 1.2 Chupu Brick in Gansu Province Gaotai City Luotuo Cheng Weijin Tomb (甘肅省高台縣駱駝城魏晉墓). (Source: Huang 2015)

Picture 1.3 Chupu Brick from Gaotai Province Xusanwan Weijin Tomb (高台縣許三灣魏晉墓室). (Source: Huang 2015)

Unlike the game of Liubo, the chessboard of Chupu does not have any route lines on it. Instead, there are three main gates (關) on the chessboard. In between the gates, there is a gap called the chasm (坑). The game strategies are to transfer all the chess through the gates to the other side of the board. During the process, the player has to obtain the "*wangcai*," which allows him to move the chess. Thus, in comparison to Liubo, Chupu does not require much cognitive skill or investment. Perhaps this was the main reason for its popularity among the common people. In the Tang Dynasty, the game gradually developed into a simple dice game. Thus, instead of moving the chess, people simply enjoyed the excitement of dice tossing. Further, the game attracted spectators, who did not actually play the game. Standing at the back of the players, these individuals would cheer and participate in the fun and excitement of the game. Very often, they would put bets on the dice. In Chinese literature, an idiom known as "呼盧喝雉" (which literally means playing Chupu and yelling on the chick) describes the excitement and fun of Chupu players and the surrounding spectators. The "chick" is one of outcomes of the combination of the "sticks." This idiom carries a negative and somewhat debasing picture of the gamblers. Later, as more people became addicted to this game, the Song (宋朝) government outlawed the game. Players were punished by the state. Thus, after the Song Dynasty, Chupu gradually disappeared from the gaming tables of ancient China.

The story of Chupu has highlighted a number of important developments in the gambling history in ancient China. Firstly, it is one of the first table games originally from foreign countries. Compared to Liubo, Chupu relies more on chance factors than cognitive skills. The outcome of the game is largely determined by the throwing of the "sticks." It is a much quicker game. Secondly, this game includes spectators who can bet and share in the fun and excitement of the game. In other words, 20 gamblers can put wager on a Chupu game, while only 2 of them throw and move the chess. The inclusion of spectators expands the numbers of eligible gamblers in a single game and contributes to the popularity of Chupu.

Contemporary gambling researchers have investigated the role of spectators in Chinese gambling. Lam (2005), in his study with casino players, found that baccarat players in Macao enjoyed gambling in a crowded table. Many of these players never touched the cards – they only followed the advice of fellow players and put bets with the persons they trust. Chan and his students, in their study of elderly gamblers in Hong Kong (Li et al. 2011), have reported similar accounts. In their observation, they found that elderly gamblers like to gamble in a park in the afternoons (Fig. 1.5). These elderly enjoyed card games and Chinese chess games. Very often, many of them were spectators who would bet with their favorite players. Chan et al. (2014) have explained why many Chinese gamblers prefer being spectators to actually playing the card games. Chinese people are more inclined to follow a strong and intelligent leader. Chinese like to conform to social norms and regulations. In other words, as Chinese, we are natural followers. Thus, in the area of gambling, we like to follow the winners. The actual playing of the game or holding the cards is not important. And if our players win, we would share the same level of fun and excitement as if we had actually played the game.

1.1.4 Gambling During Wei, Jin, and Northern and Southern Dynasties (魏晉南北朝)

During 300 years of Wei, Jin, and Northern and Southern Dynasties, China was in a state of war and chaos. This is also a very special period in Chinese history in which society suffered from prolonged instability due to political turmoil and invasion of foreigners. For example, a famous historical event known as "The Upheaval of the

Fig. 1.5 Senior male gamblers gamble in a park of a public housing estate in Hong Kong. (Photo by Li Wai Lim in September 2016)

Eight Princes (八王之亂)" took place during the Western Jin when eight feudal lords fought in ferocious battles. A famous war "Battle on the Fei-shui (淝水之戰)" occurred in A.D. 383 between Eastern Jin and Qianqin (前秦). Qianqin was defeated with 700,000 soldiers killed in this battle. After Eastern Jin perished in A.D. 420, China was split up into several northern and southern kingdoms, known as Northern and Southern Dynasties (南北朝). Wars among these kingdoms remained constant for another 170 years until Emperor Yang Jian (楊堅, A.D. 541–A.D. 604) (ruled China during A.D. 581.–A.D. 604), founder of Sui Dynasty, reunited China in A.D. 589. The warring period and the resulting poverty and social unrest made gambling a good pastime for emotional escape for the common people.

A drastic change occurred in the nature of the games during Wei, Jin, and Northern and Southern Dynasties. From the beginning of Western Jin, Liubo faded out. It was then replaced by Chupu, Backgammon (雙陸), Tan Qian (攤錢), Go (圍棋), and Archery (射箭). Among these gambling activities, Chupu was the most popular one during this period (Lau 1998).

Another reason for the popularity of the game is political instability at that time. During these 300 years, wars among the states were frequent. For a great majority of the commoners, the Confucian ideals of *Li* and morals could not solve their social problems. For them, getting rich seemed to be appropriate goals in life (Tu 2006). The following historical characters can present a hint on gambling during that period.

1.1.4.1 Xie An (謝安, A.D. 320–A.D. 385)

A prime minister of Eastern Jin, Xie An was famous for his distinguished and admirable characteristics. He purposefully expressed his unruly and open-minded traits by donating a villa obtained by gambling to others. During the Battle of the Feishui, Xie An was playing Go with his friend at home. When his nephew, Xie Xuan, the responsible general in this significant battle, sent him a victory message, he unexpectedly threw the memo to one side and continued gambling with his friend. Superficially, he did not show any excitement about winning the battle. However, after his friend had left, he was so excited that he did not find his shoe broken while rushing to his inner house to celebrate the victory (Fang and Chu A.D. 648). Xie An's attitude reflected the gambling behavior of people of the upper class – casting away materialistic concerns and worries of oneself (物我兩忘) and with no significant emotional reactions of happiness and grief (不以物喜, 不以己悲). This interesting story portrays the ideal mannerism in gambling of a noble politician – politically ambitious with emotionally controlled gambling behavior.

1.1.4.2 Seven Sages of the Bamboo Grove (竹林七賢)

Seven sages refer to Xi Kang (嵇康, A.D. 224–A.D. 263), Ruan Ji (阮籍, A.D. 210–A.D. 263), Shan Tao (山濤, A.D. 205–A.D. 283), Xiang Xiu (向秀, A.D. 227–A.D. 272), Liu Ling (劉伶, A.D.221–A.D. 300), Ruan Xian (阮咸, birthdate unknown), and Wang Rong (王戎, A.D. 234–A.D. 305). They were famous intellectuals of this period. Dissatisfied with the government and politics, they went on a passive protest by retreating into a bamboo forest at Shangyang county (currently northwestern Henan province), where they spent their days drinking, gambling, and discussing philosophical issues. Their unconventional and anti-government attitude can be seen as a disappointment in the political system and social unrest (Shum 1994). Some of the seven sages such as Xi Kang, Ruan Ji, and Liu Ling refused to compromise with the political regime, while others gradually chose to take part in the pro-establishment camp. Due to the philosophical discrepancy among them, the seven sages of the bamboo grove finally broke up. Zhong Hui (鍾會, A.D. 225–A.D. 264), a high-ranking general of Wei, later killed Xi Kang. Other members such as Shan Tao served the Jin Dynasty as a major chancellor.

Employing the Blaszczynski and Nower (2002) pathway model in the psychological analysis of the gambling behavior of the seven sages, we can see their gambling development best describes Pathway 2 pathological gamblers – emotionally vulnerable gamblers. This type of gamblers has significant emotional problems prior to their acquisition of gambling behavior. They are dissatisfied with their lives and the situational context they are living in. Thus, their excessive gambling behavior can be a form of escape from reality.

1.1.4.3 People from Lower Social Class

Most people in the lower social class lived in poverty during Wei, Jin, and Northern and Southern Dynasties. The years of social unrest and wars made traditional farming difficult. On top of this, there were famines and heavy taxation. Children were less likely to receive formal education, while adults found it hard to earn a living in a traditional farming society. For many individuals in this era, Confucian moral ideologies and Legalism such as *Li* and righteousness were no longer appealing. Instead, making fast money was the goal for many. Historical records indicated that there was heavy gambling among individuals in the lower social classes and violence arising from gambling disputes was frequent (Guo and Xiao 1995).

1.1.4.4 Gambling Development and Anti-gambling Policies

Gambling activities and types developed rapidly during these 300 years. New games such as prasena (波羅賽戲) were introduced to the working class in China. Prasena is a chess game derived from ancient India/Tianzhu (天竺). This game was popular as it combined skills and chance in the gaming process. During Wei, Jin, and Northern and Southern Dynasties, the government did not have any concrete and formal policies on gambling.

1.1.5 Gambling During Sui, Tang, Five Dynasties, and Ten Kingdoms (隋、唐、五代十國時期)

In 589, Yang Jian (楊堅), the first emperor of Sui Dynasty, conquered other states and united China. A diligent politician, he turned the country's storehouses of rice from loss to profit during his rule (March 4, 581–August 13, 604). In addition, Yang Jian was a frugal person who did not like gambling. However, there is a legend that his second son, Yang Guang (楊廣, A.D. 569–A.D. 618) (ruled China during A.D. 604–A.D. 618), once employed gambling as a tactic to win the support of others. Yang Guang and his elder brother, Yang Yong (楊勇, A. D. 568–A.D. 604), were competing for the honored position of crown prince, which in Chinese history is the heir who becomes the next emperor when the king dies. Once he discovered that the younger brother of an influential chancellor Yang Su (楊素, A.D. 544–A.D. 606) loved gambling very much, Yang Guang ordered his accomplice Zi Wen Shu (宇文述, A.D. 546–A.D. 616) to gamble with Yang Su's younger brother and intentionally lose heavily at the gambling, all for the purpose of winning the political support of Yang Su. Consequently, Yang Guang successfully made a strong connection with Yang Su, and, with the assistance of Yang Su, Yang Guang successfully defeated Yang Yong and later became the second emperor of Sui Dynasty after his father's death in 604 (Wong 2016). In this story, we can see that gambling during the feudal era in China was not only a tool for entertainment but also an effective strategy to achieve certain political purposes. Yang Guang's story is a typical example supporting our hypothesis.

Yang Guang was a cruel and unpopular emperor, and the Sui Dynasty only lasted 37 years. It came to an end on June 18, 618. It was overthrown by Li Yuan (李淵, A.D. 566–A.D. 635) (ruled China during A.D. 618–A.D. 626), who founded the Tang Dynasty. Li was the first emperor of Tang, while his son Li Shi Min (李世民, A.D. 599–A.D. 649) (ruled during A.D. 626–A.D. 649) was one of the most intelligent and successful emperors in Chinese history. The Tang Dynasty lasted nearly 300 years. This is the golden period in the history of China as during the Tang Dynasty the people lived in a relatively stable environment. In Chinese literature, a great number of famous poets came from the Tang Dynasty. Good examples are Li Bai (李白, A.D. 701–A.D. 762), Du Fu (杜甫, A.D. 712–A.D. 770), Han Yu (韓愈, A.D. 768–A.D. 824), Liu Zong Yuan (柳宗元, A.D. 773–A.D. 819), Wang Wei (王維, A.D. 701–A.D. 761), and Bai Ju Yi (白居易, A.D. 772–A.D. 846).

Gambling was popular in the Tang Dynasty, especially during the era of Sheng Tang (盛唐), which was the first 30-year rule by emperor Li Long Ji (李隆基, A.D. 685–A.D. 762) (ruled China during A.D. 712–A.D. 756). This was the most glorious age of Tang Dynasty (713–741), known as "Kaiyuan rule (開元之治)." At this time, the country was financially secure and politically stable. Drinking, partying, and gambling, especially among intellectuals, were everyday events. In fact, most of the emperors in Tang loved gambling, especially Li Long Ji and Wu Zetian (武則天, A.D. 624–A.D. 705) (ruled China during A.D. 690–A.D. 705), the only female emperor in Chinese history. Both of them were heavy gamblers. Many governmental officials and ordinary people also enjoyed or were even addicted to gambling. In an extensive review of historical records, Lau (1998) concluded that the combination of gambling and drinking was the important element during dinners and parties in Tang Dynasty. Compared with during Wei, Jin, and Northern and Southern Dynasties, gambling problems were widespread among the working class in Tang.

1.1.5.1 Anti-gambling Policies in Tang Dynasty

In A.D. 652, Zhang Sun Wu Ji (長孫無忌, A.D. 594–A.D. 659) wrote *Comments on Laws of Tang Empire* (唐律疏議) the first official law book since *Fa Jing* (法經) of Li Kui during Warring States Period. The new law book has an integrated policy on anti-gambling:

1. A person who participates in gambling will be punished by paddling (beating with wooden cane 100 times); those who gamble heavily will be sentenced to prison for 1 year.
2. A person who takes part as a banker or provides gaming tools in gambling in Changan (長安), the capital of Tang, will be sentenced to death; those who open gambling venues in areas other than Changan will be sent to a distant exile.
3. A person who obtains money or materials from others through gambling will be found guilty of the offense of larceny.

It is worthwhile mentioning that the Chinese name "gambling" and "Du Bo" first appeared together in "Comments on Laws of Tang Empire" (Wong and Yu 2006).

Notwithstanding the completed articles of anti-gambling laws, gambling was common among the elite class and the common people. The main reason is that many emperors in Tang were active gamblers. Thus, they were unwilling to strictly enforce the relevant laws.

Representatives of excessive gamblers in Tang Dynasty were as follows.

1.1.5.2 Li Long Ji (Or Named as Emperor Xuanzong of Tang (唐玄宗))

Emperor Xuanzong was not only famous for his "Kaiyuan rule" in his first 29 years of rule, but he was also notorious for his heavy gambling and later in his rule spending much of his time with concubine Yang Yuhuan (楊玉環, A.D. 71–A.D. 756). In the last 15 years of his rule, Xuanzong's policies came much under the influences of Eunuch Gao Lishi (高力士, A.D. 684–A.D. 762), prime minister Li Linfu (李林甫, A.D. 683–A.D. 753), and heavily corrupted prime minister Yang Guozhong (楊國忠). Chinese historians have pinpointed the weaknesses of Xuanzong's administration which, in many ways, contributed to the social instability of the state. During his rule, a civil war known as An Shih Revolution (安史之亂, December 16, 755–February 17, 763) broke out. This war was started by An Lushan (安祿山, A.D. 703–A.D. 757), an important provincial governor who defended the northern territory of Tang's empire. The An Shih rebellion critically undermined the internal stability of the Tang Dynasty.

In the last 15 years of Emperor Xuanzong's kingship, a number of stories demonstrate his indulgence in gambling:

1. Xuanzong loved gambling, especially the game of Chupu. Once he heard that Yang Guozhong, a distant relative of Yang Yuhuan, was an expert in gambling, he immediately summoned Yang and appointed him as an official responsible for managing the emperor's gambling account. Subsequently, Yang was promoted to a higher official rank and finally became the prime minister of Tang. This interesting story implies that Xuanzong offered high official posts solely based on his preference on gambling. Since Yang knew nearly every type of gambling, he obtained the trust of Xuanzong easily.
2. According to *Dongcheng Old Father Biography* (東城老父傳) written by Chen Hongzu (陳鴻祖), Emperor Xuanzong was also addicted to cockfighting. He owned a cock farm, which housed 1000 cocks (which might be a rounded-up figure). At that time, a teenager called Gu Chang (賈昌) was very skillful in training cocks for cockfighting. Xuanzong appointed Gu to manage his cock farm. Even though Gu lacked academic credentials, he was appointed to this important management position simply because of his excellent gambling skills in cockfighting. Consequently, at that time, there emerged a famous hymn satirizing the emperor's gambling addiction to cockfighting. It reads:

   "It's no problem that a child was born illiterate as being skillful in horse racing and cockfighting are far better than studies."

3. There was a legend that Xuanzong once gambled *cussec with his concubine Yang Yuhuan in the imperial palace. In one game set, Xuanzong would lose the game unless he could throw "four" on the dice. Extremely nervous, Xuanzong shouted "Four! Four!," and he really threw a "four." He felt extremely happy and ordered Eunuch Gao Lishi to declare that the "four" of cussec should be dyed red color. In the past, red color could not be used except when it was approved by the emperor. This interesting legend can explain why in our present time the color of "four" is painted red on every Chinese dice.

*Cussec was an ancient game in Tang Dynasty. It evolved from Backgammon. Cussec was a popular gambling type among the imperial concubines living in the royal palace. Usually, the gamblers gamble with wine and silk (Chang 1984).

Based on the contemporary criteria on gambling disorders of the *Diagnostic and Statistical Manual*, 5th edition (DSM 5; American Psychiatric Association 2013), Xuanzong was a probable disordered gambler. He spent much of his time studying and practicing gambling skills. He loved making friends with people who had an expertise on gambling. He loved gambling so much that he did not tend to the daily management meetings with state chancellors in the last 15 years of his rule. And his indulgence in gambling and lack of concern on politics in many ways contributed to the social instability at his times.

1.1.5.3 Poets and Litterateurs

The Tang Dynasty was an economically prosperous empire, especially before the An Shih Rebellion. There were many poets and litterateurs in the early and first half of the Tang Dynasty. Examples were Luo Biwang (駱賓王, A.D. 640–A.D. 684), Chen Ziang (陳子昂, A.D. 661–A.D. 702), Wang Changling (王昌齡, A.D. 698–A.D. 765), Wang Wei, Li Bai, and Du Fu. Among these scholars, gambling, drinking, and scholarly discussion of state affairs were among their favorite pastimes. And, since they wrote classical literature and poems, many of the writings were subsequently collected as part of the Chinese national treasures and heritage. A detailed reading of their poems may indicate that quite a number of them drank and gambled heavily. For instance, Du Fu wrote the poem "*Jinxi Xing*" when staying inside an inn in Xianyang (咸陽). In the poem, he described himself in a depressed mood. And the only way to entertain himself was to gamble and drink with friends. Another poem written by Li Bai described how he appreciated his luck in gambling. In order to test out his luck, he kept chasing after losses. For many of these poets, gambling was a part of the fun and pastimes that they could share with others. In their writing, they often used the word "play" (玩) and not "gamble" (賭) in describing their gambling behavior. To them and the academic class, gambling was an acceptable pastime, especially when one is in a depressed mood.

1.1.5.4 Gambling in Late Tang and During Five Dynasties and Ten Kingdoms

In late Tang Dynasty, after the An Shih Revolution, gambling was widespread. It was common to see people gamble late into the night hours. Gambling was often associated with drinking and visiting prostitutes at that time.

The Tang Dynasty ended in A. D. 907. Warlords and military leaders divided the land into zones, each with their own governments and systems. This period is known as Five Dynasties and Ten Kingdoms. Most of the monarchs during these periods were from the lower social class. They were less educated and cared less about governing with a legalistic system. Qian Liu (錢鏐, A.D. 852–A.D. 932), the first monarch of Wu Yue Guo (吳越國), was one good example. Before he seized power, he was a gang member who drank and gambled every day. He made his fortune by the salt trade (at that time, those privately trading salt could be arrested and sentenced to death) (Anonymous 2013).

1.1.5.5 Gambling Development in Tang

Gambling was very diversified in the Tang Dynasty. Traditional types of gambling including Chupu, Backgammon, chess, and kickball were popular games in Tang Dynasty. Gambling with animals such as cockfighting and horse racing were also the games of choice among commoners. New types of gambling such as cussec and leaves play (葉子戲) (Leaves play was a kind of card game, which might be the prototype for mahjong) were new favorites.

There were many books and songs describing gambling in the Tang Dynasty. For instance, *Wu Mu Jing* (五木經) is the first book which gives a description of Chupu. Similarly, "*Wo Shuo Fu*" (握槊賦) is a paper composed by Xing Yu (邢宇), which described Wu Shuo, another popular type of gambling.

*1.1.6 Gambling During Song and Yuan (*宋、元時期*)*

On February 4, 960, Zhao Kuangyin (趙匡胤, A.D. 927–A.D. 976) lodged a mutiny in Chen Qiao (陳橋) and forced the emperor of Hou Zhou (後周) to step down. Zhao established the Song Dynasty (Northern Song) and reunited China. Zhao ruled China for 16 years before his sudden death on November 14, 976. Compared to the size of Tang's territory, Song's was significantly smaller, and its political power was relatively weaker. Neighboring countries such as Liao (遼) and Western Xia (西夏)

often invaded the boundary cities of Song. On March 20, 1127, a neighboring power known as Jin (金) invaded Song and overthrew the government. This historical event was known as "Jingkang incident (靖康之變)," in which the two emperors of Northern Song, Zhao Ji (趙佶, A.D. 1082–A.D. 1135, ruled over China during A.D. 1100–A.D. 1126) and Zhao Huan (趙桓, A.D. 1100–A.D. 1161, ruled over China during A.D. 1126–A.D. 1127), were taken as hostages and sent to Jin. After this incident, Zhao Gou (趙構, A.D. 1107–A.D. 1187, ruled China during A.D. 1127–A.D. 1162), the ninth son of Zhao Ji (also the younger brother of Zhao Huan), proclaimed himself emperor on June 12, A. D. 1127. The new emperor moved to the southern part of China to re-establish a smaller independent country, which was later known as Southern Song. Southern Song only occupied about half the territory of Northern Song and could only passively defend its independence and sovereignty by signing unequal treaties for peace with Jin and later the Great Mongolia (蒙古). On March 19, 1279, Yuan (元, former name was Great Mongolia) invaded and successfully conquered Southern Song. The Yuan Dynasty was the first to have a foreign country rule China. To suppress opposition voices from local Chinese, Yuan employed very cruel policies. For instance, Chinese families were not allowed to have weapons. In some cases only one cooking knife could be shared among several families. The Yuan Dynasty ruled for only 98 years. In August 1368, Zhu Yuanchang (朱元璋, A.D. 1328–A.D. 1398), the founding emperor of Ming Dynasty (明朝), captured Da Dou (大都, same name as Beijing), the capital of Yuan, and ended its rule in China.

During the Yuan Dynasty, there were tremendous increases in business trading between China and other foreign countries. The rapid development of business encouraged residents living in rural areas to move to new cities. In many big cities, most of the newcomers were no longer farmers; they became cooks and restaurant workers, laborers, and small business entrepreneurs. The dominant job nature of the agrarian culture slowly gave way to a customer service economy. Urbanization and the subsequent increase in urban population promoted the development of new exciting games. Backgammon, kickball, cricket fighting (鬥蟋蟀), and Chu Hong (除紅), popular in Song, were originally from Liao. For the vast majority of players, the nature of gambling shifted from entertainment and recreation to mostly winning for money (Huang 2006). Legally, according to Pu (2006), the Song government strictly prohibited gambling by applying "Song Code (宋刑統)," laws drawn up by Zhao Kuangyin. However, the effective enforcement of the laws was the major problem as many people, including government officials, enjoyed gambling.

1.1.6.1 Merging of the Words "Du (賭)" and "Bo (博)"

The Chinese name for gambling is "Du Bo." "Bo" appeared much earlier than "Du." "Bo" can be defined as leisure activities. During participation in gambling, people may use money as a wager to heighten the level of involvement in games (Huang 2006). Simply put, in "Bo," the players use money to gamble, not gamble for money

(C. C. Chan 2014). The word "Bo" appeared in ancient times of China. It was not until the period of Three Kingdoms did the word "Du" get first recorded in the book *Game Theory* (博奕論), written by Wei Zhao (韋昭, A.D. 204–A.D. 273), a scholar in Eastern Wu (東吳). In this article, Wei explained in detail the negative effects of "Du." Thus, we can see that in the ancient history of China, leisure activities in which wagering was done with a small amount of money was generally acceptable. However, wagering with a large amount of money as depicted by the word "Du" was a social vice and should be strictly prohibited by law.

The earliest record of combining "Du" and "Bo" was found in the history of Song Dynasty. In A.D. 1012, Northern Song's emperor Zhao Heng (趙恆, A.D. 968–A.D. 1022, ruled China during A.D. 997–A.D. 1022) issued a decree to punish those who crossed Song's frontier and gambled in Liao's territory. In his imperial edict, Zhao mentioned "Du Bo" together (Tuo 1343). Gambling was seen as a life skill. On this aspect, Yan Shu (晏殊, A.D. 991–A.D. 1055), a famous composer of Chinese poetry, talked about his daily life with "Du Bo." He wrote:

> I am always equipped with every gambling skill when I was living in Xi Qin (家住西秦, 賭博藝隨身)." This poem implies that gambling was well received by the scholars and could be considered as a life skill. These skills could help one to socialize with friends or make a living in the community. (Yan 1967)

1.1.6.2 Secularization of Gambling in Song Dynasty

Urban development and the rapid development of international commerce in Song benefited the secularization of new games. In the latter half of Northern Song, the first gang-operated gambling houses, operated under the name "Ju Fang (柜坊)," were widespread in major cities. The management of these establishments was analogous to present-day casinos, though much smaller in scale. Many of these "Ju Fangs" employed systematic scams to cheat the customers. Firstly, they would arrange attractive young girls to invite people to participate in gambling. In the first few game sets, the participants would win a relatively small amount of money. Then, the operators of the gambling stalls would, by employing specific gambling tricks, cheat the gamblers of all their money. Then, the gang would persuade participants to borrow money to chase after their losses. At the end, participants would be heavily in debt, and some of them may even commit suicide. Worst of all, bankers of "Ju Fang" always openly solicited people including soldiers to gamble (by law, Song's soldiers were forbidden to gamble). During the last 100 years of the Song Dynasty, people not only gambled in "Ju Fangs" but also gambled heavily inside restaurants. At this time, table games that stressed speed and luck were preferred inside the gambling stalls. Good examples of these games were Guan Pu (關撲)* and Chu Hong**.

*Guan Pu was a common game in both Northern and Southern Song. The rules of the game are simple: it involves tossing coins on the floor or a plane surface. Winning depends on the combination of the coins. Another playing method of Guan Pu was called "Tan Qian (攤錢)," in which the banker shook the coins inside a container. Participants who correctly guessed the remainder would win the game.

**Chu Hong was also called Zhu Wo (豬窩), a dice game. Previously, dice was a component of Chupu and Backgammon. It became an independent game in Northern Song. Chu Hong consisted of four dice. By throwing four dice simultaneously, participant who tossed four "four" (dyed red color) would be the winner (Yang 1988).

Beginning in the Song Dynasty, for the majority of players, table games that required less cognitive skill were more preferable. Further, spectators of the games could share in the joy and excitement by simply watching others play. Contemporary researchers in casino gambling discovered that the most popular game in Macao casinos is baccarat (Chan et al. 2016). And Chinese players love to crowd around one baccarat table to play the game. Spectators also share the fun and joy by cheering and yelling at each other (Bai 1985; Lam 2005).

1.1.6.3 Consequences of the Secularization of Gambling

Contemporary researchers in gambling (Blaszczynski and Nower 2002) argue that the importance of the 3 As (acceptability, accessibility, and availability) are the key factors for the development of gambling behavior. Starting in the latter half of Song Dynasty, increased availability of gambling opportunities in restaurants and Ju Fangs attracted more people to play the games. Kato, a Japanese expert in Chinese gambling history, investigated the functions of Ju Fang. He argues that Ju Fang provided a number of important social functions: a place for gambling, accommodations (like hotels), food and beverage, prostitution services, and the manufacturing and exchange of copper coins (coin money in Song Dynasty). In other words, in Confucian ethics, Ju Fang represents a paradise for social vice for men (Kato 1976). Thus, Ju Fang was a favorite hangout for criminals and loan sharks. Consequently, in view of public law and order, Song's government prohibited the opening, operation, and management of Ju Fang in restaurants and inns.

In the literature of that period, a number of writings can give us a hint of the nature of gambling at the time. The following is a list of authors who wrote on gambling in the Tang Dynasty.

Fig. 1.6 Backgammon. (The figure was drawn by Olga, a professional artist. The copyright of this figure belongs to the authors)

1. Lu You (陸游, A.D. 1125–A.D. 1210), a famous litterateur of Southern Song, also one of the Eight Experts of Tang and Song Poetry (唐宋八大家), wrote, "there are some people who intend to cheat others' money through gambling. Every time they bet, they will absolutely win."
2. Tuo (1343), a historian on gambling, documented the following terrible event, "Once a teenager had a cock (for cockfighting gambling). His classmate asked the teenager to give the cock to him but was rejected. On revenge, that classmate stalked and intended to kill him."

1.1.6.4 Types of Gambling Commonly Practiced in Song and Yuan

Guan Pu and Chu Hong were the most favorite games in Northern and Southern Song. Other types of popular gambling in Song, Liao, Jin, and Yuan were as follows:

1. Backgammon (Fig. 1.6)

Backgammon was a popular game since Tang Dynasty. During Northern Song, several versions of the game were played in different areas. Hong Zun (洪遵, A.D. 1120–A.D. 1174), an expert in Chinese currency in Southern Song, wrote that people in the northern part of the country loved Qi Dan Backgammon (契丹雙陸) (popular in Liao, same playing method as that in Tang Dynasty), Da Jian Backgammon (打間雙陸), Qi Liang Backgammon (七梁雙陸), San Liang Backgammon (三梁雙陸), and Hui Hui Backgammon (回回雙陸). Guangzhou Backgammon (廣州雙陸) was very popular in the Southern part of China.

2. Da Ma (打馬)

Li Qing Zhao (李清照, A.D. 1084–A.D. 1155), a talented, well-known poet in Song, loved Da Ma. Da Ma, a game evolved from Chupu, was the precursor of present-day mahjong. It was played by two persons. The chess pieces in Da Ma were carved into shapes of horses. Players tossed the dice to move chess pieces. The one who reached the destination point would win the game. Li wrote a manual on how to play the game. The book is called *Da Ma Tu Jing* (打馬圖經). Da Ma was very popular until the later years of Southern Song.

3. Cai Xuan (彩選)

Cai Xuan was perhaps one of the most elegant gambling types in Song, compared with other games. It was invented by Liu Ban (劉攽, A.D. 1022–A.D. 1088), the co-editor of the classical Chinese history literature, *Encyclopedia of Enterprises and Politics* (資治通鑑) (the chief editor was Sima Guang (司馬光, A.D. 1019–A.D. 1086)). In designing this game, Liu created a diagram describing the promotion and demotion of chancellors in Western Han Dynasty. He also explained their personnel changes in the diagram so that players could literally revise Chinese history as they gambled. Song emperors emphasized imperial examination – a system of selecting suitable candidates for government service. Therefore, Cai Xuan was a popular game as the players could share the fun and fantasy of getting to the top rank of the government officialdom.

4. Kickball (Figs. 1.7, 1.8, and 1.9)

As mentioned in the above sections, kickball started as a game during the period of rivalry between West Chu and Han. During Song Dynasty, kickback was popular as it combined sports with gambling. The *Outlaws of the Marsh* (水滸傳) written by Shi and Luo (1589), one of the four Chinese classical literatures, also contained a short story on kickball. Gao Qiu (高俅), a treacherous court official active in late Northern Song during the ruling of Zhao Ji, was very skillful in playing kickball. He utilized his excellent kickball skills to entertain Emperor Zhao Ji and successfully gained his trust. Later the emperor appointed Gao Qiu as a grand army commander (太尉). Kickball continued to be a popular game in Yuan Dynasty though Mongolian imperial power strictly prohibited any type of gambling.

5. Xuan Hu Pai (宣和牌)

Xuan Hu Pai, a table game of dominoes, was very popular among commoners during the ruling period of Zhao Ji. The rules of this game are similar to the present Chinese games of Tien Gow (天九) and Pai Gow (牌九). Xuan Hu Pai was popular toward the end of Northern Song. There are historical records of a number of gamblers who gambled this game overnight and were absent from work or unwilling to return home (Huang 2006).

Fig. 1.7 Kickball in Han Dynasty

Fig. 1.8 Kickball in Tang Dynasty

1.1.6.5 Famous Active/Pathological Gamblers in the Song Dynasty

1. Li Qing Zhao

Li Qing Zhao, a famous writer in Song Dynasty, was addicted to gambling, especially Da Ma. When she was young, she enjoyed playing Da Ma with her husband, Zhao Ming Cheng. Li was proud of her excellent gambling skills as she preferred skilled-based games. Her development of gambling mirrors the Pathway 1 problem gambler according to the Blaszczynski and Nower (2002) model. She started gambling in her adolescent years. She was preoccupied with gambling as she could spend all day at the gambling table. She enjoyed gambling with her husband. However, her life made a sharp turn when Jin occupied Qing Zhou (青州, located in

Fig. 1.9 Kickball in Song and Yuan Dynasties. (The figures were drawn by Olga, a professional artist. The copyright of these figures belongs to the authors)

Shan Dong province), in A. D. 1127, where the young couple were living. The couple fled to Zhen Jiang (鎮江, located in Jiang Su province). Soon after that, Jin attacked Zhen Jiang. The couple then fled to Jiang Ning Fu (江寧府, namely, Nanjing today) in spring, A.D. 1128. Unfortunately, her husband died of malaria 1.5 years after they had settled in Jiang Ning Fu. Li lost most of her money in the war. Nevertheless, she maintained her gambling habit at this difficult time (Wang 1979), though her motivation for gambling was mostly for emotional escape. Li later moved to Jiang Nan (江南). She married again in A.D. 1132, but the marriage only lasted for 3 months when she divorced her second husband Zhang Ru Zhou (張汝舟). She continued to gamble in her last years of life. Incorporating the Blaszczynski and Nower (2002), we can interpret that Li Qing Zhao shifted from Pathway 1 to Pathway 2 pathological gamblers – emotionally vulnerable gamblers. In her last years, Li gambled mostly for obtaining emotional relief. By gambling, she was able to seek psychological comfort and solace through dissociation and mood modification (Brown 2002).

2. Emperor Zhao Ji

In Song Dynasty, there were strict laws on gambling. Zhao Kuangyin drew up the laws, *Song Code*, aimed at punishing heavy gamblers (Pu 2006). In many cases, the offenders would be given capital punishment (Ming Gong Shu Pan Qing Ming Ji 1987). Notwithstanding these severe anti-gambling laws, almost all emperors in Song history were problem gamblers. For example, Zhao Ji, the second last emperor of Northern Song, was a famous case of problem gambler. He appointed court officials such as Cai Jing (蔡京, A.D. 1047–A.D. 1126) and Tong Guan (童貫, A.D. 1054–A.D. 1126) to take up major administrative and military tasks of the imperial court. He spent his days on calligraphy, playing chess, and gambling with his concubine, Li Shishi (李師師). Zhou (1987) recorded an interesting story on Emperor Zhao Ji. Zhao Ji once gambled Backgammon and chess with Li Shishi. Losing the games, Zhao gave 2000 teals of platinum, the equivalent value of at least five houses to Li. This legend indicates that gambling was a favored pastime among the elite class.

3. Emperor Liao Daozong (遼道宗)

Gambling was also common among the ruling class of China's neighbors. Tuo (1344) recorded an event of civil promotion of Emperor Liao Daozong (original name: Ye Lu Hongji (耶律洪基), A.D. 1032–A.D. 1101, ruled Liao during A.D. 1055–A.D. 1101). This emperor was at an advanced age. He used the games of dice to decide senior civil service promotion. The suitable candidates would throw dice, and those who obtained the highest points would be promoted. This was an unprecedented event in Chinese history (Tuo 1344);

4. Gu Si Dao (賈似道, A.D. 1213–A.D. 1275)

In Southern Song Dynasty, gambling was a common activity among high-ranking officials. Among these officials, Gu Si Dao was a good example (Tuo 1344). The nickname of Gu Si Dao was called "cricket prime minister" as he loved cricket fighting. Gu came from an influential and wealthy family. His elder sister was a concubine of Emperor Zhao Yun (趙昀, A.D. 1205–A.D. 1264, ruled one half of China during A.D. 1224–A.D. 1264). Gu idled away his time during adolescence in gambling. During A.D. 1267–A.D. 1273, the Mongolian Empire invaded Xiang Yang (襄陽, a city located in present-day Hu Bei province (湖北省)). Gu was the prime minister of Southern Song at that time. However, he ignored the foreign invasion in Xiang Yang; he spent much of his time on cricket gambling with his concubines at home. Worst of all, he lied to emperor Zhao Ji (趙禥, A.D. 1240–A.D. 1274, ruled during A.D. 1264–A.D. 1274) that Song's army successfully defended Xiang Yang. Finally, Xiang Yang fell to the Mongolians in A.D. 1273.

Gu was an expert on cricket gambling. He even wrote a book called *The Book of Cricket* (促織經). This book consisted of two chapters, which described in detail how to select, feed, and train crickets, as well as strategies of cricket fighting. This book was also the first book written in history about crickets.

1.1.6.6 The Nature of Gambling in Song and Yuan

Gambling was a common social activity in Song and Yuan. Most people gambled to win money, rather than for entertainment. The art and elegance of gambling in Xia and Shang Dynasties had faded out. Games that required cognitive skills and strategies, such as Da Ma, gradually lost popularity. Instead of playing time- consuming skilled games, the majority of the commoners enjoyed quick chance games. And there were historical records of problem gamblers who committed crimes to obtain money to gamble. Gambling stalls, mostly operated as "Ju Fangs" and controlled by gangs and loan sharks, were widespread in big cities. Though there were strict laws prohibited gambling in both Song and Yuan, gambling among the commoners became out of control in the two dynasties. The major reason was that the rules were not appropriately managed and enforced by local officials. On top of this, the members of the aristocrat class including the emperors were often heavy gamblers. In addition, it was difficult to carry out anti-gambling laws as a lot of governmental officials were also shareholders of gambling stalls. In our analysis, we do believe that the culture of gambling among Chinese people nowadays presumably started from the period of Song and Yuan.

1.2 Concluding Remarks: The History of Chinese Gambling: First 3000 Years (From Xia to Song Dynasty)

We have traced the development of gambling in ancient China from Xia to the Song Dynasty. In reading the historical documents and literature, we endeavored to integrate our contemporary gambling theories in our analysis. The following is a summary of our observations:

(a) Gambling activities were initially noble cognitive pastimes for the aristocratic class in ancient China. The gaming instruments were seen as parts of national treasures and artifacts, as the recent archaeological findings have suggested. However, as the games became more popular among the working classes, these games, as in the cases of Liubo and Chupu, evolved into less complex ones which focused more on the chance factor than skills and strategies. The motivation of play has also changed from competition of cognitive skills and maneuvers to the winning of money. Thus, the nobility and elegance of the games slowly disappeared with the inclusion of wagering in the game.

(b) The earliest gaming activities were often a game of two players. However, as more people were interested in the game, spectators started to gather behind the players and put wagers on games in which they did not actually participate, as in the Chupu and Kickball. During the game, the spectators shared the fun and the excitement of the game as if they were the actual players. The inclusion of spectators added to the popularity of the games as more players, who did not actually play the game. So why didn't these gamblers actively take part in the gaming process? Some might not have had the physical ability to play, as in the case of kickball. Another reason lies with the personality of Chinese. C. C. Chan (2014) argued that the typical Chinese individual, when compared to Americans and Europeans, is more reserved, humble, and less assertive in areas of social interactions, especially in games of competition. Thus, for many Chinese, they might be more comfortable staying on the sidelines and enjoy the game from there. Also, as spectators, while they can wager their bets, they would not be blamed for any mistakes in the gaming process. Hence, we can see the spirit of Chupu in the present-day baccarat in the casinos of Macao, where a lot of spectators cheer, yell, and wager large amounts of money from behind the actual players (Lam 2005).

(c) Beginning at the Era of Spring and Autumn (春秋時代) and Warring States Period (戰國時代) gambling became more widespread among the lower working class and the poor in ancient China, especially in times of political instability and financial depression. It was apparent that more people were attracted to gambling activities in times of social instability and social unrest. Contemporary gambling researchers (Wu et al. 2014), in their prevalence study of residents in Macao, have noted that individuals who are not satisfied with their lives are more likely to participate gambling activities. This is particular apparent among males with low education and high materialistic concerns. Materialism is operationally defined as "a set of centrally held beliefs about the importance of possession in one's life" (Richins and Dawson 1992, p. 308). Further, a consistent finding in modern gambling research is that the poorest segment in a community often gamble more in their percentage of disposable income than the affluent counterparts (Chan and Wong 2012; Chan et al. 2016; Fong and Ozorio 2005; Wardle et al. 2007). On this issue, sociologist Edward Devereux (1968) asserted that gambling serves as a "safety valve" for the poor, especially for those with less education and low skill level. Through gambling, one might be able to get rich. Thus, gambling provides a hope for the poor (Friedman and Savage 1948; Ginakis and Ohtsuka 2005). Even though the majority of gamblers might not find instant riches through gambling, it is the expected utility of gambling (Hartley and Farrell 2002), i.e., getting rich in a short time with little efforts, that constitute their main motivation for gambling.

(d) Since the early years of the Tang Dynasty, gaming activities were the favorite pastimes across all social classes. The motivation of playing the games range from winning the bets and receiving validation from peers to gambling for emotional escape. Incorporating the contemporary gaming theories of Blaszczynski and Nower (2002), the pathway development of ancient Chinese problem gamblers mirrors all three pathways of development, namely, the behaviorally conditioned gamblers, emotionally vulnerable gamblers, and antisocial/impulsivist gamblers. In the academic community, we find more cases of the emotionally vulnerable gamblers. In ancient China, drinking and gambling were often means of emotional escape for the intellectuals.

(e) Since ancient times in China, the majority of Chinese have regarded gambling as a social vice. It has been considered as one of the four immoral sins of men: the other being visiting prostitutes, drinking, and smoking opium. As a sin and social disgrace, the best solution, in the eyes of many, was punishment. Thus, we see that the state laws in many of the surveyed dynasties approved severe punishment to disordered gamblers. There were few provisions for the assessment, treatment, and rehabilitation for people with gambling disorders.

1.2.1 Conclusion

In our survey of Chinese gambling history during this period, we discover that gambling activities first appeared in the historical records as noble cognitive games enjoyed by the nobility and the wealthy class. Gradually, as they became more popular among the commoners, the games' nobility and elegance disappeared. Instead, the winning of money became the most important element. Further, new games were developed to fit the diverse interests of the players. By the time of the Yuan Dynasty, gambling activities had become favorite pastimes of individuals from all walks of life. In addition, there were frequent reports of problem gamblers and violent crimes committed by them. Further, there was considerable discrepancy between public policy and the personal conduct of public officials and the aristocratic class. Chinese monarchs were often less honest, if not hypocritical, about their views on gambling. While the majority of the emperors passed harsh laws against gambling, many of them nonetheless indulged in gambling with their friends and loved ones. Maybe what Kiang Fan (2010) has suggested, some 4000 years after the Xia Dynasty, is appropriate. By the Yuan Dynasty, gambling had become the root of the Chinese civilization.

References

Aasved, M. (2003). *The sociology of gambling*. Springfield: Charles C Thomas.

American Psychiatric Association. (2013). *Diagnostic and statistical manual of mental disorders* (5th ed.). Washington, DC: Author.

Anonymous. (2013). *Fantastic story of Chinese gambling*. (不著撰人. (2013).中國古代賭博奇聞.). Retrieved August 11, 2016 from http://tw.ticaicn.com/html/6/6031.html

Bai, Y. (1985). *Ugly Chinese*. Lin Bai Publishing Co. Ltd. Taipei (柏陽. (1985). 醜陋的中國人. 林白出版社有限公司. 台北).

Ban, G. (92). *History of the Former Han Dynasty* (班固. (92). 前漢書). Retrieved June 5, 2016 from http://www.xysa.net/a200/h350/02qianhanshu/t-index.htm

Blaszczynski, A., & Nower, L. (2002). A pathways model of problem and pathological gambling. *Addiction, 97*(5), 487–499.

Brown, R. I. F. (2002). Dissociation phenomena among normal and addicted gamblers. In J. J. Marotta, J. A. Cornelius, & W. R. Eadington (Eds.), *The downside: Problem and pathological gambling* (pp. 201–222). Reno: Institute for the Study of Gambling and Commercial Gaming, University of Nevada, Reno.

Chan, C. C. (2014). *The psychology of gambling and gambling treatment.* A keynote address to the 2nd Macau Medical Association Forum-MMAF, Macao SAR, China.

Chan, Y. Y. (2014). *Last gambling in suppression in Avarice*. National Miao Li Senior High School (陳昱蓉. (2014). 壓倒貪婪的最後一場賭博. 國立苗栗高中). Retrieved June 5, 2016 from http://www.docin.com/p-807619834.html

Chan, C. C., & Wong, H. (2012, November). *Pathways to problem gambling: A summary of research from 2010–2012.* Paper presented in the first Asia Pacific conference on gambling & commercial gaming research, Macau, China.

Chan, C. C., Li, W. L., & Leung, C. I. (2014). *The psychology of gambling* (2nd ed.). Mother Mary Social Studies Centre. (陳智川、李威廉、梁頌業 (2014) 賭博心理學(第二版). 澳門高志慈社會研究中心.) ISBN 978–99937-644-9-6. Available free online: http://www.caritas.org.mo/uploads/wizpublicationdownload/201607/1977_dnnmi.pdf

Chan, C. C., Li, W. L., & Leung, C. I. (2016). *Problem gambling in Hong Kong and Macao: Etiology, prevalence and treatment*. Singapore: Springer ISBN 978-981-10-1066-8.

Chang, R. X. (1984). *Discussion of China's art*. Shanghai Literature and Art Publishing Group (常任俠. (1984).東方藝術叢談. 上海文藝出版社).

Chen, H. Z. (n.d.). *Dongcheng father biography* (陳鴻祖. 東城老父傳). Retrieved August 12, 2016 from http://leachin.blogspot.hk/2013/04/blog-post_4364.html

Chen, W. Z., & He, W. R. (2006). *Gambling history of China*. Kaohsiung Municipal Rueisiang High School (陳文智及何宛儒. (2006). 中國賭博史. 高雄市立瑞祥高級中學). Retrieved October 13, 2016 from http://lib.rssh.kh.edu.tw/essay/95essay/060.pdf

Confucius. (n.d.). *Confucian Analects* (孔子.《論語》). Retrieved June 5, 2016 from http://www.zwbk.org/zh-tw/Lemma_Show/76514.aspx

Devereux, E. C. (1968). Gambling in psychological and sociological perspective. *International Encyclopedia of the Social Science, 6*, 53–62.

Fan, Z. Y., & Zheng, X. M. (2010). On faith and custom about gambling in Chinese history. *College of Humanities and Public Administration, Huaqiao University, 362021, China, 4*, 20–29 (范正義、鄭向敏 (2010). 中國歷史上與賭博有關的信仰習俗探析.華僑大學學報(哲學社会科學版), 4, 20–29).

Fang, X. L., & Chu, S. L. (648). *The book of Jin: Biography of Xia An* (房玄齡、褚遂良等(648年).《晉書˙謝安傳》). Retrieved July 29, 2016 from https://zh.wikisource.org/zh-hant/%E6%99%89%E6%9B%B8/%E5%8D%B7079

Fong, K. C., & Ozorio, B. (2005). Gambling participation and prevalence estimates of pathological gambling in a Far-East gambling city: Macao. *UNLV Gaming Research & Review Journal, 9*, 15–28.

Friedman, M., & Savage, L. J. (1948). The utility analysis of choices involving risk. *Journal of Political Economy, 16*, 279–304.

Ge, C. Y. (1995). *The history of gambling*. Shanghai Literature and Art Publishing Group (戈春源. (1995). 賭博史. 上海文藝出版社).

Ginakis, S., & Ohtsuka, K. (2005). Problem gambling: An exploration of the role of global personal hopefulness, short-term gambling hope, and illusion of control beliefs. *Gambling Research, 17*, 7–16.

Griffiths, M. D., Hayer, T., & Meyer, G. (2009). Problem gambling: A European perspective. In G. Meyer, T. Hayer, & M. D. Griffiths (Eds.), *Problem gaming in Europe: Challenges, prevention, and intervention* (pp. xix–xxix). New York: Springer.

Gu, S. D. (n.d.). *The book of cricket* ((賈似道. (著書年份不詳). 促織經). Retrieved September 23, 2016 from https://zh.wikisource.org/wiki/%E4%BF%83%E7%B9%94%E7%B6%93

Guo, S. L., & Xiao, M. H. (1995). *Gambling history of Chinese*. China Social Sciences Press (郭雙林、蕭梅花. (1995).中華賭博史.中國社會科學出版社).

Guo, S. L., & Xiao, M. H. (1996). *The history of Chinese gambling*. Wen Chin Press, Taipei (郭雙林、蕭梅花. (1996).中國賭博史.台北文津出版社).

Han, F. (n.d.). *Han Fei Tze* (韓非.《韓非子》). Retrieved June 5, 2016 from http://www.twword.com/wiki/%E3%80%8A%E9%9F%93%E9%9D%9E%E5%AD%90%E3%80%8B

Hartley, R., & Farrell, L. (2002). Can expected utility theory explain gambling? *The American Economic Review, 92*(3), 613–624.

Huang, C. Y. (2006). Folk custom of gambling and its society construction in Song dynasty. *Journal of History of National Chung Hsing University, 17*, 105–124 (黃純怡. (2006). 宋代的賭博風習及其社會意義. 興大歷史學報, *17*, 105–124).

Huang, L. Z. (2015). Supplementary history of Chu Pu. ("樗蒲"資料補史). *Journal of Pingdingshan University, 30*, 6.

Kato, S. (1976). *Investigation of Chinese history of economy*. Huashi Press. Taipei (加藤繁. (1976). 中國經濟史考證. 台北: 華世出版社).

Kiang, F. (2010). *The gambling Chinese*. Tuan Jie Publishing Group. Beijing (江泛. (2010). 好賭的中國人.團結出版社. 北京).

Lam, D. (2005). Slot or table? A Chinese perspective. *UNLV Gaming Research & Review Journal, 9*, 69–72.

Lau, N. Y. (1998). Important questions of investigating gambling history: Bringing up from 《Gambling History of Chinese》 written by Guo, S. L., & Xiao, M. H. *Journal of Guangxi University (Philosophy and Social Science), 20*(4), 49–54. https://doi.org/10.13624/j.cnki.jgupss.1998.04.016 (柳立言. (1998).研究賭博史的重要問題–從郭雙林、蕭梅花《中華賭博史》談起.)

Li, A. (n.d.-a). *Book of five woods* (李翱. 五木經). Retrieved November 20, 2016 from http://ctext.org/wiki.pl?if=gb&chapter=482661

Li, K. (n.d.-b). *Fa Jing* (李悝. 法經). Retrieved August 19, 2016 from http://www.chiculture.net/1005/html/c03/1005c03.html

Li, Q. Z. (n.d.-c). *Da Ma Tu Jing* (李清照. 打馬圖經).

Li, Z. (n.d.-d). *Supplementary to the history of Tang Dynasty* (李肇. 唐國史補). Retrieved December 15, 2016 from https://zh.wikisource.org/wiki/%E5%94%90%E5%9C%8B%E5%8F%B2%E8%A3%9C

Li, W. L., Lee, L. F., Lo, F., Cho, K. P., & Chan, C. C. (2011). Recreational gambling among individuals in late adulthood (pp. 284–296). In: *Conference proceedings of the international conference on Gaming Industry and Public Welfare 2011*, Beijing, China, ISBN: 978-99965-2-036-5.

Lu, Y. (n.d.). *Lao Xue An Bi Ji* (陸游. 老學庵筆記). Retrieved September 16, 2016 from http://www.youscribe.com/catalogue/livres/litterature/autres/lao-shyue-an-bii-jih-48304

Luo, X. B., & Xu, R. S. (1994). *Customs of gambling in ancient China*. Shaanxi People's Publishing House. Xi'an (羅新本、許蓉生. (1994). 中國古代賭博習俗. 陝西人民出版社.西安).

Ming Gong Shu Pan Qing Ming Ji. (1987). Chungwa Bookstore. Beijing (名公書判清明集集 (1987). 北京: 中華書局).

Pu, J. (2006). *The history of legal system in China*. Central Radio and Television University Press (蒲堅 (2006).中國法制史.中央廣播電視大學出版社. ISBN 7-304-02441-0/D·209).).

Richins, M. L., & Dawson, S. (1992). A consumer values orientation for materialism and its measurement: Scale development and validation. *Journal of Consumer Research, 19*, 303–316.

Shi, X. Y. (2005). Overview of gambling in each dynasty in China. *Decision and Information, 245*, 62–63 (石肖瑜. (2005).中國歷代賭博概覽. 決策與信息, *245*, 62–63).

Shi, N. A., & Luo, G. Z. (1589). *Outlaws of the Marsh* (施耐庵, 羅貫中. 水滸傳).

Shum, Y. F. (1994, May 6). *Speech of people from three maintains: Evaluation of seven sages of the bamboo grove*. Mongpao (岑逸飛. (1994-05-16).〈三山人語.為竹林七賢評分〉.《明報》).

Sima, Q. (n.d.). *Record of the grand historian* (司馬遷.史記). Retrieved June 5, 2016 from http://www.zwbk.org/MyLemmaShow.aspx?zh=zh-tw&lid=4503

Sima, G. (1071–1086). *Encyclopedia of enterprises and politics* (司馬光 (1071–1086).資治通鑑). Retrieved October 26, 2016 from https://zh.wikisource.org/wiki/%E8%B3%87%E6%B2%BB%E9%80%9A%E9%91%91

Tu, W. X. (2006). *Gambling history*. Chinese Literature Press (涂文學.(2006).賭博的歷史. 中國文史出版社).

Tuo, T. (1343). *History of Song Dynasty* (脫脫. (1343). 宋史).

Tuo, T. (1344). *History of Liao* (脫脫. (1344). 遼史).

Wang, Z. W. (1979). *Li Qing Zhao Ji Xiao Zhu*. People's Literature Publishing House. Beijing (李清照集校注. (1979). 人民文學出版社. 北京).

Wardle, H., Sproston, K., Orford, J., Erens, B., Griffiths, M. D., Constantine, R., & Pigott, S. (2007). *British gambling prevalence survey, 2007.* Retrieved 8 July, 2015 from http://www.gamblingcommission.gov.uk/pdf/British%20Gambling%20Prevalence%20Survey%202007.pdf

Wei, Z. (243). *Game theory* (韋昭. (243年).博奕論). Retrieved September 5, 2016 from http://www.xiexingcun.com/shiciqupianqu/08/h014.htm.

Wong, T. C. (2016). *The most unreliable emperors among Chinese history*. Intelligence Culture Publishing Group (黄太子. (2016).歷史上最不靠譜的十大皇帝.智學堂文化出版社).

Wong, H. A., & Yu, T. W. (2006). Changes of perspectives in Chinese gambling and contemporary gaming management. *Macau Studies, 36*, 86–91 (黃雁鴻, 余達緯 (2006). 中國賭博觀念的演變與現代博彩管理. 澳門研究, 36, 86–91).

Wu, A. M. S., Lai, M. C. H., & Tong, K. K. (2014). Gambling disorder: Estimated prevalence rates and risk factors in Macao. *Psychology of Addictive Behaviors, 28*(4), 1190–1197.

Xing, Y. (n.d.). *Wu Mu Jing* (邢宇.五木經). Retrieved August 15, 2016 from https://zh.wikisource.org/zh-hant/%E4%BA%94%E6%9C%A8%E7%B6%93

Xu, S. (n.d.). *Shouwen Jiezi* (許慎. 說文解字). Retrieved June 5, 2016 from http://ctext.org/shuo-wen-jie-zi/zh

Yan, S. (1967). *Er Yan Ci*. WJ Bookstore, Taipei (晏殊, 二晏詞. 台北: 世界書局, 1967).

Yang, W. Z. (1988). *Book of Chu Hong*. Shanghai Classical Literature Press (楊維楨. (1988). 除紅譜. 上海古籍出版社).

Zhang, H. (n.d.). *Bowu Zhi* (張華《博物誌》). Retrieved August 15, 2016 from https://zh.wikisource.org/wiki/%E5%8D%9A%E7%89%A9%E5%BF%97

Zhang Sun, W. J. (A.D. 652). *Comments on laws of Tang Empire* (長孫無忌. (652年). 唐律疏議). Retrieved August 22, 2016 from https://zh.wikisource.org/zh-hant/%E5%94%90%E5%BE%8B%E7%96%8F%E8%AD%B0

Zhou, L. J. (1987). *Li Shishi Chuan Qi*. Shanghai Classical Literature Press (周楞伽 (1987). 李師師傳奇. 上海古籍出版社).

Chapter 2
A Cultural History of Chinese Gambling II (From Ming Dynasty to Qing Dynasty)

Rachel Volberg and Robert Williams, in an excellent review on the epidemiology of gambling, once wrote: "Gambling is a broad concept that includes diverse activities, undertaken in a wide variety of settings, appealing to different types of people, and perceived in various ways. People participate because they enjoy and obtain benefits from gambling activities. For most people, gambling is generally a positive experience; however, for a minority, gambling is associated with difficulties of varying severity and duration" (Volberg and Williams 2014, p. 26). What Volberg and Williams are arguing, contrary to traditional Chinese morals as we have seen in Chap. 1, is that gambling, as a social activity, is not a social problem in itself since a great number of individuals find joy and excitement in gambling. In this chapter, we will critically examine Volberg and Williams's assertion against the nature and scope of gambling from the Ming Dynasty to the end of Chinese feudal period, i.e., the Qing Dynasty. Our purpose is to investigate what gambling activities meant to the Chinese during these periods from cultural and historical perspectives.

2.1 Gambling During the Last Two Feudal Periods: Ming and Qing (明、清時期)

There were significant changes in the political power structure in the Ming Dynasty (A.D. 1368–A.D. 1644). The Ming emperors abolished the position of prime minister in the early years of the kingdom. Consequently, the emperors held absolute political power. There were little checks and balances on his powers and jurisdiction (Tang and Zhu 2016). To further tighten surveillance on their oppositions, Ming emperors established a department of secret police (called the secret troops (錦衣衛)) to keep a close eye on daily activities of the commoners.

The following example aptly illustrates the powers of these secret police officers. Qian Zai (錢宰, A.D. 1299–A.D. 1394), a highly respected scholar in early Ming,

C. C. Chan et al., *The Psychology of Chinese Gambling*,
https://doi.org/10.1007/978-981-13-3486-3_2

once complained about heavy workload in the imperial court. One day when he was at home, he composed a poem: "Getting up when the sky is still dark. Arriving at the main gate of the palace in the morning, the emperor complains that I am too late for work. When could I retire and enjoy my life? And when could I sleep peacefully until noon? (四鼓咚咚起著衣,午門朝見尚嫌遲。何時遂得田園樂,睡到人間飯熟時。)" On the following day, when Qian was working in his office, Emperor Zhu Yuanzhang (朱元璋, A.D. 1328–A.D. 1398, ruled China during A.D. 1368–A.D. 1398) made a joke on him, "I never said you arrive too late. Please amend your poem." Qian was shocked and immediately apologized to the emperor. In this interesting story, we can see that the emperor might have sent his secret troops to spy on his staff, including Qian Zai, every day. These undercover police would directly report to the emperor on everything unusual among his staff and people.

During the late fifteenth century, a number of emperors (e.g., Zhu Hou Zong (朱厚熜, A.D. 1507–A.D. 1567, ruled China during A.D. 1521–A.D. 1567), Zhu Yijun (朱翊鈞, A.D. 1563–A.D. 1620, ruled China during A.D. 1572–A.D. 1620), and Zhu You Xiao (朱由校, A.D. 1605–A.D. 1627, ruled China during A.D. 1620–A.D. 1627)) were inefficient in running the country administratively. Very often, they left the daily state affairs to the people around them. The eunuchs, who served as imperial servants, were often real masters of all the state affairs. Examples of these eunuchs were Liu Jin (劉瑾, A.D. 1451 A.D. 1510) and Wei Zhongxian (魏忠賢, A.D. 1568–A.D. 1627)). In 1644, the Ming Dynasty came to an end and was replaced by the Qing Dynasty.

In the area of gambling, even though all the emperors imposed strict rules and regulations on gambling, illegal gambling activities were popular across the empire. The most popular games were cricket fighting and hanging horse (馬吊), a precursor of the present-day mahjong.

2.1.1 Emperors' Attitudes Toward Gambling in Ming Dynasty

Zhu Yuanzhang, the founding emperor of the Ming Dynasty, passed a harsh law to punish lawbreaking gamblers. Punishments included chopping off the hands of criminal gamblers. In addition, he set up a house called "the free and unfettered house (逍遙樓)." The name might be a bit fancy and misleading. It was a big gambling house where the gamblers were allowed to gamble freely. However, no meal was provided inside the house. Consequently, a number of them died of hunger and dehydration. When the gamblers promised to get rid of the habit of gambling, they were released from the house. Another form of Emperor Zhu Yuanzhang's punishment was caning. According to "the Criminal Law of Ming Dynasty (大明律集解附例)," problem gamblers would be given 80 strokes of caning plus loss of the wagering money. Furthermore, their hands would be chopped off. Similar punishments were also applicable to the operators of gambling stalls. Under these strict laws, many gamblers quitted gambling.

While Zhu Yuanzhang strictly banned gambling among the commoners, he liked gambling with his chancellors. Once, he played chess with his Major General Xu Da (徐達, A.D. 1332–A.D. 1385), and he wagered "the Lake of Mochou (莫愁湖)," a lake located at the west of River Qinhuai (秦淮河), Nanjing. Xu won the bet, and Zhu rewarded him the ownership of the lake.

The laws on gambling were maintained during the rule of Zhu Jin Shen (朱見深, A.D. 1447–A.D. 1487, ruled China during A.D. 1464–A.D. 1487).

Zhu Zhanji (朱瞻基, A.D. 1399–A.D. 1435, ruled China during A.D. 1425–A.D. 1435), the great-grandson of Zhu Yuanzhang, was a successful emperor under his emperorship, as the Chinese society was politically stable and financially prosperous. However, like his grandfather, he enjoyed gambling very much. Among all games, he liked cricket fighting (Fig. 2.1) the most. He even ordered his servants to buy high-quality crickets from every corner of his empire. Hence, historians gave him a nickname "the emperor of crickets." During his rule, the selling price of crickets soared as many people were addicted to the gambling of cricket fighting. Pu Songling (蒲松齡, A.D. 1640–A.D. 1715), a well-known writer and scholar in the Qing Dynasty, wrote a chapter called "Cu Zhi (促織)" in his literature, *Strange Tales from a Chinese Studio* (聊齋志異) on this social phenomenon.

Fig. 2.1 Cricket fighting in the Ming Dynasty. (The figure was drawn by Olga, a professional artist. The copyright of this figure belongs to the authors)

2.1.2 Eunuch Wei Zhongxian's Story

A representative gambling example among the aristocratic class is the story of Li Jinzhong (李進忠). The original name of Wei was Wei Si (魏四). He changed his name to Li Jinzhong (李進忠) when he was appointed an eunuch in Ming. Unlike most eunuchs who were literally sold to the imperial court, Wei castrated himself and applied for the post of eunuch. His story is interesting as it illustrates the social problems of Chinese workers among the lower social classes during the Ming Dynasty. Wei was born into poverty. He was illiterate. In his youth, he immersed his life in the three major social Chinese sins, namely, gambling, drinking, and visiting prostitutes. Subsequently, he was heavily in debt and was forced by his debtors to separate with his wife and sell his daughter to pay the debt. Heavily in debt, he castrated himself to apply for the position of eunuch in order to escape from debtors (Chen and Xu 2005). During his service as a eunuch, he used a number of tactics to get close to the emperor to consolidate his power base in the government.

One of Wei's hobbies was gambling. In addition to gambling, Wei was also good at playing chess, music, and kickball. He loved to use these skills to win the trust of the emperor. Taking a careful study of the historical records of the Ming Dynasty, we might be able to diagnose Wei as probably suffering from antisocial personality disorder as he demonstrated the following traits (American Psychiatric Association 2013):

1. Lying, deception, and manipulation, for profit or self-amusement
2. Impulsive behavior
3. Irritability and aggression, manifested as frequent assaults on others, or engages in fighting
4. Blatantly disregards safety of self and others
5. A pattern of irresponsibility in one's behavior
6. Lack of remorse nor guilt for his problematic behavior

Wei enjoyed seeking immediate gratification of his desires. In addition to his gambling, he was impulsive and displayed a broad range of symptoms including substance abuse, criminal acts, and a series of antisocial and risk-taking behaviors. Incorporating Blaszczynski and Nower's (2002) classification, Wei could be classified as an antisocial-impulsivist gambler. This type of gamblers has a tendency to engage in a number of antisocial behaviors such as pathological lying, deception, and manipulating others for personal gains. They have little empathy for the concerns and feelings of others. As they often do not understand their own responsibility in their problems, their responses to treatment is often poor (Blaszczynski, personal communication, 2009).

2.2 Types of Common Gambling in Ming Dynasty

Several types of games were popular in Ming. Some of them might have subsequently evolved into current popular games such as mahjong, Tien Gow, and Pai Gow (Zhou 1980; Pan 1600; Feng 2007). They were:

1. Cai Xuan: It was also called "Sheng Guan Tu (陞官圖)" or literally "diagram of promotion of high government officials." This game is theoretically structured on the promotion and the demotion of chancellors according to the bureaucratic system of the Ming Dynasty. The government of Ming rested on a hierarchal system of civil servants and military officers. The players in the game would toss the dices, which determine the movement of the chesses on the diagram. Climbing up the political and social system is the focus of the game. This game was popular among the commoners as it gives the players opportunities to place themselves, in an imaginary fashion, in governmental services. In traditional Chinese culture, joining the government would mean glory for the whole family. A traditional saying captures the dream of the commoners in the Ming Dynasty: when a person enters civil services, all members of the family, including dogs and chickens, will go to heaven (一人得道, 雞犬升天).
2. Xuan Hu Pai: This table game first appeared in late Song and was popular in Ming. There were three to four players. The game later evolved into Tien Gow and Pai Gow. Tien Gow was also a very popular game in the Ming Dynasty.
3. Hanging horse: The most popular gambling tool in late Ming. Another name was "Paper Tiger (紙老虎)" as the cards were made of paper. The origin of hanging horse was not known. The game first appeared before the sixteenth century, but was uncertain whether it emerged in the early or late 1500s. Pang stated in his book *Yezipu* that hanging horse had become very popular near the end of Ming. There were 40 cards in a set of hanging horse. These cards were divided into four divisions – shi zi (十字), wan zi (萬字), suo zi (索子), and wen qian (文錢). There were four players in the game with each player taking eight cards at the beginning of the game. The remaining cards in the deck were put at the center of the gaming table. The players would draw the cards from the center deck and discard the unwanted cards. The winner of each game was the player who achieved the winning set first.

At present, it is still controversial as to whether hanging horse is a new game or evolved from table games such as Xuan Hu Pai. This game was very popular in the Ming Dynasty (Chan et al. 2014; Wu 1992). A Ming writer Feng Menglong (A.D. 1574–A.D. 1646) was a famous enthusiast of the game. He even wrote books to describe the specific skills and strategies in playing it (Feng 2007). Among contemporary researchers in gambling, it is generally believed that the modern version of mahjong evolved from hanging horse (C. C. Chan 2014; Chan et al. 2016).

2.3 The Writings on Gambling Activities in Ming Dynasty

As in Soong and Yuan, most of the people during the Ming Dynasty perceived gambling as a social sin. Some writers, however, accepted gambling as a meaningful and socially constructive pastime. For example, Feng Menglong emphasized the morals and the code of conduct in playing hanging horse. In his book *Pai Jing Shi San Pian* (牌經十三篇), he listed appropriate gaming behaviors and the "misconducts" during the gaming process. Some of the misconducts are excessive talking and superstitious behaviors (Feng 2007). He also taught skills and strategies in playing the game properly.

To sum up, gambling was strictly prohibited in early years of the Ming Dynasty. However, just like the situations in previous dynasties, very few of the anti-gambling laws were carried out as the majority of emperors and chancellors loved gambling.

2.4 Overview of Gambling History in Qing Dynasty

Rulers of Qing were Jurchen (女真族), who came from northeastern China (also called Manchu (满族)). The early emperors prohibited gambling. Kangxi, for example, (康熙, A.D. 1654–A.D. 1722, ruled China during A.D. 1661–A.D. 1722) and Yongzheng (雍正, A.D. 1678–A.D. 1735, ruled China during A.D. 1722–A.D. 1735), the two emperors in early Qing, enforced comprehensive anti-gambling policies and laws. In the history of China, Yongzheng was one of most hardworking and intelligent emperors. He also gave his best efforts on suppressing gambling activities in his young empire. Due to the efforts of these two emperors and their chancellors, there was a significant drop of gambling among the commoners (Shi 2005).

However, national economy and political stability of the Qing Dynasty began to deteriorate in the late stage of Emperor Qianlong's ruling (乾隆, A.D. 1711–A.D. 1799, ruled China during A.D. 1735–A.D. 1795). During that period, gambling became progressively more widespread over the whole country. Furthermore, China was under the attack of foreign powers in the First Opium War (A.D. 1840–A.D. 1842). The resulting defeat of the war was national shame and disgrace to the Qing Dynasty. With the ending of the war, China was forced to sign the first unfair treaty, called the Nanking Treaty, with foreign powers. China was required to pay the foreign powers, including Great Britain and France, a total sum of 21 million dollars in installments over 3 years. The provisions of the treaty also included the cessation of Hong Kong to Britain. The war and subsequent financial difficulties prompted the Qing's government to seek additional funding to finance the operating costs of the kingdom. One resulting policy was granting licenses to operate gambling houses. This was the first time Chinese governing authorities actively legalized gambling and taxed gambling activities. Establishing the legal status of gambling facilitated the accessibility, availability, and acceptability of gambling among the common people. Gambling facilities in the form of "miniature casinos" (in fact the bigger gambling stalls) and horse-racing grounds were built in Tianjin (天津) and Shanghai (上海), as well as in colonized Hong Kong and Macao (Chan et al. 2016; Wu and Lau 2014). As a result of the legalization of gambling, more people, especially the commoners, were attracted to gambling.

2.4.1 Policies Against All Types of Gambling in Early Qing Dynasty

None of the emperors in the Qing Dynasty were addicted to gambling (Chen and He 2006). However, gambling activities, especially among the commoners, were widespread since the early years of Qing. The most common games were hanging horse, Tien Gow, and animal fighting games such as cockfighting, cricket fighting, and quail fighting (鬥鵪鶉). Emperor Kangxi, in the early days of his ruling, passed the legislation to prohibit gambling. Modification of the relevant laws continued for several decades until the era of Qianlong. Compared to the laws of Ming, the anti-gambling laws in "Great Qing Legal Code (大清律例) or *the Laws of the Qing Dynasty*" were the most comprehensive legal rules in Chinese history. It covered extensive regulations and crimes on all individuals involved in gambling. The Great Qing Legal Code included provisions for case precedents. Law executors could utilize precedents as reference before making a sentence. There were several specified governmental departments authorized to execute anti-gambling laws. In Beijing, the capital of Qing, responsible governmental departments included the government office (Chinese name was "Ya men (衙門)"), magistrate of Shun Tian Fu (順天府府尹), and the imperial censor (御史). Every province and army unit also had their special officers to carry out the anti-gambling laws. A variety of punishments were recorded in the Great Qing Legal Code. For the most serious cases, the culprit guilty of the offense could be sentenced to death. Other types of punishment included corporal punishment, imprisonment, flogging, exile, and removal from the government office.

Emperors of early Qing (from Emperor Kangxi to Emperor Qianlong) were determined to ban all types of gambling. During the ruling period of Qianlong, he classified gambling as one of the four evil practices (the other three were theft, fighting, and prostitution). Notwithstanding the royal edict against gambling, the majority of commoners loved gambling. The following is a list of common games during this period:

(a) Weiqi (圍棋)

Weiqi (圍棋) is one of the famous national games in China. In Chinese, "圍" means to besiege and kill 「圍而相殺」 and 棋 means chess. Its name describes its playing method: the player has to use specific strategies to surround the opponent's chesses, and once one's chesses are being surrounded by the opponent's chesses, the player loses the game. In its early history, Weiqi was first called Yiqi (奕棋). In ancient China, it was a game as popular as another ancient game Liubo (六博). Xu Shen (許慎) in his book *Shuowen Jiezi* 《說文解字》 defined "奕" as a kind of chess game「奕,圍棋也。」. Indeed, Weiqi has a long history as its origin can be traced to the prehistorical period of the Xia Dynasty (夏朝). The book *Zhongguo Weiqi Shi* 《中國圍棋史》once mentioned that Weiqi was a common game in the Warring States Period (戰國時期), especially among the nations of Qiguo (齊國) and Luguo (魯國). On the other hand, in the Jin Dynasty (晉朝), Zhang Hua's (張華) *Bowu Zhi* 《博物誌》argued that Weiqi was invented by Emperor Yao (帝堯) or Shun (帝舜) during the Xia Dynasty, who invented the game to train his son「堯造圍棋,以教丹朱。或云舜以子商均愚,故作圍棋以教之。」. However, this assertion lacks substantial evidence. Other researchers argued that the game probably began no later than the Eastern Zhou Dynasty (東周皇朝), i.e., between the Era of Spring and Autumn and the Warring States Period (春秋戰國時期). Most likely, the game originated in the northern part of China. Historian of the Eastern Han Dynasty (東漢), Ban Gu (班固), in his book *Yi Zhi* 《奕旨》, mentioned that "奕棋" was a name commonly used by people living in the Northern region of ancient China「北方之人謂棋為奕。」. Given that people gambled heavily on both Liubo (六博) and Yiqi (奕棋), the term "Boyi" (博奕), a literal combination of the two games in Chinese, originates primarily from the two games. The name is commonly used to describe gambling behaviors in the early Chinese communities.

While the earliest players of Weiqi were mostly nobles and princes in the upper social circle, the game was slowly spread to all social classes. To many Chinese, Weiqi is not only a game but is also essentially a piece of art. He (2001) in his book *Weiqi and Chinese Culture* 《圍棋與中國文化》 asserts that "Arts" represented human desires. Arts should be nonmaterialistic – they signify freedom, happiness, and harmony「藝術是非功利的,以自由、快樂、和和諧為指歸」(He 2001, p.15). The game was invented during the period of the Zhou Dynasty (周朝), when most people in the community enjoyed relative political stability and economic prosperity. Starting in the Zhou Dynasty, the game was considered as one of the six kinds of artistic activities (六藝) which included music (琴), chess (棋), calligraphy (書), drawing (畫), horse riding (馭), and archery (射). These games were considered as the arts of life and were widely enjoyed by people from all walks of life.

Ma Rong (馬融), a famous scholar in the Eastern Han Dynasty, wrote a poem called "*Weiqi Fu*" 《圍棋賦》, in which he described that each set of Weiqi was played on a 3-feet squared chessboard and the game was like a real battle between two parties. He wrote: "略觀圍棋兮,法於用兵;三尺之局兮,為戰斗場." (Playing chess is like fighting in a war; the players need to employ specific strategies and tactics in the game.) There was a Chinese idiom"一子棋錯滿盤皆落索," which means a slight mistake in the chess game can cost ultimate defeat. This idiom later becomes a famous Chinese proverb, advising everyone to be careful in every step we take and in every decision we make.

From a cultural perspective, Weiqi carries some of the core Chinese traditional beliefs. For instance, the rounded chess pieces and squared chessboard symbolize the sky and the Earth, i.e., the Chinese concept of "天圓地方"or, literally, the round sky and the square land. He (2001), in a rather subtle tone, asserts that the game set of "squared against the rounded" and the "black and white chess pieces" demonstrates the beauty of harmony and the concept of *Yin-Yang* (陰陽). On a similar vein of thought, Liu (2007) in his book "The History of Chinese Weiqi" 《中國圍棋史》suggests that the design of Weiqi is more than simple cognitive strategies – it is a game about mathematics and astronomy. The rules of Weiqi involve the application of strategic calculations such as the placement of chess pieces, the sequence of moving them, and positional judgments. The game requires rigorous employment of special attentional processes and cognitive strategies. In essence, the game is more complex than Liubo.

Throughout Chinese history, players often took Weiqi as an excellent game of wisdom. It was a game for the emperors and the aristocratic class. Legend has it that the founding emperor of the Han Dynasty Han Gaozu Liu Bang (漢高祖劉邦) loved the game very much. One important key to the success of Weiqi was the element of self-improvement in cognitive skills, patience, and mental attention and control. Ban Gu (班固) in his writing "*Yi Zhi*" 《奕旨》clearly distinguished the difference between Weiqi and Liubo. The gaming structure of Liubo depends on one's luck, while a player's success in Weiqi is largely determined by his/her use of skills and strategies during the game. In the Han Dynasty, Weiqi was taken as a training tool for *Li* or social etiquette. Liu (2007) argues that the characteristic of Weiqi in the Han Dynasty was about "communication or conversation between the two players in the game." It is a special form of "hand-conversation" (手談). In this regard, instead of having verbal conversation, the game is a communication with another person using the hands. Furthermore, He (2001) contends that the game is carried out as a competition embedded in silent language. It is an elegant skill game that challenges the players.

In Northern and Southern Dynasty (魏晉南北朝), with the development of international commerce, Chinese merchants took Weiqi to Korea, Japan, India, and other Western regions through the Silk Road (絲綢之路). In the Tong and Song Dynasties (唐宋時期), skillful players of Weiqi could obtain an official position named "Officer of Chess" (棋待詔) in governmental services. Their duties were to study the skills of Weiqi and to play the game with the emperor. An officer in the Song Dynasty (宋朝), Xu Xuan (徐鉉), published an article called *The interpretation of Weiqi examples* 《圍棋義例詮譯》, which summarizes a total of 32 common terminologies in the game. His publication greatly contributed to the standardization of the rules in Weiqi. The basic rule of Weiqi is rather simple, i.e., to besiege and kill (圍而相殺). A standard set of Weiqi includes a 19 × 19 square chessboard and two boxes of rounded chess pieces (180 black and 180 white). The chessboard consists of 19 horizontal and vertical lines. The chess pieces should be placed on top of the crossing points. There are in total nine dots being marked on the chessboard for a player to locate the chess, which are called "stars" (星), and the dot in the middle is called "Tianyuan" (天元). He (2001) argues that the earliest chessboard should be at least 7 × 7 instead of the current arrangement. In order to raise the level of excitement and competitiveness, chessboard was further expanded into 13 × 13 and then to the modern-day 19 × 19 one. In 1971, archeologists discovered a Tong Dynasty tomb with a 15 × 15 celadon chessboard in the Hunan Xiangyang (湖南湘陽) province. Liu (2007) believes that 19 × 19 chessboard might be adopted as early as the Period of Three Kingdoms (三國時期). Most likely, the 17 × 17 chessboard was more common in the Northern areas, while the Southern area preferred using the 19 × 19 chessboard. The number of chess pieces depends on the number of lines on the chessboard; for example, 17 × 17 requires 289 chess pieces, while 19 × 19 requires 361 chess pieces. During the early development of the game, Weiqi tools were made of broken woods or stones. Later, the instruments were refined with different precious materials such as celadon.

2.4.2 Ambivalence and Conflict Regarding the Enforcement of Anti-gambling Laws in Qing Dynasty

Gambling was popular in Qing despite the harsh anti-gambling laws. The reasons are many:

1. Disconnection between the anti-gambling laws and social life

   The Qing's laws treated all gamblers as a homogenous group. In other words, heavy punishment would be given to gamblers no matter whether he or she gambled recreationally or compulsively. As the majority of gamblers gambled for fun to kill time during festivals and holidays, the punishment led to much resentment among commoners. In their leisure hours, many commoners gambled in the corners of backyards to escape the police's surveillance. Moreover, a number of governmental officials (especially those local magistrates) were reluctant to prosecute the gamblers who were their friends or relatives.
2. Corruption was severe in the Qing Dynasty. Gamblers could pay off the officials by sending them gifts or money. One of the Chinese idioms best described the attitudes of local government authorities on gambling laws:

   > "The authorities have policies from above while the local law enforcers have their own ways of getting around them (上有政策,下有對策)." The majority of operators of large gambling houses had connection with the local magistrates. In order to escape prosecution, they often offered bribes to governmental officials.

3. The popularity of gambling among the people

   People from all walks of life, ranging from the highest social class (e.g., kinsmen of the emperor) to those who lived in extreme poverty (e.g., beggars), participated in gambling in late Qing (Pan 2008). Gambling also became social events among government officers. The province of Guangdong was notorious for being a gambling hub in late Qing.

2.5 Legalization of Gambling and Features of Gambling Houses in Late Qing

In early Qing, gambling was illegal. However, after the Qing government lost in the Opium Wars to foreign powers (First Opium War happened from A.D. 1840 to A.D. 1842; Second Opium War lasted from A.D. 1856 to A.D. 1860), and spent a significant amount of manpower and financial resources to suppress the rebellion of Taiping Heavenly Kingdom (太平天國) from A.D. 1851 to A.D. 1864 (not until A.D. 1872 did the last military force of Taiping was wiped out), its national finances were drained. The Qing government needed to collect new source of taxes to maintain its regular expenditure and to subsidize the "Westernization Movement (洋務運動, A.D. 1861–A.D. 1895)." The Westernization movement was the Qing government's major attempt to modernize the country and industrialize the military. Out of these concerns, tax from legalized gambling was taken as a viable option. The province of Guangdong (廣東), the area notorious for illegalized gambling, was the first target area of legalized gambling. In A.D. 1885, Zhang Zhidong (張之洞, A.D. 1837–A.D. 1909), the viceroy of Guangdong and Guangxi (廣西), proposed collecting gaming tax by legalizing gambling in Guangdong. Later, Zhang enforced similar legislation in Hubei (湖北) in order to raise money for huge cost in purchasing foreign cannons and warships. In A.D. 1900, Li Hongzhang (李鴻章, A.D. 1823–A.D. 1901), viceroy of Guangdong and Guangxi, declared a total legalization of gambling in Guangdong. On January 27, 10 days after he had arrived Guangdong, the Qing government abolished restrictions on all types of underground gambling activities such as *fantan* (番攤), underground lottery, *Shan Piao* (山票), *Pu Piao* (鋪票), and *Weixing* (闈姓). The Qing government legalized all types of gambling by issuing licenses to those who won the tenders (Liang 2000).

Among these games, *fantan* was very popular among the working class. The game is simple. The gaming instruments consist of a big bowl, a gaming stick, and around 200 coat buttons. Each game set begins as the banker puts a random number of buttons under a big bowl. The players have to wager on the number of buttons under the bowl. They are not required to find out the actual number of buttons as the buttons are counted in the multiples of four. Thus, for instance, if there are 99 buttons in the bowl, the winning number is three (99/4 = 24 + 3). The choices of the bets are 1, 2, 3, and 4. Winners will get three times minus 5% of their bets if they win. Thus, if a player wagers $100 on three and this number comes out as the winning number, he/she will receive $285 ($100 × 3 − $15).There are three factors behind the popularity of *fantan* in the late Qing Dynasty. Firstly, this is a simple game to master and does not require language or cognitive skills. Secondly, this is a fast and continuous game with each set lasted less than 10 min. Thus, an illiterate day laborer, after receiving his salary in the late afternoon, could gamble half an hour in the gambling stall before he goes home for dinner. Thirdly, the game is a table game where the players can compete with each other. We have mentioned that since ancient times, Chinese love games where they can compete with the opponents. Winning of the games is not just about money – it is the glamor and excitement of beating other players in the game. *Fantan* is still available in some casinos in Macao.

The legalization of gambling in China in late Qing was the first governmental measures to openly endorse legalized gambling in the history of China (Pan 2008). However, strictly speaking, the legalization of gambling in Chinese communities began during the British colonization of Hong Kong (where the present authors are compiling this writing). The Qing Dynasty ceded Hong Kong to Great Britain in 1941 after the Opium War. On June 17, A.D. 1844, Governor Sir MacDonnell of Hong Kong proposed gaming tax through licensing and legislation. The Legislative Council of the Hong Kong Government passed the "Maintain Social Order and Weathered Regulations." This law gave police the power to grant licenses to the operation of gambling houses. The regulations were effective until A.D. 1872, when Governor Sir Kennedy was committed to ban gambling in Hong Kong (Chan et al. 2016; Cheung 2009). The Qing Dynasty also gave Macao, a Chinese small island off the southern part of China, to Portugal. In 1847, the Portuguese Macao government legalized gambling in Macao through the introduction of a licensing system. The law marked the beginning of Macao's gaming industry.

Not long after the formal legalization of gambling in China, the number of gambling houses increased at a very fast rate. The profits of gambling houses were enormous. Shrewd Chinese merchants soon built large gambling houses, operated on an accounting and administrative system. These casinos were run with a modern system of staff management. In these establishments, there were specific recruitment and training for dealers, cashiers, security guards, receptionists, and promoters (Lau 1998). These gambling houses attracted people from all walks of life. The following are a number of characteristics of these gambling houses:

1. There were no upper or lower limits of wagers.
2. All were welcome to gamble in these houses. There were neither entrance fees nor dress codes.
3. These gambling houses operated all games in a simple and organized manner. Duration of each game set was short.
4. Operators used high payoff ratio to attract customers.
5. Gambling operators pretended to run the games in a fair manner.
   Gang leaders owned the majority of these gambling houses. Very often, they would set up brothels and opium rooms adjacent to these gambling areas. In many ways, legalized gambling houses epitomized the essence of the four moral sins of men: visiting prostitutes, gambling, drinking, and smoking opium.

2.5.1 Government Lotteries

The last 15 years of the Qing Dynasty witnessed a series of political crises and economic difficulties. China was at war against a coalition of eight countries (八國聯軍) (Japan, Russia, the British Empire, France, the United States, Germany, Italy, and Austria-Hungary) in 1900. With the invasion of the coalition in Beijing in the summer of 1900, China was forced to sign another unfair treaty – Boxer Protocol (辛丑條約), one of the most humiliating political treaties in the history of China. China had to pay a huge amount of money to the eight countries. As the government had little financial reserves, it had to raise extra taxes by issuing lotteries. Beginning in A.D. 1901, the Qing government issued lotteries in Guangdong, Hubei, and Zhejiang (浙江) under the pretext of raising charity fund. Cities like Shanghai, Guangzhou (廣州), Hangzhou (杭州), and Wuhan (武漢) became lottery issuing centers. Three years later, the Qing government issued lotteries in Fujian (福建), Henan (河南), Sichuan (四川), and Liaoning (遼寧) under the slogan of "promoting new policies and restoring the economy." But in fact, taxes collected were mainly used for the war reparations and the everyday expenditure of each province, instead of for the use of charity purposes or economic development. In 1910, 1 year before the ending of the Qing Dynasty, the issuing of lotteries was banned (Min 2000).

2.5.2 Integration of Chinese and Western Gambling Tools in Late Qing

Compared with the previous dynasties, types of gambling in Qing were numerous. Pan (2008) records the following games in the Qing Dynasty:

1. Traditional gambling activities: Pitch-pot games, a game with a long history, received popularity among the commoners in Qing (Ding 2002).
2. Archery: Manchu Bannermen (八旗兵) was the major military force of Qing. All soldiers in Bannermen were from Manchu. The majority of these soldiers were proficient in equestrian archery. At the beginning of the Qing Dynasty, the emperors banned all types of gambling except equestrian archery as they saw this game as a competition rather than a type of gambling. Equestrian archery has a long tradition in Manchu. While the focus of the game is a competition of speed and accuracy, some riders utilize their skills of archery to gamble during competition. This game has never been popular among the commoners as the game required a number of horses and large racing field. Furthermore, this is a violent, and somewhat, dangerous game as serious injuries would happen during the competition. This game disappeared from historical records after Emperor Jiaqing (嘉慶, A.D. 1760–A.D. 1820, ruled China during A.D. 1796–A.D. 1820) assumed office in A.D. 1796.

3. Mahjong: Mahjong became one of the most popular types of gambling in late Qing. Chan et al. (2016) give a good description of the game. They write:

   > It is commonly played by four players (with some three player variations found in South Korea and Japan). The game is played with a set of 144 tiles based on Chinese characters and symbols, although some regional variations use a different number of tiles. In most variations, each player begins by receiving 13 tiles. In turn players draw and discard tiles until they complete a winning hand using the 14th drawn tile to form four groups (each with 3 tiles) and a pair. There are standard rules about how a piece is drawn, the use of simples (numbered tiles) and honors (winds and dragons), the kinds of groups, and the order of drawing the tiles. There are many regional variations in the rules, with the most popular version being the Cantonese version. (p. 4)

   In the Qing Dynasty, people from all walks of life enjoyed mahjong. Empress Dowager Cixi (慈禧太后, A.D. 1835–A.D. 1908), the most powerful political figure in late Qing, was addicted to mahjong. While it is basically a chance game, the players can employ skills and strategies to maximize one's probability in winning the game. During the game, the players often gossip on their personal issues and relationships. During the Qing Dynasty, a lot of governmental officials and rich people loved playing mahjong. Legend has it that some players wagered more than 50,000 ingots of gold in each game (Xu Year unknown).
4. Pacapio (白鴿票): Pacapio evolved from pigeon racing in Guangdong Province in Mainland China in the late Qing Dynasty. Upon their discussion on gambling in Macao, Chan et al. (2016) record the history of this game:

   > In the earlier version of the game, birds were identified with names based on traditional Chinese literature known as "Qianziwen"(千字文, Thousand-Character Essay). The players can place bets on the competing pigeons. This racing later evolved to a game similar to a lucky draw, in which players wagered on 10 of 80 characters written on a piece of paper. The players won if five or more chosen characters matched the drawn characters. Today, the game employs numbers instead of text and the manual control balloting has been replaced by computerization…………Pacapio games are still available in Macau in Hotel Lisboa (葡京酒店) and in Wing Hing Pacapio Centre (榮興電腦白鴿票投注站). (p. 13)

   Thus, Pacapio is largely a chance game, where the player has to pick 10 characters out of a list of 80. As almost no skill is involved in the game, it is very popular among farmers and working-class laborers.
5. Cockfighting (鬥雞)
   As a game, cockfighting (Fig. 2.2) is one of the special games only found in ancient China. Even now, it is a popular game in many regions of China. This section will examine the origins and the development of this game in ancient China.

Gambling with animals and insects were common in many countries for centuries. Bullfighting in Spain (corrida de toros), spider fighting in the Philippines, and cockfighting in China were good examples of cultural heritages in these countries. In China, the history of animal sports might begin with the transformation of a nomadic economy to a farming economy. In a farming community in ancient China, people started to breed their own poultries for food or as a commercial product for sale. Leisure activities were few. Thus, the first animal games often involved house-

Fig. 2.2 Cockfighting remained popular in several dynasties in China. (The figure was drawn by Olga, a professional artist. The copyright of this figure belongs to the authors)

hold pets. In Europe, dog racing and horse racing were noble games in medieval times. In China, cockfighting (鬥雞) and cricket fighting (鬥蟀) were among the first games recorded in Chinese history.

As a leisure game, the history of cockfighting might begin as early as the Zhou Dynasty (周朝). In rural communities, farmers often chose male cocks for the cockfighting game. The rules of the game were extremely cruel. Cocks had to fight until they passed out during the fighting. The owners of the cocks often provided special armor to the cocks to enhance their fighting ability. Furthermore, citing from "Zuo Zhuan" 《左傳》, Robert Cutter (1989) in his book *The Brush and the Spur* writes: "When the cocks of Ji and Hou fought, Ji put mustard on his gamecock, while Hou made metal spurs for his. '季郈之鬥雞,季氏介其雞,郈氏為之金距'(p.10)." This short story clearly describes the scene of cockfighting. The mustard was intended to make the cocks excited and angry during the fighting. Guo and Xiao (1995) in their book *The History of Chinese Gambling* argue that cock owners often applied different tricks to enhance their chances of winning. The most common methods are to put "wolf's grease" on the fighting cocks and the use of armor to cover the claws of the cocks. Prince Cao Zhi (曹植) in the Era of Three Kingdoms (三國時期) once wrote a poem called *Cockfighting* 《鬥雞篇》. He vividly described the game: "The cock tweeted loudly to the sky and spread its wings. It is hoped that, with the help of the wolf's grease, it can always win the fight." 《長鳴入青雲,扇翼獨翱翔。願蒙狸膏助,常得擅此場。》. The employment of the grease of wolf in the game might need more explanation. Ancient Chinese believed that in the animal world, wolves hunt cocks for food. Thus, the male cocks would feel threatened by the smell of wolf's grease (狸膏). Consequently, the cocks would escape from the other fighting cocks. This procedure of covering cocks with wolf's grease, though irrational from the eyes of modern men, might well illustrate how illiterate farmers in ancient rural China projected personal control, though illusory, over a gambling situation. Contemporary theories of gambling may explain that gamblers employ, rather unconsciously, subjective strategies to increase their probability of winning (Ohtsuka and Chan 2010). Such measures, including personal superstitious beliefs and behaviors, might not be efficient in increasing their chances of winning.

In the Zhou Dynasty, many players trained their own fighting cocks to compete in the game. In "*Liezi Huangdi*" 《列子.黃帝篇》, a story described the training process of fighting cocks. The training took nearly a month. Each cock was trained to be ruthless and fearless in the face of threats from other cocks. There is a Chinese idiom known as 「呆若木雞」, literally meaning "as fearless and emotionless as a wooden cock," which describes a person being emotionless and standing still. This idiom might originate from the training of cockfighting.

The popularity of cockfighting in Chinese communities reached its peak in the Tong Dynasty (唐朝). At that time, players established a high standard in cockfighting. Even the emperors loved cockfighting. Among the most famous players was Emperor Tang Xuanzong (唐玄宗). Li ordered his councilors to establish cock training centers and cockfighting venues for his entertainment. Guo and Xiao reported that Xuanzong collected thousands of male cocks in his nurturing centers. He also had 500 servants to take care of and train the cocks. A brief story in *The New Book of Tang* 《新唐書》records: "As the Emperor loved cockfighting, the aristocrats and individuals in the upper class loved the game as well. Commoners could only play with wooden cocks" (as there were not many male cocks available in the community) 「玄宗好鬥雞,貴臣戚皆尚之,貧者或弄木雞。」《新唐書.五行志》.

Cock trainers in the Tong Dynasty had a special status in the royal palace. Among those cock trainers, the most famous one was Jia Chang (賈昌), the son of Jia Zhong (賈忠). Legend has it that he could communicate with the fighting cocks, though at present it is difficult, or even impossible, to validate such claims. The Emperor Xuanzong (唐玄宗) loved his skills and talents and granted him the title of "Cock General"《雞將軍》. A poem composed in the Tong Dynasty placed a sarcastic view on the popularity of cockfighting at that time. In *Dongcheng Father Biography* 《東城老父傳》, where the author Chen Hongzu (陳鴻祖) (n.d.) wrote: "A man does not need to learn to write. Rather, obtaining knowledge and skills in cockfighting and horse riding grant better opportunities than acquiring knowledge in books."《生兒不用識文字,鬥雞走馬勝讀書。》

However, cockfighting, as a game, lost its popularity after the Tong Dynasty, though it remained as a game of choice among the commoners in the Yuan (元朝), Ming (明朝), and Qing Dynasty (清朝) till the present age. Hon (2007) in *The Gaming Cultures of Ancient China: The Leisure Game of Chess* 《中國古代游戲文化-閒敲棋子落燈花》reports that at present cockfighting is classified into four main categories: Central Cockfighting (中原鬥雞), Zhangzhou Cockfighting (漳州

鬥雞), Tu Lufan Cockfighting (吐魯番鬥雞), and Xishangbanna Cockfighting (西雙版納鬥雞). In particular, Zhangzhou Cockfighting is the biggest group in southern China, while Central Cockfighting dominates northern China. The Kaifeng Cockfighting (開封鬥雞) is the most well-known group among those in Central Cockfighting. Every year, a national cockfighting competition is held on the second of the first month of the lunar calendar (正月初二), and three more competitions will be arranged before Ching Ming Festival (清明節) in March or April. The venue is known as "cockfighting crater" (鬥雞坑), as the fighting platform is built lower than the ground surface. The general rule for cockfighting is simple. Two cocks have to be of similar weight, similar head size, and similar age. Like kickboxing, before the competition, two cocks greet each other ritually. After the judge rings the bell and signals the players to "release the cocks" (撒雞), the competition begins. Each round of fighting lasts for approximately 15 min. The owner of the cock can request for a rest after one to two rounds. Sometimes, a cockfighting competition may take a whole day, and its champion represents a huge pride to the owner. In order not to disturb the cocks' fight, the spectators of the game are not allowed to yell at the cocks.

Why is cockfighting popular in Chinese society throughout the years? In examining Chinese business culture, De Mente (1994) argues:

> In Confucian terms, the ideal man was described as a 'gentleman,' meaning one who was upright and moral in all things and observed the proper rituals of etiquette in his behavior… Propriety, as espoused by Confucius, is based on three principles: Respect for human dignity, fairness (what is unfair to one is unfair to all) and "reversibility" (willingness to be the recipient of one's own manners and actions). Another ingredient always added to these principles is 'duty' – one's duty to parents, to employers, to customers, and to the state. (p. 21)

There is a famous idiom in Chinese culture: "君子動口不動手," meaning a gentleman should refrain from hurting others physically and impersonal conflicts should be dealt with by words rather than violence. This demonstrates the basics of *Li* in Chinese culture. This principle is evident in Chinese Kung Fu training and competitions. Kung Fu masters often teach their disciples propriety and respect for human lives and dignity in fighting. Thus, the contemporary mix of martial arts and boxing, where hurting the opponents severely is the rule of the game, is never a popular spectator sports among ethnic Chinese. However, the principle of *Li* and respect do not extend to animals. Even today, the Western principle of animal rights is alien to the majority of Chinese people. In Chinese contemporary diet, we eat almost any type of insects and animals – snakes, roaches, cats, dogs, bears, etc. The list is endless. This can explain why the cruel and inhumane treatment of cocks in cockfighting is generally acceptable in ancient China.

Secondly, as a spectator sport, cockfighting is an excellent cognitive game as the owners of the cocks have to employ specific breeding methods, diets, and skill and strategies during the game. The game also does not require a specific level of literacy and mathematical skills. Thus, it is a fun game for the illiterate rural farmers.

2.6 Conclusion on Chinese Gambling History: From Ancient China to the End of Feudal Period

In Chap. 1 and this chapter, we have traced the development of gambling from ancient China until the end of the Qing Dynasty, the last imperial period in China. In these 4000 years, we have seen gaming activities going through periods of changes and adaptations to the needs, crises, and social and cultural developments of the Chinese people. Incorporating contemporary psychological theories of gambling, we have a number of interesting observations:

(a) From *Bo* to *Du*: The Chinese word for "gambling" comprises of two parts: wagering (*Du*) and competition (*Bo*). *Du* carries a connotation of betting and winning, while *Bo* emphasizes more on the entertainment value of the gaming activity. From ancient China to the Tang Dynasty, for the majority of Chinese gamblers, the main motivation of gambling was for fun and leisure. For instance, most of the players in games like *Liu Bo*, *Chu Pu*, *Go*, and kickball participated in the activities for leisure or recreational purpose. For these players, the motivation for joining the gaming activities was the excitement and fun of the game. For them, the wagering and winning of money was secondary to the entertainment value of the game. In other words, the early Chinese gamblers gambled with money and not for the money (C. C. Chan 2014). For many of these players, the gaming activity represented a fun and shared social activity where they found meaning and purposes in life. A good example was the game of kickball. This game was probably one of the first spectator games that attracted a wide audience. The game probably became popular for the soldiers who left home for wars during the Han Dynasty. To the soldiers, the game was a leisure activity where they could temporarily escape from the worries and pains of wars. On this issue, contemporary gambling researchers have provided an excellent observation:

> Alienation, as the term is used by sociologists, refers to a condition in which certain individuals are removed from the decision-making processes which govern the greater part of their daily lives. .... Many sociologists believe that the advent of modern industrialization, with its time clocks, monotonous assembly line labor, and large bureaucratic organizations, has caused workers to feel uncreative, isolated, unable to exercise any initiative, and lacking any meaning of control in their lives. Consequently, many of the first sociologists to consider gambling attributed it to the strong feelings of alienation encountered by a large segment of society. (Aasved 2003, p. 27)

Thus, the majority of players in ancient China did not describe their activities as "gambling" or "賭" in Chinese but as "playing" or "玩."

However, the nature of gambling gradually shifted from "*Bo*" to "*Du*" during the Song Dynasty, as there was an increase in large-scaled urbanization and the development of commerce and trading at that time. Gambling stalls known as "Ju Fangs," usually run by gangs and criminals, started to appear in major cities.

Gambling became more widespread among the commoners. The main motivation for gambling evolved from fun to monetary gains.

(b) From noble cognitive games to games of chance: The first Chinese games of *Liubo* and *Chupu* were originally games enjoyed by the aristocratic class. The players had to employ cognitive strategies and tactics to win the game. During the process of the game, the players usually assumed a quiet and noble manner. In other words, the early were "gentlemen's games" designed for the leisure fun of the noble class. However, as gambling activities became more secularized, the meaning of the games slowly evolved to a competition of beating the opponents and winning the money. Cognitive games, which required longer time to play, were replaced by quick chance games. One example was "*Fan Tan*," where the players had to guess the numbers of buttons in a bowl. Technically, no skills were involved in this game. In addition, as more players were involved in spectator games such as cockfighting and cricket fighting, the process of the games involved more violence as the players often yelled at each other during the games. In other words, the nature of "*Li*" and the nobility of the games slowly disappeared.

(c) From prohibition to regulation: In our review on the cultural and historical developments of gambling in China, we have witnessed a process of active governmental prohibitions with severe punishments to the process of decriminalization and regulation. We have asserted in Chap. 1 that gambling, as a social behavior, has been considered as one of the four major sins of Chinese men – the other being visiting prostitutes, smoking opium, and drinking. Thus, it comes to no surprise that almost all imperial governments levied severe punishments on gamblers. One of the cruelest punishments was cutting off the hands of gamblers in the early Ming Dynasty. However, governmental attitude in the later years of the Qing Dynasty changed drastically as the government needed to collect gambling taxes. The move from prohibition to regulation and taxation mirrors the development of the gaming industry in Australia (McMillan 1996). Furthermore, in the Qing Dynasty, the Chinese community became more tolerant on gambling activities provided they were carried out peacefully and under governmental control. It should be noted that the majority of Chinese players were recreational players, who found gambling a leisure and fun activity. Maybe what Volberg and Williams (2014) argue is appropriate in describing the cultural and historical developments of gambling in China: The majority of people participated in gambling because they enjoyed and gained benefits from these activities. For these individuals, especially farmers and illiterate laborers, gambling was generally a positive experience. Only, for a minority of players, gambling was associated with difficulties of varying severity and duration. To understand the problems and severity of these disordered gamblers, we need to obtain studies on the prevalence and state of gambling, which will be discussed in our next chapter.

References

Aasved, M. (2003). *The sociology of gambling*. Springfield: Charles C Thomas.

Blaszczynski, A. (2009). Problem gambling: We should measure harm rather than 'cases. *British Journal of Addiction, 104*(7), 1070–1074.

Blaszczynski, A., & Nower, L. (2002). A pathways model of problem and pathological gambling. *Addiction, 97*(5), 487–499.

Chan, C. C. (2014a, July). *A model on the pathways development of Chinese problem gamblers in Hong Kong and Macau*. Paper presented at the international conference on Gaming, Leisure and Entertainment, Macau, China.

Chan, Y. Y. (2014b). *Last gambling in suppression in aavarice*. National Miao Li Senior High School (陳昱蓉. (2014). 壓倒貪婪的最後一場賭博. 國立苗栗高中). Retrieved from http://www.docin.com/p-807619834.html

Chan, C. C., Li, W. L., & Leung, C. I. (2014). *The psychology of gambling* (2nd ed.). Mother Mary Social Studies Centre. (陳智川、李威廉、梁頌業. (2014). 賭博心理學(第二版. 澳門高志慈社會研究中心). Retrieved from http://caritas.org.mo/zh-hant/publication/other-publications

Chan, C. C., Li, W. L., & Leung, C. I. (2016). *Problem gambling in Hong Kong and Macao: Etiology, prevalence and treatment*. Singapore: Springer.

Chen, H. Z. (n.d.). *Dongcheng father's biography* (陳鴻祖. 東城老父傳). Retrieved from http://leachin.blogspot.hk/2013/04/blog-post_4364.html

Chen, W. Z., & He, W. R. (2006). *Gambling history of China*. Kaohsiung Municipal Rueisiang High School (陳文智及何宛儒. (2006).中國賭博史.高雄市立瑞祥高級中學). Retrieved from http://lib.rssh.kh.edu.tw/essay/95essay/060.pdf

Chen, S. L., & Xu, W. J. (2005). *Narrating the sixteen emperors of Ming Dynasty*. Taipei: Linking Publishing. (陳時龍及許文繼. (2005).正說明朝十六帝. 台北聯經出版社).

Cheung, L. H. (2009). *Twenty-eight Governors in Hong Kong*. Hong Kong: Joint Publishing. (張連興. (2009). 香港二十八總督. 三聯書店(香港)有限公司).

Criminal Law of Ming Dynasty. (1374). (大明律集解附例 (1374)). Retrieved from https://zh.wikisource.org/zh-hant/%E5%A4%A7%E6%98%8E%E5%BE%8B

Cutter, R. J. (1989). *The brush and the spur: Chinese culture and cockfight*. Hong Kong: The Chinese University Press.

De Mente, B. L. (1994). *Chinese etiquette & ethics in business* (2nd ed.). Chicago: NTC Business Books.

Ding, R. K. (2002). *Liu Hu*. Hong Kong: Chungwa Bookstore. (丁柔克. (2002). 柳弧. 中華書局).

Feng, M. L. (2007). *Feng Meng Long Quan Ji*. Jiangsu: Phoenix Publishing House. (馮夢龍 (2007). 馮夢龍全集. 鳳凰出版社. 江蘇).

Great Qing Legal Code. (1644–1971). (大清律例. (1644–1971). Retrieved from https://zh.wikisource.org/wiki/%E5%A4%A7%E6%B8%85%E5%BE%8B%E4%BE%8B/%E5%88%91%E5%BE%8B#.E5.88.91.E5.BE.8B.C2.B7.E9.9B.9C.E7.8A.AF

Guo, S. L., & Xiao, M. H. (1995). *History of gambling in China*. Beijing: China Social Sciences Press. (郭雙林及蕭梅花. (1995). 中華賭博史.中國社會科學出版社).

He, Y. P. (2001). *Weiqi and the Chinese culture*. Ren Min Press. (何云波. (2001). *圍棋與中國文化*. 人民出版社.). ISBN 9787010034621.

Hon, M. W. (2007). *Chinese ancient gambling culture: The leisure game of chess*. Yunnan, China: Yunnan People's Publishing House. (韋明鏵. (2007). 中國古代游戲文化-閒敲棋子落燈花.雲南人民出版社).

Lau, N. Y. (1998). Important questions of investigating gambling history: Reflections from *History of gambling in China* (S. L. Guo, & M. H. Xiao, Eds). *Journal of Guangxi University (Philosophy and Social Science), 20*(4), 49–54. https://doi.org/10.13624/j.cnki.jgupss.1998.04.016 (柳立言. (1998).研究賭博史的重要問題–從郭雙林及蕭梅花《中華賭博史》談起).

Liang, Q. C. (2000). *Biography of Li Hong Zhang*. Tianjin: Tianjin Baihua Literature and Art Publishing House. (梁啟超. (2000).李鴻章傳.天津百花文藝出版社).

Liu, S. C. (2007). *The history of Chinese Weiqi*. Chengdu Times Press. (劉善承. (2007). *中國圍棋史*. 成都時代出版社). ISBN 9787807055433.

McMillan, J. (1996). *Gambling cultures: Studies in history and interpretation*. London: Routledge.

Min, J. (2000). Flooding and outlaw of lotteries in late Qing Dynasty – A hundred year's history of lotteries. *Bai Nian Chao, 11*. (闵杰 (2000). 清末彩票的泛滥与取缔—彩票百年史之三. 百年潮,第*11*期).

Ohtsuka, K., & Chan, C. C. (2010). Donning red underwear to play mahjong: Superstitious beliefs and problem gambling among Chinese mahjong players in Macau. *Gambling Research, 22*(3), 18–33.

Pan, H. G. (2008). Gambling and anti-gambling in Qing Dynasty. *Jianghan Tribune, 9*, 61–66. (潘洪鋼. (2008). 清代的賭博與禁賭. 江漢論壇,*9*, 61–66).

Pang, Z. H. (1600). *Yezipu*. (潘之恆 (1600s). 葉子譜). Retrieved from http://www.5ebook.net/html/122-7/7078.htm

Pu, S. L. (1740). *Strange tales from a Chinese studio*. (蒲松齡. (1740). 聊齋志異).

Shi, X. Y. (2005). Overview of gambling in each dynasty in China. *Decision and Information, 245*, 62–63. (石肖瑜. (2005).中國歷代賭博概覽. 決策與信息, *245*, 62–63).

Tang, G., & Zhu, Y. Y. (2016). *History of Ming*. Hong Kong: Chung Hwa Book. (湯綱 及朱元寅. (2016). 明史. 中華書局(香港)有限公司.

Volberg, R. A., & Wiliams, R. J. (2014). Epidemiology: An international perspective. In D. S. C. Richard, A. Blaszczynski, & L. Nower (Eds.), *The Wiley-Blackwell handbook of disordered gambling* (pp. 26–48). New York: Wiley. https://doi.org/10.1002/9781118316078.ch2.

Wu, W. Y. (1992). *Huan Kou Ji Lue*. Shanghai: Shanghai Classical Literature Press. (吳偉業. (1992). 綏寇紀略. 上海古籍出版社).

Wu, A. M. S., & Lau, J. T. F. (2014). Gambling in China: Socio-historical evolution and current challenges. *Addiction, 110*, 210–216. https://doi.org/10.1111/add.12710.

Xu, S. (100–121). *Shouwen Jiezi*. (許慎. (100–121年). 說文解字). Retrieved from http://ctext.org/shuo-wen-jie-zi/zh.

Xu, Y. (Year unknown). *The interpretation of Weiqi examples*. 徐鉉(年代不詳). *圍棋義例詮譯*.

Zhang, H. (n.d.). *Bowu Zhi* (張華《博物誌》). Retrieved from https://zh.wikisource.org/wiki/%E5%8D%9A%E7%89%A9%E5%BF%97.

Zhou, S. (1980). *Huang Hun Xiao Pin*. Shanghai: Shanghai Classical Literature Press. (周劭. (1980s).黃昏小品.上海古籍出版社).

Chapter 3
The State and Prevalence of Gambling in Chinese Communities

While writing on the future of commercial gambling in Macao, Chan et al. (2016) conclude:

> We do look forward to seeing the transformation of Macao from a city of gambling to a metropolitan city of global tourism and leisure destination – An Asian icon of gaming and prosperity. And as long as commercial gambling is carried out responsibly and morally, it can offer hopes and dreams of a better livelihood for the 640,000 residents in the small enclave in the southern part of China (p. 152).

The authors are optimistic about the development and contribution of gambling to Macao. As a special administrative region (SAR) in the People's Republic of China (PRC), Macao sees commercial activities as the heart and soul of the city's economy. In the last 15 years, Macao government's conscious efforts in building integrated casino resorts as a means of business development have created and initiated progressive epigenetic differentiations of economic opportunities for this small city and its neighboring areas. Ironically speaking, gambling is illegal in China; except for state-owned lotteries which are operated under the blessings and close monitors of state officials, all types of gambling are outlawed by the Communist regime. Hence, should the PRC extend the Macao model to all areas in China? Should casino resorts be built in other major cities of China? Why does the Chinese government outlaw all gaming opportunities except state-sponsored lotteries? Before we can realistically respond to these daunting questions, we need to have a clear understanding of the state and prevalence of gambling in China. In this chapter, we will first explore the current state of gambling and the prevalence of problem gambling in China. Then, we will survey on the state of gambling in two special administrative regions in the PRC, namely, Hong Kong and Macao. We will finally conclude this chapter with a study on Taiwan, the largest Chinese community outside the PRC.

C. C. Chan et al., *The Psychology of Chinese Gambling*,
https://doi.org/10.1007/978-981-13-3486-3_3

3.1 From Gambling to Lottery Betting: Gaming Development During the Recent 30 Years in Mainland China

Gambling is illegal in China. Thus, if the police find two individuals playing a card game with money in a small restaurant after lunch, the state officials can charge them with a criminal offense. At present, only public lotteries are sanctioned by the Chinese government. There are two types of lotteries issued by the government of the PRC: China sports lottery (中國體育彩票) and China welfare lottery (中國福利彩票). These lotteries are issued by the State Sports General Administration of Sports Lottery Management Center (國家體育總局體育彩票管理中心), also known as the China Sports Lottery Management Center (中國體育彩票管理中心) and Chinese Welfare Lottery Center (中國福利彩票發行中心), respectively. Under bureaucratic hierarchy, the China Sports Lottery Management Center is placed under the direct supervision of the State Sports General Administration (國家體育總局), while Chinese Welfare Lottery Center belongs to the Ministry of Civil Affairs (民政部) (Li 2009). Both governmental agencies are run by civil servants. Thus, it is fair to say that all the gaming policies and operations are strictly monitored by the central government. As such, gaming policies have to abide by the regulations and interests, both socially and economically, of the state (Fig. 3.1).

3.1.1 Developmental History of Lottery in Mainland China

The origin of lottery can be traced all the way to the banking system during the early years of the PRC. In the 1950s, in order to encourage people to save money, the Agricultural Bank of China (中國農業銀行) and the People's Bank of China (中國人民銀行) issued certificates of deposit or regular small saving rewardable plan (定期定額有獎儲蓄存單). In these plans, the investors, usually humble farmers with

Fig. 3.1 (**a, b**) Welfare lottery selling venues in Shenzhen. (Photos taken by Li Wai Lim on June 9, 2017)

meager income, could put in a small amount of money in these certificates, which carried a small chance of winning a larger amount of money. By investing in these certificates, the farmers could have the benefit of locking the money in a bank. Certificates of deposit or regular small saving rewardable plan were the earliest lotteries since the establishment of the PRC (Cai Piao Jiu Jiu 2016). The sole purpose was to help the commoners, especially poor farmers, to save money. By investing in these certificates, the farmers could always receive the principal they invested. There was no financial provision for any loss in this kind of investment (Figs. 3.2a and 3.2b).

These figures were drawn by Olga, a professional artist. The copyright of these figures belongs to the authors.

This first saving/lottery plan was prematurely aborted by the Chinese government with the outbreak of the Cultural Revolution in 1966. During these years, the ruling aristocracy, headed by Mao Zedong, attempted to eradicate capitalism in China. Ruthless measures and punishment were inflicted on entrepreneurs. Business companies were shut down. Buddhist temples and churches were destroyed, and thousands of businessmen were sent to undergo the so-called labor reform (勞動改造) and cognitive reform (思想改造). The movement was initially a political campaign, but the 10 years' political and social unrests took away the lives of millions of Chinese, as well as the budding business system of the young Republic. Economic recession and extreme poverty were the two major social consequences of the Revolution. In the area of gaming, the disruption of the country's economy and the

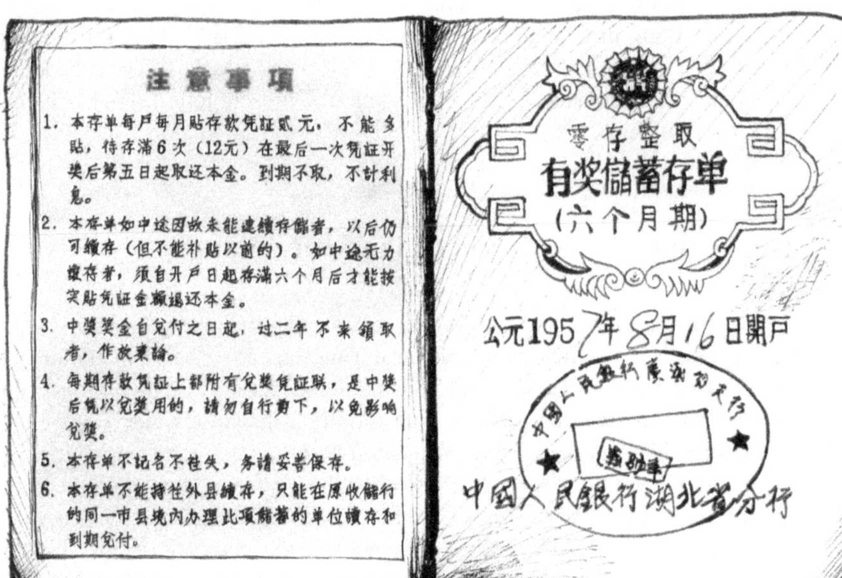

Fig. 3.2a Regular small saving rewardable plan issued by the People's Bank of China in 1957, Hubei. (Source: He, X. (December 12, 2011). Yan Zhao Wan Bao)

Fig. 3.2b The front side of a small saving rewardable plan, with a face value at RMB 50. (Source: He, X. (December 12, 2011). Yan Zhao Wan Bao)

bank system resulted in the cessation of the rewardable saving plans. The Cultural Revolution ended in 1976. In 1980, President Deng Xiaoping enforced new economic reforms, known as "Four Modernization," setting out strategic developments in agriculture, industry, national defense, and technological advancement. The new policies, based more on the principle of capitalism, brought in new reforms and measures that revitalized the Chinese economy. In 1981, the People's Bank of China and Agricultural Bank of China resumed issuing the scheduled saving rewardable plan (按期有獎儲蓄存單), with face values at RMB 5 and RMB 10. The scheduled rewardable plan can be considered as the forerunner of present lotteries in Mainland China (Cai Piao Jiu Jiu 2016).

3.2 Developmental History of China Sports Lottery

Sports lottery has a long history. The earliest recorded sports lottery was horse racing sweepstakes (馬票), which were popular during the early twentieth century in big cities such as Shanghai, Tianjin, and Wuhan. Horse racing, with its origins from Medieval European aristocratic nobility, was initially a spectator game. During the early 1920s, foreign businessmen in China started horse racing in the major cities of China. At that time, betting was relatively simple: the players could bet on the winners of each race, named "win" (獨贏), or the first three fastest horses in the race named "place" (位置). One interesting observation is that the majority of Chinese players had never tried horseback riding; some never saw a running horse before they bet on the game. For the majority of Chinese players, winning the sweepstakes was the major motivation for participating in this European spectator game. Horse racing is the first major game in China that combined a healthy and elegant sports event with gambling. However, horse racing was banned after the establishment of the PRC in 1949. We believe the main reason for the banning of the game is that the new Communist regime could not accept gambling and horse racing, which were considered as Western capitalist pastime.

After the cessation of the Cultural Revolution in 1976, China experienced serious financial difficulties. When President Deng Xiaoping assumed office in 1980, the new young government had to find new ways to finance the various reform programs. In the minds of the administrators of the new government, lotteries were the probable solutions. Among the first major lotteries, one was the financing of "Beijing International Marathon" in 1984. The Chinese Athletic Association (中國田徑協會) and Chinese Sports Service Company (中國體育服務公司) issued lotteries for the Marathon event from October 10, 1984 to the noon of October 13, 1984. The drawing of winning numbers was held at 10 a.m. on October 14, 1984. The front side of the lottery ticket showed the drawing of seven athletes running side by side. The size of the lottery was 12.5 cm x 7 cm. The amount of issuance was 50,000. Two weeks later on November 1, 1984, in order to raise money for the construction of Fujian Province Sports Center, the Fujian government issued sports lottery, named as "Fujian Province Sports Center Memorial Lottery of Construction (福建省體育中心建設紀念獎券)." Since then, local governments of several provinces (such as Guangdong, Zhejiang, Sichuan, Hubei) successively authorized lotteries for the purpose of collecting money for the building of infrastructures. However, there was no formal regulation to monitor lottery issuance at that time. Consequently, some industrial and commercial enterprises, as well as some local governments, often regarded lottery issuance as a viable venue to collect money from the general public. This resulted in the excessive issue of lotteries. Consequently, the State Council (國務院) passed the "Notice on Stopping Excessive Lottery (國務院關於制止濫發各種獎券的通知)" in order to closely monitor the issuance of different types of lotteries on March 4, 1985. Furthermore, the State Council also requested local governments to administer close supervision on the use of money collected from the sales of lotteries. The law successfully prohibited private enterprises from over-issuing lotteries, but it had little influence on local governments.

The first Chinese sports lottery, named "The Sixth National Lottery Fund," was launched in 1986. Its main purpose was to raise fund for the Sixth National Games (第六屆全國運動會). Between 1988 and 1990, there were 898 types of sports lottery related to "The Eleventh Asian Games (第十一屆亞洲運動會)," which was held in Beijing from September 22, 1990 to October 7, 1990. This was also the first time China organized such a major international sports event.

The year of 1994 witnessed a monumental milestone in the development of China sports lottery. On April 5, 1994, the National Sports Commission Sports Lottery Management Center was established and was endowed by the State Council the sole right to issue sports lottery. The major task of the newly established official Sports Lottery Management Center was to unify management, printing, and issuance of sports lottery in Mainland China. On May 31, the State Council commissioned the People's Bank of China to be the sole institution in charge of the official lottery issued in China. In the same year, the sports lottery was also officially renamed as "China Sports Lottery." About 2 months later, national sports director Mr. Wu Shao Zu (伍紹祖) signed the "Twentieth Orders (第20號令)," which established the legitimate status of the sports lottery industry. Since then, funds raised from sports lottery would be used for subsidizing sports events and the development of sports in China. Between 1994 and 1995, the face value of sports lottery was RMB 2 (About US $1.3). At that time, types of sports lottery included the traditional type (傳統型), the instant type (即開型彩票), and the combined (traditional plus instant type (即開與傳統結合型) ones. Sales of sports lottery between 1994 and 1995 are worth RMB 1 billion. In 1999, sports lottery sales increased tremendously to RMB 4 billion. One year later, it further skyrocketed to RMB 9 billion (Qianzhan Research Institute of Products, March 18, 2014).

In 2000, the authority responsible for managing official lottery rested in the Ministry of Finance (財政部) (originally managed by the People's Bank of China) (Li 2009). The Ministry of Finance is responsible for auditing the issuance of lotteries, determining locations, and the supervision of sales. It operates directly under the authority of the State Council (Chen et al., December, 2013).

Figure 3.3 illustrates the structure of the two types of lottery administration.

In 2001, the State Council expanded the size of lottery issuance and adjusted the proportion of public welfare fund (公益金). In general, the expenditure of sports lottery can be divided into three parts: winning bonus, administrative costs, and public welfare funds:

1. Winning bonus: It is paid to lottery buyer(s) who win(s) the bet. The percentage of bonus should not be less than 45% of the sports lottery fund.
2. Administrative costs: The costs are kept at 25% of the sports lottery fund, including 4% of sports lottery printing fees, 1% of sports lottery issuing fee by the China Sports Lottery Management Center, and 20% of retail and sales of sports lottery fee by local authorities.

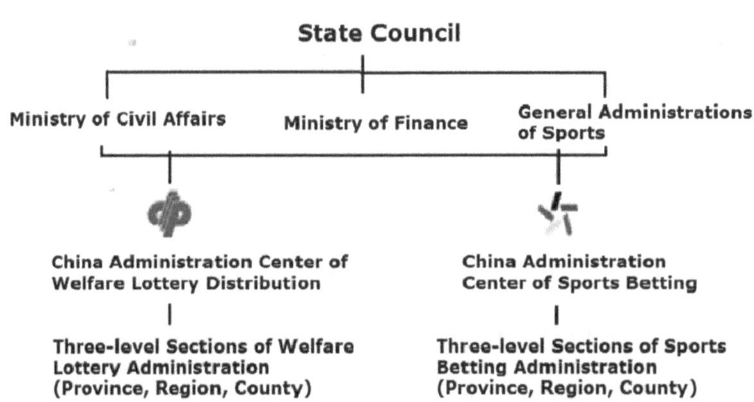

Fig. 3.3 Structure of the administration of two lottery systems in Mainland China. (Source: Chen et al., December, 2013). Challenges Mainland China faces when lotteries are allowed to be distributed and sold through the Internet/telephone

3. Public welfare funds: About 30% (or more) of sports lottery fund is used for social welfare, education, sports development, and medical services. The central and the local (provincial) financial authorities are responsible for managing the public welfare fund and spending it in the services mentioned above.

The proportion of public welfare funds devoted to social, sports, and medical projects varied from year to year. For example, the "Olympic Glory Project" and "National Fitness Program" shared over 60% of the fund's expenditure (Han 2013). In 2004, the State General Administration of Sports utilized 60% of the public welfare fund in the "national fitness program" to build nationwide sports facilities (e.g., fitness paths, table tennis tables, basketball stands, and physique testing equipment) in urban and rural areas. Additional fitness centers and sports clubs were built in remote and backward areas (BBC Monitoring Asia Pacific, July 2005).

Since 1994, the development of sports lottery has been growing steadily. Between 2000 and 2003, the sales of sports lottery exceeded that of welfare lottery. In 2003, one famous incident known as "Fake BMW case in Xian (西安寶馬體育彩票舞弊案)" caught the attention of the general public. On March 23, a young man named Liu Liang won the first prize of the sports lottery (instant-type lottery). The prize was a BMW sports car (valued at RMB 480,000) and cash of RMB 120,000 as rewards. A few days later, the Xian Sports Lottery Management Center declared Liu's ticket as fake and nullified his winning qualifications. Liu and his family members suspected local officials had replaced his ticket and sued the relevant government officials. In response to this incident, in May, 2004, the nationwide sales of instant-type sports lottery was temporarily suspended. After a few months' investigation, Xian's police force discovered that Liu's scenario was not an outlier – there were several complaints reporting similar scenarios. Liu's fake BMW case was a major notoriety in China sports lottery industry. Finally, the police force arrested several government officials and salesmen of sports lottery, whom were charged of bribery. Two individuals were also arrested for manufacturing fake lottery tickets. All of them were heavily fined and sent to jail from 6 months to 13 years in December 2004 (Wu, December 3, 2004).

In June 2004, another major fraud in sports lottery was disclosed and extensively reported by the mass media. Shenzhen Cai Shi Ta Investment and the Development Company Limited (深圳市彩世塔投資發展有限公司) produced false documents on lottery sales. The amount of money involved was about RMB 44,488,000. The Cai Shi Ta Company was involved in fraudulent operations in 17 major cities such as Guangzhou, Shanghai, Shenzhen, Hangzhou (杭州), and Chongqing (重慶) between December 2001 and November 2002. One of the fraudulent cases is illustrated in Fig. 3.4. In a lottery draw, Cai Shi Ta Company designed special draw box to manipulate the outcomes of the draw. The instruments were simple. Magnets were stacked on the interior of the draw box. Thus, certain numbers would definitely not come out in the draw. This strategy aimed to increase the winning chances of a group of numbers. On March 25, 2004, the Yangzhou Intermediate People's Court (楊州市中級人民法院) found the 15 defendants guilty of unlawful business operation (SinaChina, January 4, 2008).

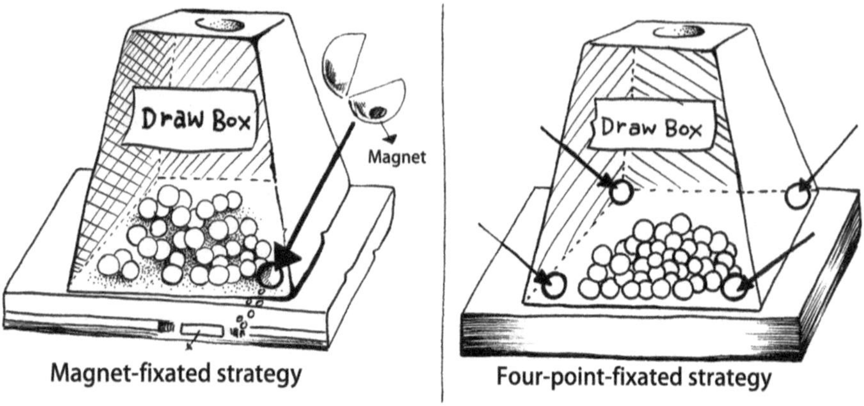

Fig. 3.4 Strategies of fraud during "lucky drawing". (Source: SinaChina, January 4, 2008. Retrieved on March 4, 2017 from http://news.sina.com.cn/c/2008-01-04/143014668254.shtml. This figure was drawn by Olga, a professional artist. The copyright of this figure belongs to the authors)

In 2004, probably due to the fraudulent cases in 2003, sports lottery sales dropped to RMB 15.4 billion. In response to the fraudulent problems, China Sports Lottery Management Center started to reform both the operation of lottery tickets and playing strategies of sports lottery. Consequently, computerized sports lottery betting gradually replaced the traditional lucky draw system. In addition to the instant- (即開型) and lottery-type (樂透型) products, the authority also started the issuance of quiz-type lottery (競猜型). In 2007, annual sales of all types of sports lottery reached RMB 38.6 billion.

Table 3.1 shows amounts of annual sports lottery sales from 2008 to 2016.

Current available types of sports lottery in Mainland China include "Super Lotto (超級大樂透)," "Arrangement of 3 (排列3)," "Arrangement of 5 (排列5)," Seven Colors (七星彩)," "22 Choose 5 (22選5)," "31 Choose 7 (31選7)," and "Soccer Winning Color (足球勝負彩)." Super Lotto is the most popular type among sports lottery, contributing to more than 60% of the annual sports lottery sales. Moreover, there are multiple betting methods in the Super Lotto. Buyers can select single betting (單式投注) by choosing 5 numbers from a set of 35 numbers, plus selecting 2 more numbers from another set containing 12 numbers (RMB 2 for each single bet). Another way to bet is multiple betting (複式投注). The maximal betting amount for single betting should not exceed RMB 20,000, while the upper limit of other ways of betting is RMB 30,000. The highest winning in the history of Super Lotto was recorded on August 4, 2014, won by a lottery buyer from Zibo, Shandong (山東淄博), who was awarded more than RMB 497 million. The second highest payout was recorded from Wuhan, Hubei, on January 19, 2015, with the winning being RMB 267 million. This amount is more than the earnings of 10,000 factory workers in a lifetime. The purchasing of lottery via the Internet or apps on mobile phones is common in Western countries. In 2013, the Chinese government passed the law entitled "Administrative Rules Governing Lottery Distribution and Lottery Sales (彩票發行

Table 3.1 Annual sports lottery sales (2008–2016)

Year	Amount of sports lottery sales (RMB in billion)
2016	188.15
2015	166.373
2014	176.41
2013	132.797
2012	110.492
2011	93.785
2010	69.446
2009	56.873
2008	45.615

Source: Ministry of Finance of the People's Republic of China. Retrieved on March 4, 2017 from http://www.mof.gov.cn/index.htm

銷售管理辦法)" to legalize selling lottery through the Internet and telephone (Chen et al., December 2013). Hence, it is fair to say that lottery gambling is a highly accessible game in China.

3.3 Developmental History of China Welfare Lottery

As written above, all kinds of gambling including lottery were banned during the first several decades of the PRC. Until 1981, the Agricultural Bank of China (中國農業銀行) and People's Bank of China (中國人民銀行) issued certificate of timed deposit small saving rewardable plan (定期有獎儲蓄存單), with face value of RMB 5 or RMB 10. This was a prologue to the subsequent China welfare lottery. The Ministry of Civil Affairs (民政部) requested issuance of welfare lottery during a regular meeting of State Council in December 1986. In 1987, the State Council permitted the request of the Ministry of Civil Affairs, aimed at collecting funds for social services such as child and elderly care, disability assistance, and alleviating poverty. The issue management center was then set up on June 3, 1987 (the issue center was renamed as China Administration Center of Welfare Lottery Distribution in December 1994). The first China welfare lottery ticket was printed and tested in Tianjin City Coinage Factory (天津市造幣廠). The ticket was printed in six colors: purple, green, black, light tan, dark, and light blue. On July 27, the first set of China welfare lottery was on sale in Shijiazhuang (石家莊), Hubei. Three days later, Shanghai established ten selling venues and began to sell welfare lottery tickets. The sales were further expanded to other cities or provinces rapidly, which established a strong foundation for the welfare lottery industry in China. The selling record was continuously broken since the public sales of welfare lottery. In early

December 2001, Shenzhen (深圳), a city just next to Hong Kong in Guangdong Province, recorded the sales of RMB 190 million in 9 days at ten selling points. The growth of welfare lottery sales dramatically surged as China's economy bloomed after it was qualified to become a member of the World Trade Organization (WTO) on December 11, 2001.

Table 3.2 displays the annual welfare lottery sales from 2008 to 2016 (Ministry of Finance of the People's Republic of China 2008–2016).

By the end of the first decade of the twenty-first century, China welfare lottery issue system had progressed from traditional counter sales to sales via hotline system. Hotline system ensured the accuracy of lottery issuance and extended the time of sales up to the moment before drawing of lottery. A few years later, the online lottery system was developed. With the help of the Internet and computerization of lottery sales, the monitor of illegal lottery sales by the welfare lottery management center was more effective. As information technology became more advanced, operation of online lottery sales was also getting more efficient. According to Chen et al. (2013), the number of Chinese netizens reached 591 million by the end of June 2013. With an increasing concern for network safety and broader penetration of network in Mainland China, the Chinese government is putting more effort into protecting the privacy of electronic lottery buyers and fighting crimes against fraud related to lottery sales through the Internet.

Current available types of welfare lottery in Mainland China include high-frequency games, rapidly drawn games, and scheduled (regular) draw lottery (source: http://www.cwl.gov.cn/ (China Welfare Lottery Official Website,中國福利彩票官方網站)):

Table 3.2 Annual welfare lottery sales (2008–2016)

Year	Amount of welfare lottery sales (RMB in billion)
2016	206.492
2015	201.511
2014	205.968
2013	176.34
2012	151.032
2011	127.797
2010	96.802
2009	75.606
2008	60.398

Source: Ministry of Finance of the People's Republic of China. Retrieved on March 12, 2017 from http://www.mof.gov.cn/index.htm

(a) High-frequency games:

1. Instant scratch cards: It costs RMB 5 to RMB 30 per ticket, with various playing methods. Another name of instant scratch cards is Fucai ji kaipiao (福彩即開票).
2. Video lottery terminals (VLTs): VLTs are computer-based games. Similar to the operation of slot machines, it also appears as a stand-alone machine driven by a random number generator (RNG). Types of games include virtual scratch cards, various slot games, and virtual sports games (e.g., virtual lucky racing in the format of Formula 1 style).

(b) Rapidly drawn games:

1. Keno 8 (also known as Happiness 8, 快樂8): Beijing Happiness 8 lottery is an online lottery game based on the official results of the games released by Beijing Welfare Lottery Web. The 20 winning numbers are randomly generated from 80 numbers (1–80). There are various playing modes derived from the 20 numbers, and different bonuses may be awarded according to the number of betted codes or playing modes. For example, players can bet on selected numbers, total value, sing, tenth and hundredth digit of the winning numbers, odd or even value, big/small and odd/even parlay, or even elements (metal, wood, water, fire, earth (五行:金木水火土)). The maximum winning prize could be up to RMB five million as that spot is a progressive payout (as Happiness 8 is a progressive keno). The cost of each bet is RMB 2. New games start every 5 minutes on the official website.
2. PK pickup (PK拾): The cost of each bet is RMB 2. Drawings are held online every 5 minutes. Lottery buyers can select the order of numbers from 1 to 10 to predict the pattern of the draw. Similar to Keno 8, PK Pickup has a number of prizes based on how many numbers selected are correct.

(c) Scheduled draw lottery:

1. 3D lottery (福彩3D): Resembled the playing method of electronic slot machine, 3D lottery is the simplest game among various welfare lottery games. With a cost of RMB 2 per bet, lottery buyers simply need to choose three numbers (each 0–9), who would win RMB 1000 if the numbers and order are exactly the same as the buyers' chosen ones.
2. Double chromosphere (also called Shuangseqiu or Union Lotto,雙色球): It commenced in February 2003. Regular draw is held every Tuesday, Thursday, and Sunday night. Players pick 6 from 33 (1–33) red balls plus one from 16 blue balls (1–16). Lottery buyer who has won the first prize (6 red balls +1 blue ball) would be rewarded RMB ten million. There are other fixed prizes which make double chromosphere the most popular game across the lottery industry in Mainland China.
3. The Seven (七樂彩): The playing method is very similar to Mark Six (六合彩) in Hong Kong. It is drawn every Monday, Wednesday, and Friday at 21:15. Lottery buyers simply select seven numbers (1–30). The lotto draws eight numbers (the eighth number is called the extra number). The jackpot is

set at 70% for seven numbers, 20% for six numbers plus the extra number, and 10% for six numbers. The jackpot is up to a maximum of RMB five million. There are also some fixed odds prizes: five numbers plus the extra number (RMB 200), five numbers (RMB 50), four numbers plus the extra number (RMB 10), and four numbers (RMB 5).

It is worth noting that provinces, autonomous regions, or municipals are authorized the right to issue their own local lottery.

Due to the complex types of lottery available in Mainland China, flaws and controversies seem to be inevitable. One example happened on January 25, 2015, which raised much public concern – a delayed drawing of double chromosphere (2015011). Usually, double chromosphere is drawn at 21:30 every Tuesday, Thursday, and Sunday, broadcasted live by China Education Television (中國教育電視台). At 21:10, January 25, 2015, 20 min before lottery drawing, Chongqing City's (重慶市) Welfare Center reported glitches in data index and failed to process them. Nationwide statistics of the total sales of double chromosphere were therefore not being calculated. The drawing procedure was forced to postpone. According to the reporter from Xinhua Agency, the drawing procedure was done 2 hours later without direct broadcast, and the results were released on Twitter only (Yang, January 26, 2015). The delay triggered extensive public controversy. Some people doubted whether the results were fabricated by certain officials, while others criticized if there was a formal supervision during the drawing procedure. People's courts in some cities or districts subsequently accepted the lawsuits filed by local notary offices.

3.4 Problems in Chinese Lottery Development

While Chinese lottery industry continues to boom in the last decade, Li (2015) identified three major problems in sports lottery:

1. Inefficient management system and operation mechanisms – The current state-run lottery system has significant operational problems. Two examples can aptly demonstrate the existing flaws in the management system. In October 2007, two bank staff members in the northern city of Handan (邯鄲) (a city located in Henan province) were convicted of stealing RMB 50.95 million from their workplace to buy lottery tickets. The two defendants were sentenced to death. One month later, a 36-year-old lottery vendor in Anshan (鞍山), a city in Liaoning province, stole RMB 28 million from lottery sales. The offender was arrested and sentenced to jail (BBC Monitoring Asia Pacific, December 2, 2007). These two incidents demonstrate the lack of efficient supervision of the lottery system and sales operations.
2. Insufficient policies and regulations – Unlike foreign countries (e.g., Australia and Singapore), where a complete set of policies and laws on responsible gambling were passed before their casinos were formally open, there was no set of complete regulations overseeing the overall lottery operation and accounting

systems. For instance, existing regulations imposed by the State Council seem not efficient enough to stop illegal online soccer betting. Provinces like Guangdong (廣東) and municipals such as Chongqing (重慶) had uncontrollable underground gambling in the past decade (Li 2014). In fact, the CCP government does have policies and penalties targeted at striking those who practice underground gambling. However, the actual execution of policies is difficult as government officials are involved in underground gambling business (further details will be discussed in Chap. 7 of this book).

3. The underlying reason of insufficient supervision may be due to the enormous size of the lottery market. There are 29 provinces in China, with a total area larger than the United States. It is difficult, if not impossible, for the central government to monitor regions far away from Beijing – the PRC's capital. In other words, local governments might make significant changes on the gaming policies for the sake of making profits for themselves without seeking approval from the central government. Li (2015) stated that some local governments willfully disclosed misleading lottery information to the public. Illegal gambling is common in China. In almost every major city, there are secret underground casinos, mahjong houses, and private lotteries. Chinese gaming operators are ingenious in their design of illegal games. For example, in major cities of Southern China, some operators design their own Hong Kong "Mark Six" game. The players select their own numbers on these tickets. These operators would serve as the banker. It was estimated that transactions in the black gambling market was as high as RMB 1 trillion in 2014 (PR Newswire, June 25, 2015).

In addition to the above problems, unfair or fraudulent competition in sports events has been a serious concern as a result of sports lottery issuance. Match fixing, black whistle (referees' unfair judgment), and corruption of soccer clubs' administrative were prevalent (Li 2009). Until recent years, the General Administration of Sports of China reformed Chinese premier league and achieved significant improvement in its administration and management system to guarantee fair competition among soccer matches.

Notwithstanding efforts being undertaken by the Chinese government, the proliferation of lottery gaming has created a number of social problems, one of which being the increased prevalence rate of disordered gambling. In 2012, a survey entitled "Internet survey among Chinese lottery buyers' behaviors," reported by the Lottery Research Center of China[1], Beijing Normal University (北京師範大學中國彩票事業研究中心), indicated that there were over 200 million regular lottery buy-

[1] Found in July 2009, the Lottery Research Center, Beijing Normal University, provides consultation to the Chinese government in Chinese lottery development and policy-making. It also carries out academic research and market analyses in order to provide expert opinions to relevant government authorities (Lottery Research Center of China, Beijing Normal University 2017). Cooperated with Asia Pacific Association for Gambling Studies (APAGS), the center organized the Third Asia Pacific Conference on Gambling & Commercial Gaming Research (APCG2015) on April 12–14, 2015 in Beijing. Scholars of the center also participated and presented their academic papers in other international gaming conferences and important activities such as Global Gaming Expo (e.g., G2E Asia held in the Venetian Macao, May 17–19, 2016).

ers in China. On average, they spent RMB 85 per month to buy lottery. Seven million of them could be classified as problem lottery buyers, and around 430,000 were in severe level (prevalence rate is about 3.2%). Professor Chen Haiping of the Lottery Research Center of China, Beijing Normal University, reported that 80% of the sample (number of questionnaires collected = 176,213; number of valid sample $\simeq$ 38,000) in the above research study come from the lower socioeconomic level in the community, who frequently dreamed of becoming rich through winning the grand lottery. The symptoms of Chinese problem lottery buyers, according to Chen, included loss of personal control over gambling, tolerance, chasing, and withdrawal, which were more or less the same as problem gamblers diagnosed as having gambling disorder in DSM-5 (American Psychiatric Association 2013). Most of the problem lottery buyers were aged between 18 and 45, with a monthly salary between RMB 1500 and RMB 3000, who had achieved a basic secondary school education (Chen 2012). As the research data were collected on the Internet, the age groups of responders were relatively younger, as the majority of elderly in China usually do not have computer skills and knowledge. Furthermore, it is very difficult to assess the validity of the responses. Despite these problems, the study was by far the most comprehensive gambling study in China to date, in which findings were similar to those gambling research conducted in Western countries (Griffiths and Parke 2010; Tsitsika et al. 2011). These findings include:

(a) Males are more likely to develop gambling problems.
(b) People from low-socioeconomic status buy more lottery tickets to sustain their hope of getting rich.
(c) Adolescents are more vulnerable to become addicted in online gambling.

3.5 Conclusion on Modern Chinese Gambling

As we have argued in Chap. 1, gambling is an integral part of Chinese culture. Throughout the history of China, nearly every feudal government had their strict policies and harsh laws aiming to prohibit gambling. Punishment could be very severe such as hand chopping in the Ming Dynasty. On top of the legal sanctions against gambling, traditional Confucian teaching classified gambling as one of the four cardinal sins of men, with the other being visiting prostitutes, drinking, and smoking opium. Notwithstanding these measures, gambling activities flourished throughout the history of China. One might ask why Chinese people love gambling so much despite all these social and legal sanctions. As an ethnic Chinese and a psychologist working in Hong Kong and Macao for over 25 years, I see that gambling is the most preferable and common pastime in Chinese communities. The reasons for the popularity of gambling can be the following:

(a) When compared to Westerners, the majority of ethnic Chinese, especially elderly, do not enjoy sports and physical games. For the majority of Chinese, boxing, *Kung Fu* fighting, American football, and baseball are never popular sports. In many Chinese communities in Hong Kong and Macao, we do not have the luxury of large football fields and gymnasium. In fact, golf, as a sport, is a game for the rich and celebrities in China. Thus, for the vast majority of ethnic Chinese, gambling is a relatively safe and convenient pastime in a small community. Take the example of mahjong. It is an excellent pastime for housewives, who can spend an afternoon playing mahjong with neighbors (Chan et al. 2016).
(b) Secondly, for the majority of Chinese, the dream of getting rich is their primary motivation in life. The principal author of this book has been teaching college in Hong Kong since 1997. In his experiences working with young people, he finds that over 80% of college students choose college majors out of monetary concerns. Most of them pick a career not out of passion nor social impact, but how much money the career would bring them every month. A college major that has narrow career opportunities would not interest students. In 2017, the University of Hong Kong has decided to abolish astronomy and joint mathematics/physics as college majors. In Hong Kong, good college education is the first step to starting an economically profitable career. However, for the individuals without college education, gambling might be a quick and fast approach to obtaining personal riches.
(c) Gambling presents a hope for the socially disadvantaged groups. Over half a century ago, Noble Prize laureate Milton Friedman argued that individuals in the lower socioeconomic class are more likely to buy lottery tickets (in order to get rich), while individuals in the upper social class are more prone to protect their wealth (Friedman and Savage 1948). Thus, legalized gambling could help maintain the status quo and social stability. Evidence supporting this assertion can be found in a prevalence study in England. Wardle et al. (2007) found that 68% of respondents in the survey ($N = 9003$) participated in gambling in the previous year. Fifty-seven percent of interviewees said they once bought lottery. Those with low-socioeconomic status gambled significantly more. Seventy-three percent of interviewees with their educational level secondary or below gambled in previous year, compared with 61% of counterparts with bachelor degree or above. The findings may imply that people who were poor, had lower monthly income, and the less educated would participate more frequently in gambling activities. Chan et al. (2016) also shared similar findings in Hong Kong and Macao. The authors argue that legalized gambling provides a safety valve to the lower social class, as gambling gives them "hope" to get rich. This observation is also applicable to lottery buyers in Mainland China.

3.6 A Review on the Problems and Challenges in Gambling Research in China

(a) Research in gambling studies is only in its infancy stage in Mainland China. Most of the reported studies were written in Chinese. While much has been said about gambling problems in China (Chen 2015), majority of the reported studies were carried out by nonacademic organizations. Their methodologies in data collection and analysis lack scientific validation. Most of these studies collected data from online sources. Very often, they would post the questionnaires on the Internet and ask the respondents to report their gambling behaviors and problems. The researchers would then make inferences and draw conclusions from these data. There is a lack of justification and verification on the collected questionnaires. Thus, the results and conclusions of these investigations might be biased.

(b) Many of the reported investigations employed testing instruments that lack empirical validation. For instance, Wang (2006), in a study of 299 players in sports lotteries, reported that the prevalence of problem gambling was 0.3%. Li et al. (2011), drawing samples of over 5000 respondents from five major cities including Shanghai, reported the prevalence rate of problem gambling to be 2%. Both studies, however, employed a "self-made" instrument for their respective study. It is difficult, if not impossible, to compare the findings across these investigations.

(c) Many of the reported studies were investigations based on interviews conducted in lottery betting outlets (Chen 2015). The majority of these research projects were carried out on players of sports lotteries. There are very few reports on recreational gamblers in China.

(d) The sampling problem may be a main reason that contributes to the broad range of reported prevalence rate of problem gamblers. For instance, Wang (2011), in a sample of 1600 respondents in Shanghai, reported a prevalence rate of 14.2%, the highest among all reported investigations. At the lower end of the spectrum, Wang (2006) reported a rate of 0.3% from a sample of 299 participants, and Ceng (2010) obtained a prevalence rate of 1.2%. This range of differential prevalence can be attributed to sampling bias.

We have outlined the development and state of gambling in Mainland China. We now turn our focus to the two major special administrative regions (SAR) of China, namely, Hong Kong and Macao. Both SARs share a common heritage with that of Mainland China. However, the two special regions were once ruled under foreign jurisdictions: Hong Kong was governed under British power, and Macao was a Portuguese colony. The sovereignty of both places was returned to China in the last 20 years. The following sections will outline the state of gambling in these two SARs.

3.6.1 Hong Kong

When compared to Mainland China, Hong Kong has conducted relatively more extensive research on the state and prevalence of gambling. The first extensive study was done by the researchers of the Hong Kong Polytechnic University (Hong Kong Polytechnic University 2002). In a random sample of 2004 participants aged between 15 and 64, 78% of the sample had participated in some form of gambling in the previous year. For the respondents, the most favored form of gambling was Mark Six (a form of lottery tickets) (64.2%) and social gambling (45.9%). Among the gamblers, 1.85% of the participants could be considered as "probable pathological gamblers" according to DSM-IV (American Psychiatric Association 1994). Their most favorite game was horse racing. Moreover, the study also included a questionnaire survey of 2000 students. Among these young students (all under 18), a sizable number of them (49.2%) participated in gambling activities in the previous year. Most of them learned gambling from their friends and families. An interesting finding was that gambling was a favorite pastime as they often shared gambling experiences with their families during festive holidays. The prevalence rate of pathological gambling among underage students was 2.6%.

Three years later, researchers at the University of Hong Kong launched a follow-up study on the state and prevalence of gambling in Hong Kong (The University of Hong Kong 2005). The methodology of this study was similar to that of the study in 2002. The major part of this study was a random sampling of 2093 residents aged 15–64. In the structured interviews, the respondents were asked about their gambling behaviors in the previous year. This study yielded similar findings with that of the investigation in 2002. As a group, 81.1% of the respondents admitted having participated in some forms of gambling in the previous year. There was a significant decrease in the participation rate in horse race betting (30.4% in 2001 to 25.5% in 2005). The researchers speculated that this was the consequence of the legalization of soccer betting in 2003 as some players in horse racing might choose to wager on soccer matches. 16.3% of the respondents have participated in football betting with the Hong Kong Jockey Club. Using the DSM-IV (American Psychiatric Association 1994) as the clinical assessment tool, the prevalence rates for pathological gamblers and problem gamblers were 2.2% and 3.1%, respectively (the figures in the study in 2002 were 1.85% and 4%, respectively).

This study also included a survey of 2095 young students from secondary schools and institutes of the Hong Kong Vocational Council. The students were given questionnaires to assess their gambling behaviors and habits. The findings indicated that the participation rate of gambling activities among youths aged 12–17 was 29.8%, showing a significant drop of participation rate in Mark Six lotteries and horse race betting (from 19.4% in Mark Six and 9.2% in horse racing in 2001 to 15% and 4.4%, respectively). Besides, this study witnessed a decrease in problem gambling among the youths. Using DSM-IV as the clinical assessment tool, the rates of pathological gamblers and problem gamblers were both 1.3% (compared to 2.6% and 4.5%, respectively, in 2002).

The researchers in the Hong Kong Polytechnic University (2011) reported a follow-up prevalence study on gambling. This investigation employed a similar methodology to that of the previous two prevalence studies. In this investigation, the researchers interviewed 2024 respondents on the telephone. The participants were asked about their gambling behaviors and preferences in the previous 12 months. In this recent investigation, the respondents' gambling participation rate was 62%, indicating a significant drop when compared to the study conducted in 2005 (81.1%). With fewer people participated in gambling, the prevalence rates of possible problem and possible pathological gamblers were 1.9% and 1.4%, respectively, with both rates being significantly lower than the corresponding rates of the 2005 study. Among the gamblers, the most preferred games were Mark Six lottery, social gambling, horse racing, games in Macao casinos, and football betting. 0.3% of the respondents reported joining illegal gambling activities in the previous year. This figure might be misleading as ethnic Chinese are often reluctant in disclosing their personal problems, especially their illegal behaviors to others (Chan et al. 2016). In their experiences of working with gamblers in Hong Kong, the authors speculate that the prevalence of illegal gambling should be much higher in this community.

These major investigations also sought to understand the personality and pathways development of gamblers. From their qualitative interviews with the participants, the findings indicated that the majority of the problem gamblers in the studies learned to gamble with families and friends when they were young. They often gamble during Chinese festivals and holidays. For them, gambling was their favorite pastime since young. Very often, they reported an early win in the early stage of their gambling career. Their involvement with gambling could last more than 20 years before they realized they had gambling problems.

Chan and his research team have reported a series of qualitative studies on the personality development of Chinese gamblers (Chan 2014; Chan and Ohtsuka 2013). Utilizing the pathways development model of Blaszczynski and Nower (2002), Chan attempted to investigate the pathways of personality and social development of gamblers, especially problem gamblers. Most of the problem gamblers came from Pathway One of the Blaszczynski and Nower (B/N) model. For these gamblers, they often reported learning gambling at home or with their friends. For them, gambling activities were significant parts of their childhood lives. The majority of these gamblers did not report significant behavioral and emotional problems during childhood. Thus, gambling was very much a learned habit from childhood or in B/N terms, behaviorally conditioned pattern earlier in one's life. For many of these gamblers, their gambling behaviors were often reinforced by early wins. Most would often associate personal skills and luck with gambling. As these gamblers develop, they would often learn new game skills and might take gambling as their favorite pastimes. Pathway Two gamblers were emotionally maladjusted prior to the development of gambling problems. Their development demonstrates distinct developmental differences with that of the gamblers in Pathway One. These gamblers usually reported personal emotional problems such as depression and anxiety. These gamblers often took gambling as a type of emotional escape from their personal problems. Women gamblers who experienced childhood traumas and family problems might gamble more in the face of stress. On this issue, Jacobs (1986) and Brown (2002) share similar views as they argue that gambling is a type of ego defense mechanism for these individuals. Thus, treatment planning for these gamblers should include measures and strategies to alleviate their emotional problems. New coping skills should be taught. In contrast to the first two types of problem gamblers, Pathway Three gamblers usually had behavioral problems and antisocial behavioral patterns in their childhood. These patterns include truancy from school, smoking, irresponsible sexual behavior, and gambling. In other words, gambling was only one of their antisocial behaviors during childhood. As they matured into adulthood, their involvement in gambling became more varied and intense. Many of these gamblers would take part in illegal gambling as well. Very often, they might not lead a responsible lifestyle as they seldom reported having a socially appropriate employment. They are also characterized by their pathological lying and lack of conscience. Treatment for these gamblers is guarded as they often fail to see problems in their gambling (Blaszczynski 2009).

In reviewing the various research on the state of gambling in Hong Kong, Chan et al. (2016) pointed out the following problems and inadequacies:

(a) Majority of the existing investigations were carried out by short telephone interviews (mostly under 1 hour). Very often, ethnic Chinese in Hong Kong are reluctant to disclose personal information to strangers, especially issues of shame and personal problems which problem gambling would often entail. As such, the refusal rate of interviews is high, as evidenced in the three major prevalence studies (Hong Kong Polytechnic University 2002, 2011; The University of Hong Kong 2005). Moreover, it is difficult, if not impossible, to validate the gathered information from the telephone interviews.
(b) There have been very few reported studies that employ validated psychological inventories to investigate the personality and psychological states of the respondents (Chan 2014). Take the three major prevalence studies as examples. Even though all three major investigations interviewed participants on their emotional states, they did not employ objective psychological testing in their evaluation. Very often, the investigators would draw conclusions from structured interviews. For instance, the interviewers might ask the participants whether they have depression or anxiety problems. Clinically, this diagnostic approach lacks professional judgment and clinical validation.
(c) The recent prevalence study indicates a drop of general participation in gambling activities. To date, there has been little research in Hong Kong on the reason behind the recent decrease in gambling participation. The recent drop of problem gambling prevalence rate in Hong Kong parallels the findings of gambling research in other major jurisdictions (Williams et al. 2012). In an excellent review on the literature on prevalence studies worldwide, Williams and his colleagues discover that problem gambling rates peaked in the mid-to-late 1990s for North America and in the early 2000s for Australia and other nations. The rates leveled off in the mid-2000s. One possible explanation is the adaptation

hypothesis proposed by Storer et al. (2009). The researchers argue that the decrease in prevalence rate can be due to a number of factors such as natural recovery or professional intervention, adjusting to gambling opportunities, increase in government-sponsored treatment, or increasing awareness of potential harms among the participants. Future gambling research on Hong Kong should address this issue.

3.6.2 Macao

Macao, a special administrative region (SAR) of the People's Republic of China, is a small island located at the southern tip of China, some 60 kilometers southwest of Hong Kong. In 1557, the small island was given to Portugal by the Qing imperial government. While some Portuguese came to settle in this small island, the majority of residents were ethnic Chinese. The Portuguese government appointed administrators to manage the small colony. Portuguese-styled governmental system, schools, and legal rules were installed. As the Qing government never intended to retrieve the colony politically, Portuguese culture slowly took root in this small enclave in the southern part of China. Portuguese-styled buildings, Western government system, and Catholic schools were built. Casino gambling, an initially European gaming concept, was introduced to Macao when the first casino monopoly was granted to the Tai Xing company in 1937. In 1962, an operating monopoly was given to STDM, a company headed by Dr. Stanley Ho. This privilege gave the gambling giant the rights to develop a variety of games including casinos, greyhound racing, and horse racing in Macao. On December 20, 1999, the Portuguese government returned Macao to Chinese sovereignty. It is now, similar to Hong Kong, a special administrative region in the People's Republic of China. Macao is governed under a specific law system, known as the Basic Law of Macao, which protects the capitalist system and a high level of political autonomy that the local residents have been enjoying since the Portuguese rule. However, the change of government does not bring much social and economic changes to the majority of Macao residents. In terms of gambling, Western gaming conglomerates were invited to bid on new gambling licenses. American companies such as Las Vegas Sands and Wynn have been successful in developing resorts in Macao, either on their own or as a joint venture with other local investors. These integrated resorts consist of five-star hotels, exhibition and conferences facilities, luxury shops and boutiques, elegant restaurants, and Las Vegas entertainment shows. At the time of writing, there are 41 casinos in Macao.

Fong and Ozorio (2005) of the University of Macao undertook the first gambling prevalence study in Macao. In this pioneer investigation, 1121 participants, randomly recruited in the community, were interviewed over the telephone. The participants were asked, in addition to the basic demographic information such as age and gender, about their gambling history and patterns. The findings indicated that about two thirds of the respondents had gambled during the previous year. Their most favorite games were Mark Six (a form of public lottery operated by the Hong Kong Jockey Club in Hong Kong), mahjong, and sports betting. The participants were assessed on items of DSM-IV (American Psychiatric Association 2000). It was found that 1.78% of the respondents were classified as probable pathological gamblers and 2.5% were considered probable problem gamblers. Problem gamblers were noted to be those being male and having a monthly income of approximately MOP 8000 (roughly equivalent to US$1000). Among the participants, the most popular games were mahjong (43.8%), Mark Six (38.7%), sports betting (21.9%), and casino (21.2%). This finding contrasted with a group of help-seeking problem gamblers. For these individuals ($N = 108$), casino gambling (68%) and sports betting (32%) were the most preferred games.

In 2010, another prevalence study was reported by the researchers from the University of Macao (Fung and Ng, August 2010). In this study, 2011 local residents, aged between 15 and 64, were randomly selected and interviewed on the telephone. Based on the *Diagnostic and Statistical Manual of Mental Disorders* fourth edition, text revision (DSM-IV-TR) (American Psychiatric Association 2000), 2.8% of the participants were found to be potential pathological gamblers. This rate was higher than that of previous studies. A subsequent major investigation undertaken by the Social Welfare Bureau of the Macao government (University of Macao 2014) yielded a significantly lower prevalence rate of problem gamblers. The methodology of this study was similar to that of the previous studies, with 2158 Macao residents, aged between 15 and 64 years of age, randomly selected. The prevalence rate of probable pathological gamblers was 0.9% (compared to 2.8% in 2010). The rate of gambling participation was also found to be lower than that of previous studies. Macao residents' gambling participation rate in 2013 was 49.5% (55.9% in 2010 and 59.2% in 2007). Among the gamblers, the monthly median gambling spending and monthly average gambling spending both demonstrated a significant drop when compared to those of previous studies (MOP 755 in 2010 and MOP 505 in 2013). Compared to the 2010 survey, the respondents' participation rate of all gambling activities decreased significantly. The five most preferred gaming activities were "Mark Six" (33.1%), "social gambling (e.g., mahjong)" (21.7%), "Macao casino" (11.9%), "slot machines" (7.2%), and "sports betting" (4.5%). The findings showed that 1.9% of the respondents could be classified as probable problem gamblers and 0.9% could be classified as probable pathological gamblers. The data indicated that there is a significant drop of problem gambling prevalence rate in the jurisdiction in the last few years. The researchers did not explain the reasons for such a drastic decline. A similar drop in the number of probable pathological gamblers was evidenced in the investigations conducted during the same period in Hong Kong. Thus, the present authors speculate that intensified government efforts in raising public awareness regarding gambling problems and their efforts in combating illegal gambling might be the most possible reasons for such drop. Future research has to look into this aspect.

In 2013, major changes were made in the diagnosis of problem gambling in the *Diagnostic and Statistical Manual of Mental Disorders*, fifth edition (DSM-5) (American Psychiatric Association 2013). In the new classification, the "Illegal

Act" criterion was removed, and the threshold for the diagnosis of gambling disorder was lowered to four instead of the former five criteria. Based on the new criteria, Wu et al. (2015) interviewed a random, representative sample of 1018 Macao residents on the phone. This study found that the estimated prevalence rate of gambling disorder was 2.1% among the Macao adult population. This figure was higher than the findings of previous investigations. The researchers speculated that this might be due to the differences in samples. Moreover, by lowering the criteria in the diagnosis of gambling disorder, it would make the diagnostic assessment more sensitive. Consequently, more gamblers would be diagnosed as having gambling problems. Detailed analysis on the demographic information suggested that the personal risk factors of gambling disorder were being male, having low education, a preference for casino gambling, and high degree of materialism (i.e., personal desires for material possessions in one's life, Richins and Dawson 1992).

Social researchers have reported studies on underage gambling in Macao. Kam and Wong (2014) performed a study on soccer betting among Macao's college students. Among 880 participants recruited from universities in Macao, 39.8% had bet on soccer matches in the preceding 12 months. When asked about their motivation for gambling, the respondents expressed the following reasons: entertainment (15.5%), killing time (12.65), and peer influence (12.3%). Statistical analysis on the personality characteristics of the participants indicated a significant positive correlation between severity of problem and sensation seeking ($r = 0.615$, $p < 0.01$). Employing the Problem Gambling Severity Index (Ferris and Wynne 2001) as the assessment tool, ten of the participants could be classified as problem gamblers. About 90% of moderate- and high-risk gamblers were males. The researchers concluded that gambling problems among young people are severe.

In reviewing the research conducted on the state of gambling in Macao, we have the following observations:

(a) Majority of the existing research are prevalence studies. Very often, these quantitative studies aimed at measuring the prevalence rates of gambling disorders, as well as personality of gamblers and their motivations of gambling. There are few research that investigate the treatment needs of gamblers. To date, no randomized controlled studies on treatment with disordered gamblers have been undertaken in Macao. This issue should be the focus of concern in future research on Macao.

(b) The recent prevalence studies indicated that the rate of disordered gambling is higher in Macao than that in Hong Kong and many other jurisdictions. One possible explanation is the increased accessibility and availability of gambling opportunities in the area. As of 2017, in an area smaller than one third of Las Vegas, Macao houses 39 casinos. The Blaszczynski and Nower (2002) pathways model of problem gambling, which stresses that the three As (availability, accessibility, and acceptability) of gambling opportunities are the necessary conditions for the development of problem gambling among individuals, can explain this finding.

(c) Most disordered gamblers choose casino gambling as their game of choice. This would reflect the special characteristics of Macao. The gaming industry brought more than 33 billion USD of gross revenue in 2011. It constitutes two fifths of Macao's GDP and 23.0% of the total employment in Macao (Wu et al. 2015). There are few qualitative research studies specifically conducted on casino gamblers in Macao (Chan 2014). Chan and Ohtsuka (2013) reported a qualitative study on 15 gamblers in Macao. The researchers discovered a unique pathway of the casino gamblers. For many of these gamblers, casino is their home, where they find their work, excitement, food, and, most importantly, their meaning in life. As all casinos in Macao operate 24/7, most of these gamblers stay in the casinos every day. Psychological treatment for these gamblers is difficult, if not impossible, as they have little insight into their own problems.

3.6.3 Taiwan

Taiwan, formally called the Republic of China, is an independent state off the coast of the People's Republic of China. In the fifteenth century, Taiwan was under Dutch control. Later, the Qing Dynasty established sovereignty of the island and included it as a part of the imperial empire. In 1895, following the defeat of the Sino-Japanese War, the Qing Dynasty, in addition to paying Japan a huge amount of monetary compensation, ceded Formosa, the name of Taiwan in the nineteenth century, to Japan. In the early years of the twentieth century, Japan instituted a number of changes in the cultural, social, and educational systems in Taiwan. After their defeat of the Second World War in 1945, Taiwan was returned to Chinese sovereignty. Later, civil war between the Nationalist government and the Communist army headed by Mao Zedong broke out in China in 1945. In 1949, Mao and his Communist army conquered Beijing. Remnants of the Nationalist government fled to Taiwan and established an independent regime known as the Republic of China.

In the new regime, the first priority was national security. Thus, the Republic of China, since its early days of establishment, formed military alliance with the United States. In the previous decades, Taiwan bought enormous amount of military installations from the United States. This has been a point of contention between Taiwan and the People's Republic of China.

In the area of culture, the change in political sovereignty has not significantly impacted the daily lives of the commoners. The majority of Taiwanese people are Chinese, and they share the same Chinese cultural heritage with their mainland counterparts. The Confucian culture of *Li*, or etiquette, family care, and respect are regarded as the fundamental virtues in Taiwan. In the area of gambling, Taiwanese hold similar Confucian attitudes as the people in Mainland China. Gambling is a social vice; it is one of the four major sins of Chinese men, with the other three being visiting prostitutes, drinking, and smoking opium. Thus, since the beginning of the Republic of China, gambling, with the exception of government-sponsored lotteries, is illegal in Taiwan. However, illegal gambling is very common. The following is a brief summary of the state of gambling in Taiwan:

(a) Public lotteries: The Uniform Invoice or Unified Invoice (統一發票), first introduced in 1951, is a state lottery organized under the Ministry of Finance of the Republic of China. The lottery was first intended to raise funds for public infrastructure expenditure and the provision of social services for the poor. In the last 50 years, lottery has been a success in achieving its goals as lottery is a popular gaming option among the majority of Taiwanese. One reason is its easy accessibility and availability. Players can buy the lottery tickets in major convenience stores, an option not available in Hong Kong. Furthermore, if the players win an amount of NT 200 (about US$7), they can redeem the prize money at major convenience stores. In 2011, the "special prize" was NT$2 million (US$63000). The "first prize" of NT$200,000 (USD $6200) is the tickets that match all the eight-digit numbers drawn. Subsequent prizes are valued at NT$40,000 (US$1300), NT$10,000 (US$313), NT$4000 (US$136), NT$1000 (US$31), and NT$200 (US$7), which are given to tickets bearing the matching 7, 6, 5, 4, and 3 numbers, respectively. More prizes make the lottery more appealing as more players are reinforced by the variable reinforcement ratio (Skinner 1971). All in all, lotteries give people hope, especially individuals at the lower socio-economic end of society (Friedman and Savage 1948).
(b) Illegal gambling: Except for lotteries organized by the government, all other forms of gambling are illegal in Taiwan. The only legal provisions are mahjong and card gambling during Chinese festivals. However, illegal gambling is rampant. Mahjong houses and illegal gambling, often run by gangs, are common in major cities in Taiwan. Shrewd Taiwanese merchants set up connections with casinos in Macao to help players to transfer funds to Macao. In January 2013, Taiwanese police investigated the alleged transfer of US$180 million from Taiwanese gamblers to casinos in Macao through the Australia-based Melco Crown Limited.
(c) Casino: In 2009, Taiwan legislature passed amendments on the Offshore Islands Development Act which gave three outlying islands, namely, the communities of Kinmen (金門), Matsu (馬祖), and Penghu (澎湖), the authority to build casinos if more than 50% of local residents agreed in a local referendum. Shortly after the Act, the residents of the Penghu voted against the development of casinos. Up to now, there are no legal casinos built in Taiwan.

On July 7, 2012, the residents of the Matsu Islands voted by a ratio of 57–43% in favor of allowing the construction of a casino on the island (turnout rate was 40.76%). Matsu is a small island with about 10,000 residents only. A casino with the development of business and infrastructure would boost the tourism industry of the island. However, the final decision to authorize the building of the casino would need the approval and blessing of the Taiwanese government. Originally, it was expected that Matsu would have its first casino opened in 2019 by Weidner Resorts, run by former Las Vegas Sands Corp President and Chief Operating Officer William

Weidner (Stone 2013). However, at the time of writing, the Taiwanese government has not sanctioned the building of a casino. Some government officials even said that Matsu is more suitable for developing tourism with its local features instead of constructing a casino.

In reviewing the state of gambling in Taiwan, we noticed the state of gambling in Taiwan shares some of the characteristics with their counterparts in PRC. As a state built on Confucian moral principles and social responsibilities, gambling, among the majority of ethnic Chinese, is considered as a social vice. Thus, it is difficult, if not impossible, for governmental authorities to initiate policies and legislations for the development of commercial gambling even in rural islands like Penghu and Matsu. Having said that, the authors of this publication still believe that casino integrated resorts and related business development are vital means for economic development. Maybe Chan et al. (2016) are right: As long as commercial gambling is carried out responsibly and morally, it can offer hopes and dreams for a better livelihood to the people in Macao and possibly for our friendly neighbors in Taiwan.

References

American Psychiatric Association. (1994). *Diagnostic and statistical manual of mental disorders* (4th ed.). Washington, DC: Author.

American Psychiatric Association. (2000). *Diagnostic and statistical manual of mental disorders* (4th ed., text-revision). Washington, DC: Author.

American Psychiatric Association. (2013). *Diagnostic and statistical manual of mental disorders* (5th ed.). Washington, DC: Author.

BBC Monitoring Asia Pacific. (2005, July). Most money from China's sports lottery goes on national fitness – Official. *Xinhua News Agency*.

BBC Monitoring Asia Pacific. (2007, December 2). China to issue first national regulation on lotteries next year. *Xinhua News Agency*.

Blaszczynski, A. (2009). Problem gambling: We should measure harm rather than 'cases. *British Journal of Addiction, 104*(7), 1070–1074.

Blaszczynski, A., & Nower, L. (2002). A pathways model of problem and pathological gambling. *British Journal of Addiction, 97*, 487–499.

Brown, R. I. F. (2002). Dissociation phenomena among normal and addicted gamblers. In J. J. Marotta, J. A. Cornelius, & W. R. Eadington (Eds.), *The downside: Problem and pathological gambling* (pp. 201–222). Reno: Institute for the Study of Gambling and Commercial Gaming/ University of Nevada, Reno.

Cai Piao Jiu Jiu. (2016, April). *Developmental history of lottery in new China*. Retrieved from http://caif866.com/post/383.html

Ceng, W. B. (2010). *Investigation on problematic lottery buyers in sports lottery in Shanghai*. Shanghai University of Sport. (曾雯彬 (2010).上海市體育彩票問題彩民研究.上海體育學院).

Chan, C. C. (2014, November). *The psychology of gambling and gambling treatment*. Keynote address at the 2nd Macau Medical Association Forum-MMAF, Macao SAR, China.

Chan, C. C., & Ohtsuka, K. (2013). The clinical and social construction of the paichais of Macau. *The Asian Journal of Gambling Issues and Public Health, 3*, 6, 1–11. Retrieved from https://doi.org/10.1186/2195-3007-3-6.

Chan, C. C., Li, W. L., & Leung, C. I. (2016). *Problem gambling in Hong Kong and Macao: Etiology, prevalence and treatment*. Singapore: Springer.

Chen, H. P. (2012). *Internet survey on Chinese lottery buyers' behaviors*. Lottery Research Center of China, Beijing Normal University (陳海平 (2012). 中國彩民行為網絡調查. 北京師範大學中國彩票事業研究中心). Retrieved from http://www.71.cn/2012/0422/665711.shtml

Chen, H. P. (2015). *Prevalence of Chinese problematic lottery buyers – Internet survey and analysis on cases reported by mass media*. Liaoning University Press (陳海平 (2015). 中國問題彩民流行率- 網絡調查與媒體案例分析. 遼寧大學出版社.).

Chen, H. P., Li, K., & Fan, L. S. (2013, December). *Challenges China mainland faces when lottery is allowed to distribute and to sell through internet/telephone*. Paper presented in the second Asia Pacific conference on gambling and commercial gaming research (APCG 2013), December 1–4, 2013, Kaohsiung.

Ferris, J., & Wynne, H. (2001). *The Canadian problem gambling index: User's manual*. Toronto: Canadian Centre on Substance Abuse.

Fong, K. C., & Ozorio, B. (2005). Gambling participation and prevalence estimates of pathological gambling in a Far-East gambling city: Macao. *UNLV Gaming Research & Review Journal, 9*, 15–28.

Friedman, M., & Savage, L. J. (1948). The utility analysis of choices involving risk. *Journal of Political Economy, 16*, 279–304.

Fung, K. C., & Ng, M. P. (2010, August). *Report on "Survey on Macao people's participation in gaming activities"*. University of Macao. (馮家超博士及伍美寶 (2010年8月). 「澳門居民參與博彩活動調查 *2010*」研究報告. 澳門大學博彩研究所).

Griffiths, M. D., & Parke, J. (2010). Adolescent gambling on the internet: A review. *Journal of Adolescent Medicine and Health, 22*(1), 59–75.

Han, G. X. (2013). Research on developmental history of Chinese sports lottery. *Shanxi Sports Science and Technology, 4*. (韓國星. (2013). 中國體育彩票發展史研究. 山西體育科技, *4*).

He, X. (2011, December 12). A citizen owns a RMB 10,000 note of regular small saving rewardable plan: The value is not high but worth collecting. *Yan Zhao Wan Bao* (賀霞 (2011年12月12日).市民有1953年萬元存單,不算巨額但有收藏價值.燕趙晚報). Retrieved from http://finance.people.com.cn/bank/BIG5/16576895.html

Jacobs, D. F. (1986). A general theory of addictions: A new theoretical model. *Journal of Gambling Studies, 2*, 15–31.

Kam, S. M., & Wong, I. L. K. (2014, July). *Study on soccer betting among Macao's college students*. Paper presented in the International Conference on Gaming, Leisure and Entertainment, 2014, Macao. (甘雪媚及黃麗娟 (2014年7月). 澳門大專學生參與足球賭博之研究. 博彩•休閒•娛樂國際學術研討會,澳門,中國).

Li, H. J. (2009). Experience of sports lottery issuance in mainland China. *National People's Sports, 38*(1). (李豪傑. (2009). 中國大陸發行體育彩票之經驗. 國民體育第三十八卷第一期).

Li, G. (2014). Research on the sales fairness of Chinese lottery industry. *Journal of Shanghai Normal University (Philosophy & Social Sciences Edition), 43*(4), 33–45. https://doi.org/10.13852/J.CNKI.JSHNU.2014.04.004.

Li, C. L. (2015). *Reviews on issuing history of China's sports lottery and research in legislation countermeasures*. Paper presented in the international conference on management science, education technology, arts, social science and economics (MSETASSE 2015). Atlantis Press.

Li, H., Wu, Y., Li, H. M., & Chen, J. (2011). Investigation on the current situation of problematic sports lottery buyers in China. *Journal of Shanghai Physical Education Institute, 37*(5), 9–13 (李海,吳毅,李宏民,陳敬 (2011).我國體育彩票問題彩民現狀調查.上海體育學院學報).

Lottery Research Center of China, Beijing Normal University. (2017). *Objectives of the lottery research center*. Retrieved from http://chinalottery.bnu.edu.cn/ABOUT/

Ministry of Finance of the People's Republic of China. *Annual Sports Lottery Sales* (2008–2016). Retrieved from http://www.mof.gov.cn/index.htm

PR Newswire. (2015, June 25). *China's casino and gambling industry outlook to 2019 – Growth led by surge in foreign tourists*. New York: ABI/INFORM Dateline.

Qianzhan Research Institute of Products. (2014, March 18). *Sports Lottery*. (前瞻產業研究院 (2014年3月18日). 體育彩票). Retrieved from http://big5.baike.qianzhan.com/detail/bk_81c9dd7c.html

Richins, M. L., & Dawson, S. (1992). A consumer values orientation for materialism and its measurement: Scale development and validation. *Journal of Consumer Research, 19*, 303–316. Retrieved from https://doi.org/10.1086/209304.

SinaChina. (2008, January 4). The mystery of Cai Shi Ta fraud. *Xinghua News Agency*. Retrieved from http://news.sina.com.cn/c/2008-01-04/143014668254.shtml

Skinner, B. F. (1971). *Beyond freedom and dignity*. New York: Knopf.

Stone, F. I. (2013). The big bet. *Foreign Policy, 202*, 66–70.

Storer, J., Abbott, M., & Stubbs, J. (2009). Access or adaptation? A meta-analysis of surveys of problem gambling prevalence in Australia and New Zealand with respect to concentration of electronic gaming machines. *International Gambling Studies, 9*, 225–244. https://doi.org/10.1080/14459790903257981.

The Hong Kong Polytechnic University. (2002). *Report on a study of Hong Kong People's participation in gambling activities*. Hong Kong: The Hong Kong Polytechnic University. Retrieved from http://www.hab.gov.hk/file_manager/en/documents/whats_new/gambling/report-eng.pdf

The Hong Kong Polytechnic University. (2011). *The study on Hong Kong people's participation in gaming activities*. Hong Kong: The Hong Kong Polytechnic University. Retrieved from http://www.hab.gov.hk/file_manager/en/documents/policy_responsibilities/others/gaming_report_2011.pdf

The University of Hong Kong. (2005). *Report on a study of Hong Kong people's participation in gambling activities*. Hong Kong: The University of Hong Kong. Retrieved from http://www.hab.gov.hk/file_manager/en/documents/whats_new/gambling/KeyStat_200514_e.pdf

Tsitsika, A., Critselis, E., Janikian, M., Kormas, G., & Kafetzis, D. A. (2011). Association between internet gambling and problematic internet use among adolescents. *Journal of Gambling Studies, 27*(3), 389–400.

University of Macao. (2014). *Report on a study of Macao people's participation in gambling activities 2013*. Macao: Institute for the Study of Commercial Gaming.

Wang, Y. Y. (2006). *Study on pathological gambling among the consumption on sports lottery*. Dalian University of Technology. (王艷耘 (2006). 體育彩票消費中病態賭博問題研究.大連理工大學).

Wang, Y. (2011). *Studies on problematic lottery buyers' personality traits in Shanghai's sports lottery consumption*. East China Normal University. (王燕 (2011).上海市體育彩票消費中問題彩民的人格特徵研究.華東師範大學).

Wardle, H., Sproston, K., Orford, J., Erens, B., Griffiths, M. D., Constantine, R., & Pigott, S. (2007). *British gambling prevalence survey 2007*. Retrieved from http://www.gamblingcommission.gov.uk/pdf/British%20Gambling%20Prevalence%20Survey%202007.pdf

Williams, R. J., Volberg, R. A., & Stevens, R. M. G. (2012). *The population prevalence of problem gambling: Methodological influences, standardized rates, jurisdictional differences, and worldwide trends*. Report prepared for the Ontario Problem Gambling Research Centre and the Ontario Ministry of Health and Long Term Care.

Wu, H. (2004, December 3). The origin and end of "fake BMW case in Xian". *Xinhua News Agency*. (吳皓(2004年12月3日).西安寶馬彩票案始末.新華社). Retrieved from http://www.people.com.cn/BIG5/shehui/1062/3030951.html

Wu, A. M. S., Lai, M. H. C., & Tong, K. K. (2015). Internet gambling among community adults and university students in Macau. *Journal of Gambling Studies, 31*, 643–657. https://doi.org/10.1007/s10899-014-9451-8.

Yang, T. (2015, January 26). China Administration Center of Welfare Lottery Distribution explained the whole picture about the delay of double chromosphere draw on January 25, 2015. *Xinhua News Agency*. Retrieved from http://news.xinhuanet.com/politics/2015-01/26/c_1114137623.htm

Chapter 4
The Motivation of Chinese Disordered Gamblers: A Cultural Perspective

In a recent prevalence study conducted on Macao, gambling researchers Wu et al. (2014) concluded that "materialism may continually promote people's gambling motive to win money in order to satisfy their materialistic need, thus making them vulnerable to gambling disorder" (p. 1196). Here, the authors argued that the major motivation of gambling for the majority of Chinese gamblers is winning money. Materialistic concerns are the basic reasons for Chinese to participate in gambling activities. This assertion negates the psychodynamic explanation of gambling to displace inferiority in childhood (Rosenthal 1986) and the behaviorist view of gambling to escape from personal problems (Brown 2002; Jacobs 1986). Is winning money the principal motivation among the majority of Chinese disordered gamblers? What are the factors that make gambling the favorite pastime in Chinese communities? Before we can realistically approach this question, we need to have an understanding of the particular cultural aspects of Chinese heritage that contribute to the development of gambling. The present chapter will address the list of questions from a cultural perspective.

4.1 Gambling as a Socially Acceptable Pastime in Traditional Chinese Communities

In traditional Confucian teaching, a good person should be hardworking and devoted to his/her career; play brings no benefits to the moral integrity of a person (勤有功, 戲無益). In other words, in Chinese culture, play and leisure, especially in the form of gambling, is not preferred. Throughout history, Chinese parents teach their children to be productive and useful to their families and country. Hence, while the American psychiatric professionals describe disordered gamblers in terms of gambler's personality and adverse consequences of gambling (DSM-5, American Psychiatric Association 2013), Chinese people see play, especially excessive gambling, as an ontological social vice.

C. C. Chan et al., *The Psychology of Chinese Gambling*,
https://doi.org/10.1007/978-981-13-3486-3_4

However, play is an important part of our lives (Smith and Abt 1984). Classical studies on the play behaviors of children (e.g., Parten 1932) propose that children love to play at a very young age. In Chap. 1, we have highlighted the historical development of gambling in China. One important observation we discovered is that gambling has been a favorite pastime throughout the centuries among Chinese communities. The ancient games like *Liubo* and *Hanging Horse* (the earliest version of the present-day mahjong) were all common family games. There are two salient characteristics of these games. Firstly, these table games require specific cognitive skills and strategies by which the players use to compete with each other. As the players invest more efforts in the games, their winning probability would be significantly enhanced. Secondly, monetary element is not the most important part of gambling – it is the excitement and the related entertaining process that attract the players to the game. The game is a fun pastime. This is why the first author believes that most Chinese gamblers, especially those recreational gamblers, gamble with the money and not for the money (Chan 2014).

Narratives regarding Chinese gamblers indicated that the majority of gamblers first learned about gambling from their parents and childhood peers (Chan 2014; Ohtsuka and Chan 2014). In fact, gambling is a common family pastime during festivals and Chinese holidays. Figures 4.1, 4.2, and 4.3 show gambling activities among Chinese people during Lunar New Year festivals. The game they were playing was called *Hoo Hey How* (魚蝦蟹). In this game, the banker throws dices in a large bowl and asks the players to wager on the outcomes of the combination of dices. The winner of the game is the one who can correctly estimate the winning number(s)/symbol(s). This game requires minimal skills. Thus, it is a highly favored game among illiterate laborers working in factories, construction sites, and food markets and the elderly living in community centers or residential homes. Children can also share the fun and excitement of this game, especially during holidays and family festivals as the pictures clearly demonstrate.

Figure 4.4 is a photo exhibiting a housewarming party. The guests are playing a game of *Cussec*, a popular table game in Hong Kong. Figures 4.5 and 4.6 capture

Figs. 4.1, 4.2, and 4.3 Family gathering during Lunar New Year. Family members enjoying the game of *Hoo Hey How*. (Photos taken by the second author on January 31, 2017)

Fig. 4.4 People participated in gambling during housewarming party. (Photo taken by Cheung Wing Chi on February 1, 2017)

Figs. 4.5 and 4.6 Elderly gambled in nursing homes in Hong Kong. (Photos taken by Li Wai Lim on October 17, 2016)

elderly playing Chinese poker in nursing home. Chinese poker games and mahjong are integral elements in the daily schedules of most nursing. For the retired elderly, especially those confined to wheelchairs or indoor walking, recreational gambling is a meaningful pastime. For many, it delivers an existential meaning to life in communal livelihood (Ohtsuka and Chan 2014). These pictures support the assertion that gambling activities are favorable entertainment in Chinese communities.

4.2 Behaviorally Conditioned Problem Gamblers: Disordered Gambling as a Favorite Pastime that Gets Out of Control

Blaszczynski and Nower's (BN) (2002) pathway model of problem and pathological gambling is an empirically based model that addresses the personality development of gamblers. The fundamental premise of this model is that the 3As of gambling opportunities, namely, early accessibility, availability, and acceptability, are crucial to one's development of gambling behavior. Problem gamblers often report early gambling experiences with family members and peers. Very often, these activities are their favorite pastimes in childhood. Many of them recall early winning experiences that reinforce their continued involvement in gambling in early adulthood.

The importance of the 3As of gambling can help us understand the motivation and personality development of Chinese disordered gamblers. In Hong Kong and Macao, Chan and his colleagues (Chan 2014; Chan and Ohtsuka 2013; C. C. Chan et al. 2012; Chiu and Chan 2015) reported a series of validation studies on the BN (2002) model. In these studies, participants were recruited from various occupational groups and social background in Hong Kong. There were groups of working-class housewives, cargo laborers, sex workers, taxi drivers, retirees, Macao casino players, investors in the stock market, and female Filipino domestic helpers. The participants were interviewed by structured questionnaires, built on DSM-IV-TR (American Psychiatric Association 2000) and Problem Gambling Severity Index (PGSI) (Ferris and Wynne 2001). The interview protocols included enquiries into the respondents' developmental histories, their careers and social relationships, and gambling habits. Major findings indicated that the BN (2002) model can adequately explain the personality and gambling development of problem gamblers. Most of the problem gamblers reported early experiences of gambling. Very often, they, as the BN model stipulates, learned to gamble from family and friends during childhood. Gambling was their favorite pastime. An early winning experience was often reported. As they matured into adulthood, their involvement in gambling activities became more intensive. Many even considered gambling as their only hobby and pastime in life.

The narratives of players on soccer betting provide excellent illustrations on these disordered gamblers (Au Yeung et al. 2011). As children, almost all of these gamblers loved the game of soccer. They participated in soccer betting as they wanted to have more involvement in their pastimes. It was not until they developed gambling problems that they saw the need for counseling and treatment. For these gamblers, their emotional problems such as depression and anxiety are the consequences of their gambling. Blaszczynski and Nower (2002) termed this type of gamblers as behaviorally conditioned gamblers. For them, disordered gambling is a favorite pastime that gets out of control.

In addition to early acceptability and early availability of gambling opportunities, Chinese gamblers also find gambling activities to be easily accessible all over Mainland China, as sports and welfare lottery tickets are commonly sold in major convenience stores. Moreover, there are numerous underground casinos and gambling houses in major cities (Chen and Zhang 2012). Players can also wager, illegally of course, on horse racing and underground Mark Six through telephone. In the special administrative regions of Macao and Hong Kong, gambling opportunities are even more easily accessible. At the time of writing, there are currently 41 casinos in Macao (with an area less than one third of Las Vegas) operated by 6 licensed enterprises. All casinos are open 24/7. Literature on problem gambling evidenced a positive association between the proximity of casino venue and increased gambling prevalence (Korn and Shaffer 1999; Productivity Commission 2010; Tong and Chim 2013). Thus, easy accessibility to gambling opportunities can be related to an increase in problem gambling.

Started as a childhood hobby, motivations for gambling for these gamblers are very diverse (Chan 2014). Some gamble to socialize with friends, while others play the games for materialistic gains. For the majority of Chinese gamblers, especially those who belong to the lower socioeconomic class, gambling can be an inexpensive game. While the rich and the famous can make expensive travels and spend millions on cars and luxury items, individuals living in a poor neighborhood, especially those retired elderly, can find meaning and fun in a game of mahjong (Ohtsuka and Chan 2014). They do not gamble for materialistic gains. In other words, they gamble with the money, not for the money (Chan and Ohtsuka 2011). From a sociological point of view, Cavion et al. (2008) wrote: "This suggests that gambling maybe one of a general constellation of coping behaviors employed by marginalized groups, or, less pejoratively, is one of a cluster of historically condemned behaviors more easily or openly adopted by groups with weaker affiliation to the dominant power structure (In the pursuit of winning" (p.112-113). In this vein of thought, gambling can be taken as a meaningful activity for those who feel alienated from the more affluent social groups. It is only when this pastime gets out of control that these gamblers develop problems.

4.3 The Emotionally Vulnerable Gamblers: Disordered Gambling as an Emotional Escape from Personal Problems

In contrast to behaviorally conditioned gamblers whose gambling starts early in childhood and is a favorite pastime with peers, emotionally vulnerable gamblers seek emotional escape, usually unconsciously, through gambling activities. Qualitative studies on the motivation of Chinese emotionally vulnerable gamblers are few. Disordered gamblers scored significantly lower in all domains on quality of life (Mythily et al. 2011). Life dissatisfaction may lead to negative emotions and thus serve as a motivation for gamblers to gamble for boredom alleviation, mood alternation, and escape (Tao et al. 2011; Wu et al. 2012). In Hong Kong and Macao, the first author of this publication has carried out a number of research projects on women and gambling. In one of the qualitative studies with female sex workers, C. Y. Chan et al. (2012) found that women with emotional problems sought gambling as a means of emotional escape. The participants were interviewed on their gambling histories, careers, and relationship development. Majority of the female sex workers were found to have significant emotional problems prior to their acquisition of gambling habits. Many of them suffered from depression and anxiety for a lengthy period of time. In response to these problems, they sought gratification and emotional escape from addiction, which was gambling in their case. For these sex workers, gambling was a source of defense mechanism for their personal problems, a finding suggested by Brown (2002), who argued that gamblers with depressed moods are more prone to employ gambling, often unconsciously, as a means for emotional dissociation and regulation.

Wood and Griffiths (2007) have provided support for this assertion. Fifty problem gamblers, aged from 18 to 63, participated in the study. The participants were interviewed on a protocol. The results suggested that the majority of gamblers were emotionally vulnerable gamblers. A detailed thematic analysis on the participants' responses indicated that problem gamblers gambled to escape from personal problems. Such an escape is achieved through mood modification. Therefore gambling, for these individuals, serves the function of filling their emptiness in life.

This assertion has been supported by a literature review on Chinese female gamblers. Leung (2017) argued that Chinese women are more prone to employ gambling as a means to escape from stress and negative emotions. These gamblers neither gamble to win more money nor materialistic gains but to divert, rather unconsciously, their attention away from everyday problems and frustration. On this issue, Jacobs' (1986) general theory of addiction suggests that gambling addiction serves to regulate emotions. Thus, gambling for these women is a means to obtain emotional relief, being a psychological oasis where gamblers seek psychological solace through momentary sensory stimulation and mood modification (Ohtsuka and Chan 2009). In other words, gambling is a form of defense mechanism for these female gamblers. It is a sort of self-medication through which they attempt to help themselves. Successful treatment for these clients, therefore, has to incorporate therapy and counseling catered for their emotional vulnerabilities and concerns.

4.4 Antisocial/Impulsive Gamblers: Disordered Gambling as an Aspect of a Deep-Rooted Antisocial Personality Style

The third group of disordered gamblers is the antisocial/impulsive gamblers. For this group of disordered gamblers, gambling is an integral aspect of their personality and lifestyle. Physiologically, they might have inborn neurological and/or neurochemical biological deficiencies in controlling impulses, though they also possess similar psychosocial vulnerabilities as the emotionally vulnerable gamblers (Blaszczynski and Nower 2002). The majority of them can be described as antisocial and impulsive (Blaszczynski and McConaghy 1994; Blaszczynski and Steel 1998; Tse et al. 2012). Their failure to control impulses and to seek immediate gratification of wants and desires without carefully evaluating the resulting consequences may begin at childhood. Looking for constant stimulation from their environment, these gamblers tend to be impulsive and manipulative in their social relationships. Behaviorally, they display a broad range of conduct problems, usually starting in teenage years or even earlier, which include stealing and fighting, truancy, cruelty to animals, substance abuse, fire setting, and involvement in criminal acts. Their ability to achieve insight into their problems, even after a series of severe punishments, is poor, and they show no remorse. Irresponsible and excessive gambling is a part of their antisocial behavioral patterns. In other words, their conduct problems existed prior to their disordered gambling. Their failure to control impulses in gambling results in chasing their losses (Blaszczynski and Steel 1998; Chan and Ohtsuka 2013). Moreover, they usually display superficial charm and perform pathological lying in order to cheat their families and friends out of money. Thus, the chief motivation of these gamblers is the seeking for excitement and constant stimulation. Many of them, of course, would gamble for the winning; nevertheless, it is the excitement that attracts and keeps them in the games.

The lifestyles of the antisocial gamblers are different from those of the behaviorally conditioned gamblers. While majority of the behaviorally conditioned gamblers have stable employment and career development, the antisocial/impulsive gamblers see little shame nor guilt in living off the savings of family and friends. For them, excitement, play, and stimulation are the primary concerns of life. As such, many antisocial gamblers preoccupy themselves with gambling and other risky activities every day. Some even take gambling venues as their second homes. In a study on mahjong houses in Hong Kong, Khiatani et al. (2013) found that many of these gamblers visit gambling venues a few times a week. Some even go every day. It is a place where they can relax and socialize with their friends. In other words, the gambling houses are, as the researchers argued, their "third places," a living and entertainment hub after their homes and workplaces.

A similar observation has been reported by Chan and Ohtsuka (2013) in their study on disordered gamblers in Macao. Many antisocial/impulsive gamblers never leave the casinos. Some of them find a living in the casinos by working illegally as middlemen for loan sharks. Some live off the complimentary foods and drinks provided by the casinos. Almost all of them do not have a socially responsible career.

Locals in Macao call them *Paichai* (扒仔), a sarcastic name which literally means "illegal takers" or "loan sharks' servant boys." These disordered gamblers, like their counterparts in the mahjong houses in Hong Kong, enjoy a lifestyle of which gambling and other socially inappropriate behaviors such as drinking and visiting prostitutes are blended together. To this kind of gamblers, gambling is a common language and activity they can relate to with their peers. Their motivation of gambling can be very diverse: the excitement of the games, the validation from peers, the winning of the money, or simply the meaning of their lives (Chan and Ohtsuka 2013). As they do not see the need for treatment on their gambling problems, they would not seek professional help voluntarily. On rare circumstances, they are forced to come to treatment, either by their family members who help them pay off debts (usually negotiated with their family members before they are "willing" to come to treatment) or by government authorities on court orders. However, their compliance rates are usually poor (Chan 2014).

4.5 The Materialistic Gamblers: Disordered Gambling as a Consequence of Greed

Richins and Dawson (1992) defined materialism as "a set of centrally held beliefs about the importance of possession in one's life" (p. 308). Put in simpler terms, individuals who put priority on materialism consider monetary gains and acquisition of material possessions such as nice houses, expensive cars, and luxury their chief concerns in life. In studies conducted on Chinese gamblers, materialism is found to be positively associated with the gamblers' problems (Tao et al. 2011; Wu et al. 2012). Almost in all prevalence studies on Chinese gamblers, one consistent finding is that people participate in the game for the winning of money (e.g., Zeng and Forrest 2009; Zeng and Zhang 2007). Put in more succinct terms, winning money is the major motivation in Chinese gambling (Kale and Spence 2009). This assertion is supported by Chan, Wan, and Wong (2015), who found that 70.2% of Hong Kong Chinese gamblers in their study (N = 118) and 54.7% of Mainland Chinese gamblers (N = 110) aimed to win money in their gambling.

The first author has been serving as a psychologist in Hong Kong and Macao for over 25 years. In his research studies, he has asked numerous lottery players the motivation behind their gambling. The predominant answer is winning the big prize (Chan 2014). In their responses, they would often describe how their lives and their loved ones would be changed with the winning. The majority would say they would buy a luxurious apartment with their money. Others said they would stop working and travel around the world. When these gamblers talked about their winning wishes, which, I trust, none of them might ever achieve, they sounded hopeful and joyful. It is precisely this hope and the love of money that give them the impetus to buy lotteries every week. For them, gambling is not a favorite pastime – it is a means for making more money.

The materialistic gamblers differ from the behaviorally conditioned gamblers in that the former may not come from a childhood that encourages gambling activities; nor do they have any emotional problems prior to the acquisition of gambling habits as the emotionally vulnerable gamblers do. Instead, materialism and the desire to get rich and to improve one's livelihood may be the main motivation of the disordered gamblers who came from economically disadvantaged groups. It has been a consistent finding among prevalence studies that gamblers with lower income are more likely to gamble a larger proportion of their income in their wagering (e.g., The Hong Kong Polytechnic University 2011; Wardle et al. 2007). So why do the poorer people gamble more? What is the motivation of gambling for the socially disadvantaged groups? Arguing from a sociological perspective, Devereux (1968) believed that gambling is socially functional for the poor as it serves as a safety valve for these individuals in modernized capitalist society, where education, expertise, social connections, and hard work are the fundamentals for success. An educated professional engineer or medical doctor can expect to earn HK$100,000 (or US $13,000) a month in Hong Kong, while a manual laborer makes less than $10,000 (US $1300) per month. For these individuals and those who are unable to achieve these materialistic goals in a capitalistic society, gambling would provide a means to achieve personal riches and advancement in a quick way. Thus, from a social viewpoint, gambling is functional as it helps maintain the status quo in society. In essence, it renders the less fortunate the opportunities to social mobility and advancement. Winning the grand prize in lottery can help one to live the dreams of a lifetime. Put it more succinctly in psychological language, gambling gives a materialistic wish for the poor. On this issue, the Friedman-Savage model of gambling and social climbing (Friedman and Savage 1948) proposes that gambling offers hope for the poor, while life and property insurance protects the wealth of the rich and famous. Hence, buying a welfare lottery of RMB$2 (about US 30 cents) would bring materialistic hope for a poor Mainland Chinese factory worker. It is exactly this expected utility of gambling (Hartley and Farrell 2002) that makes it socially functional. Unlike the antisocial/impulsive gamblers, materialistic gamblers often maintain a stable career. They do not have problem behaviors, and they usually have a positive perspective on life and work. To them, gambling is neither a sin nor a pastime; it is a meaningful activity to achieve riches in life.

The materialistic gamblers and the behaviorally conditioned gamblers are not mutually exclusive groups. In the first author's experiences while working with disordered gamblers in Hong Kong, he has identified several interesting features in the motivation of Chinese behaviorally conditioned gamblers. Many a time, the initial motivation of these gamblers is the excitement and fun of the games. This is especially true for the young players in soccer betting (Au Yeung et al. 2011). For these young gamblers, the wagering is secondary to the enjoyment of the games (love the games, not the odds). Nevertheless, with increased involvement in gambling, their motives on gambling become more diverse. The nature of gambling evolves from the enjoyment of a pastime and hobby to wagering for monetary gains. Another good example is a qualitative study on cargo laborers reported by Chan and Chan (2012). In this investigation, the researchers interviewed a number of manual laborers working in the cargo terminals. All of them gambled on horse racing and soccer matches. Some of them first started as recreational gamblers. However, as they spent more time and efforts on the games, their chief motivation in the wagering was winning the sweepstakes and the jackpot. The fun and the joy were secondary to the materialistic motives of gambling. One interesting finding among Chinese behaviorally conditioned gamblers, especially the punters in horse racing, is that as they begin to lose, their interest and enjoyment in the games slowly disappear. In other words, their continued involvement in gambling manifests their desire of chasing over their losses rather than the love of the games (love the odds, not the games).

Hence, the fundamental motivation of the materialistic gamblers is the hope for monetary gains. Ginakis and Ohtsuka (2005) asserted that everyone needs hope, which can be classified into two types: long term and short term. Unable to attain any long-term hope, wagering on horse races at least provides an unemployed restaurant worker with a short-term hope, a hope that the person cannot receive in his everyday job. It is this hope that motivates him to gamble persistently, albeit repeatedly frustrated by his many losses.

In delineating the motivation of problem gamblers, we see Chinese gamblers' motivation as diverse and shifting over their development of gambling history. In the first author's experiences with Chinese gamblers (Chan 2014), the majority of Chinese gamblers start as recreational gamblers. Their interest in gambling often starts in early childhood with friends and family. When asked about their motivation in gambling, they would declare "killing time" and "fun, excitement and interest" in their responses. However, when they are more involved in excessive gambling, many of them would say "winning money" as their major or only goal. By then, some disordered gamblers might even take gambling, rather unconsciously, as a compulsive behavior through which they feel a need to engage in daily gaming activities. Starting from this moment, the fun and joy they once enjoyed is gone. Instead, they gamble to chase over their losses and to escape from the withdrawal symptoms, such as anxiety and depression, of gambling disorders. Maybe what Wu et al. (2014) asserted is too simplistic in our portrayal of Chinese gamblers' motivation in gambling. We trust that materialism is only one of the factors that contributes to why people gamble. There are a host of other factors that we need to look into in order to understand the motivation of these gamblers.

References

American Psychiatric Association. (2000). *Diagnostic and statistical manual of mental disorders* (4th ed., text rev.). Washington, DC: Author.

American Psychiatric Association. (2013). *Diagnostic and statistical manual of mental disorders* (5th ed.). Washington, DC: Author.

Au Yeung, C. S., Lam, P. Y., & Chan, C. C. (2011). *Soccer betting in Hong Kong – A profile of young bettors* (pp. 276–283). In Conference proceedings of the international conference on Gaming Industry and Public Welfare 2011, Beijing, China.

Blaszczynski, A., & McConaghy, N. (1994). Criminal offences in gamblers anonymous and hospital-treated pathological gamblers. *Journal of Gambling Studies, 10*(2), 99–127. https://doi.org/10.1007/BF02109935.

Blaszczynski, A., & Nower, L. (2002). A pathways model of problem and pathological gambling. *British Journal of Addiction, 97*, 487–499.

Blaszczynski, A., & Steel, Z. (1998). Personality disorders among pathological gamblers. *Journal of Gambling Studies, 41*, 51–71.

Brown, R. I. F. (2002). Dissociation phenomena among normal and addicted gamblers. In J. J. Marotta, J. A. Cornelius, & W. R. Eadington (Eds.), *The downside: Problem and pathological gambling* (pp. 201–222). Reno: Institute for the Study of Gambling and Commercial Gaming/University of Nevada, Reno.

Cavion, L., Wong, C., & Zangeneh, M. (2008). Gambling: A sociological perspective. In M. Zangeneh, A. Blaszczynski, & N. E. Turner (Eds.), *In the pursuit of winning: Problem gambling theory, research and treatment* (pp. 95–117). New York: Springer.

Chan, C. C. (2014, November). *The psychology of gambling and gambling treatment*. A keynote address at the 2nd Macau Medical Association Forum-MMAF, Macao SAR, China.

Chan, Y. Y., & Chan, C. C. (2012, March). *Pathways development of problem gamblers: Validation of Blaszczynski and Nower (2002) model*. Paper presented at the Asian Conference on Psychology and the Behavioral Sciences, Osaka, Japan.

Chan, C. C., & Ohtsuka, K. (2011). Pathways to development of problem gambling among Chinese gamblers in Hong Kong: Validation of the Blaszczynski and Nower (2002) model. *The Asian Journal of Gambling Issues and Public Health, 2*, 17–28.

Chan, C. C., & Ohtsuka, K. (2013). The clinical and social construction of the Paichais of Macau. *The Asian Journal of Gambling Issues and Public Health, 3*, 6, 1–11. Retrieved from https://doi.org/10.1186/2195-3007-3-6.

Chan, C. C., Ohtsuka, K., & Chan, K. I. (2012). *Pathways to recreational gambling and problem gambling: A summary of eight studies*. In Conference Proceedings of the International Conference on Gaming Industry and Public Welfare 2012, Beijing, China (pp. 54–63). ISBN: 9789996520600.

Chan, C. Y., Yick, K. S. C., Khiatani, P. V., Tse, T. H. M., & Chan, C. C. (2012). *Problem gambling among female sex workers in Hong Kong*. Paper presented at the 22nd National Association for Gambling Studies Annual Conference, Launceston, Australia.

Chan, S. H. J., Wan, Y. K. P., & Wong, I. K. A. (2015). Exploring the differences among Chinese casino gamblers' characteristics, motivations, and behaviors. *Journal of Vacation Marketing, 21*(1), 23–36.

Chen, X. Q., & Zhang, J. J. (2012). Motivation of private lottery buyers. *China Journal of Health Psychology, 20*(3), 363–365 (陳秀芹及張積家(2012). 私彩彩民的心理動機. 中國健康心理學染志, 20(3), 363–365).

Chiu, A. S. L., & Chan, C. C. (2015). Meta-analysis of problem gambling in Hong Kong: Using qualitative approach. *Journal of Gambling, Tourism & Leisure Research, 1*, 90–101.

Devereux, E. C. (1968). Gambling in psychological and sociological perspective. *International Encyclopedia of the Social Science, 6*, 53–62.

Ferris, J., & Wynne, H. (2001). *The Canadian problem gambling index: User's manual*. Toronto: Canadian Centre on Substance Abuse.

Friedman, M., & Savage, L. J. (1948). The utility analysis of choices involving risk. *Journal of Political Economy, 16*, 279–304.

Ginakis, S., & Ohtsuka, K. (2005). Problem gambling: An exploration of the role of global personal hopefulness, short-term gambling hope, and illusion of control beliefs. *Gambling Research, 17*, 7–16.

Hartley, R., & Farrell, L. (2002). Can expected utility theory explain gambling? *The American Economic Review, 92*(3), 613–624.

Jacobs, D. F. (1986). A general theory of addictions: A new theoretical model. *Journal of Gambling Studies, 2*, 15–31.

Kale, S., & Spence, M. T. (2009). Casino customers in Asian versus Western gaming jurisdictions: Implications for Western casino operators. *Worldwide Hospitality and Tourism Themes, 1*(4), 320–331.

Khiatani, P. V., Yick, K. S. C., Chan, C. Y., Tse, T. H. M., & Chan, C. C. (2013, December). *The quasi-legitimate 'third place': A qualitative investigation into the culture and context of gambling houses in Hong Kong*. Paper presented at the 2nd Asia Pacific conference on gambling & commercial gaming research, Kaohsiung, Taiwan.

Korn, D., & Shaffer, H. J. (1999). Gambling and the health of the public: Adopting a public health perspective. *Journal of Gambling Studies, 15*, 289–365.

Leung, A. (2017). Gambling problems among the female populations in Hong Kong. In H. Bowden-Jones & F. Prever (Eds.), *Gambling disorders in women: An international female perspective on treatment and research* (pp. 87–96). London/New York: Routledge.

Mythily, S., Edimansyah, A., Qiu, S. J., & Munidasa, W. (2011). Quality of life in pathological gamblers in a multiethnic Asian setting. *Annals Academy of Medicine Singapore, 40*, 264–268.

Ohtsuka, K., & Chan, C. C. (2009). Desperate housewives: An analysis of the characterizations of female gamblers portrayed in gambling movies in Hong Kong. *International Journal of Mental Health and Addiction, 7*, 229–238. https://doi.org/10.1007/s11469-010-9274-5.

Ohtsuka, K., & Chan, C. C. (2014). Senior gambling in Hong Kong: Through the lenses of Chinese senior gamblers – An exploratory study. *Asian Journal of Gambling Issues and Public Health, 4*(4), 1–12 Retrieved from https://ajgiph.springeropen.com/track/pdf/10.1186/s40405-014-0004-y.

Parten, M. B. (1932). Social participation among preschool children. *Journal of Abnormal and Social Psychology, 27*(3), 243–269. https://doi.org/10.1037/h0074524.

Productivity Commission. (2010). *Gambling*. Canberra: Productivity Commission.

Richins, M. L., & Dawson, S. (1992). A consumer values orientation for materialism and its measurement: Scale development and validation. *Journal of Consumer Research, 19*, 303–316.

Rosenthal, R. (1986). The pathological gambler's system for self-deception. *Journal of Gambling Behavior, 12*(2), 108–120.

Smith, J. F., & Abt, V. (1984). Gambling as play. *Annals of the American Academy of Political and Social Science, 474*, 122–132.

Tao, V. Y. K., Wu, A. M. S., Cheung, S. F., & Tong, K. K. (2011). Development of an indigenous inventory GMAB (Gambling Motives, Attitudes and Behaviors) for Chinese gamblers: An exploratory study. *Journal of Gambling Studies, 27*, 99–113.

The Hong Kong Polytechnic University. (2011). *The study on Hong Kong People's participation in gaming activities*. Hong Kong: The Hong Kong Polytechnic University Retrieved from http://www.hab.gov.hk/file_manager/en/documents/policy_responsibilities/others/gaming_report_2011.pdf.

Tong, H. H. Y., & Chim, D. (2013). The relationship between casino proximity and problem gambling. *Asian Journal of Gambling Issues and Public Health, 3*(2), 1–17. https://doi.org/10.1186/2195-3007-3-2.

Tse, T. H. M., Khiatani, P. V., Yick, K. S. C., Chan, C. Y., & Chan, C. C. (2012, November). *More than a simple game of 'Cops and Robbers': What marks the differences between law-enforcement personnel and individuals with a criminal background with gambling problems?* Paper presented at the 22nd national association for gambling studies annual conference, Launceston, Australia.

Wardle, H., Sproston, K., Orford, J., Erens, B., Griffiths, M. D., Constantine, R., & Pigott, S. (2007). *British gambling prevalence survey 2007.* Retrieved from http://www.gamblingcommission.gov.uk/pdf/British%20Gambling%20Prevalence%20Survey%202007.pdf

Wood, T. A., & Griffiths, M. D. (2007). A qualitative investigation of problem gambling as an escape-based coping strategy. *Psychology and Psychotherapy: Theory, Research and Practice, 80*, 107–125.

Wu, A. M. S., Tao, V. Y. K., Tong, K., & Cheung, S. F. (2012). Psychometric evaluation of inventory of gambling motives, attitudes and behaviors (GMAB) among Chinese gamblers. *International Gambling Studies, 12*, 331–347.

Wu, A. M. S., Lai, M. C. H., & Tong, K. K. (2014). Gambling disorder: Estimated prevalence rates and risk factors in Macao. *Psychology of Addictive Behaviors, 28*(4), 1190–1197.

Zeng, Z., & Forrest, D. (2009). High rollers from Mainland China: A profile based on 99 cases. *UNLV Gaming Research & Review Journal, 13*(1), 29–43.

Zeng, Z., & Zhang, D. (2007). A profile of lottery players in Guangzhou, China. *International Gambling Studies, 7*(3), 265–280. https://doi.org/10.1080/14459790701601430.

Chapter 5
The Personality of Chinese Gamblers

Personality refers to a person's consistent patterns of feeling, thinking, and behaving (Pervin et al. 2005). In the 1980s, researchers in addiction proposed that there are certain types of personality and attributes that predispose a person to substance and behavioral addictions. Among these researchers, Alan Lang (1983) put forward the concept of addictive personality. In his description, individuals with this personality style have an inborn and genetic propensity to addictive behaviors. Their notable behavioral characteristics include introversion and enjoyment of solitary pursuits, impulsiveness, and risk-taking. This proposition, though intriguing, is deterministic in nature as the model places the origins and etiology of addictive disorders on the genetic dispositions of a person. It neglects environmental influences, including the roles and attitudes of a person's family and friends. More importantly, the assertion disregards one's personal choices and discretion in governing one's gambling behavior. Scientific studies validating the concept of addictive personality have been very few (Myrseth 2011; Petry 2005). On this issue, Blaszczynski (Blaszczynski and Tempel 2008), in his keynote address at the National Association of Gambling Studies (NAGS), argued that an individual should have control over his/her gambling behavior and decisions. In this vein of thought, the responsibility of gambling should rest upon the judgment and decisions of the gambler rather than the genetic predisposition the person may have. In reviewing the literature on the personality of gamblers, Chan et al. (2016), in their recent book *Problem Gambling in Hong Kong and Macao: Etiology, Prevalence and Treatment*, came to the conclusion: "Bearing in mind that problem gamblers often come from diverse backgrounds with different motivations for gambling, there should not be one single type of addictive personality as Lang (1983) has proposed" (p. 71). The authors analyzed the personality and development of gamblers from Blaszczynski and Nower's (2002) model and presented a detailed account on the personality development of gamblers from an ecological-social-cognitive perspective. Nonetheless, the book failed to discuss the similarities and differences between Chinese gamblers and Western gamblers. The current chapter thus intends to fill this gap. Our purposes are to understand the personality characteristics of Chinese

C. C. Chan et al., *The Psychology of Chinese Gambling*,
https://doi.org/10.1007/978-981-13-3486-3_5

gamblers and the empirical differences in personality patterns, if any, between the Chinese gamblers and Western gamblers.

5.1 Local Studies on Chinese Gamblers' Personality

One of the major difficulties in reviewing existing literature on this topic is a lack of empirical studies on the personality of Chinese gamblers. Existing literature on Chinese gamblers was mostly published by researchers with training in social work, business, economics, and public administration (e.g., Chen 2012; Wong 2010). In many of these studies, the focus of investigation was often placed on prevalence rate, demographics, and social characteristics of gamblers (e.g., The Hong Kong Polytechnic University 2002, 2011, 2017; The University of Hong Kong 2005). Very few of the existing research have explored the personality characteristics of gamblers in depth. For instance, Cheng (2006) reported a qualitative study on eight Chinese female gamblers. Her investigation was based on a social work paradigm, within which the respondents were interviewed according to a structured protocol. The procedure did not include the use of validated psychological inventories. The findings concluded that the female gamblers reported gambling out of boredom and emotional problems. When compared to male gamblers, women gamblers often gambled with less money. For many of these participants, successful rehabilitation often did not come from psychological intervention as very few of them would voluntarily seek professional help. Instead, peer support was vital to their recovery processes.

The methodology of this investigation is prototypical of the majority of the qualitative studies reported in Hong Kong and Macao (e.g., Lam 2005; Wong et al. 2015). In these research projects, the researchers often recruited participants from gambling treatment centers. There was a lack of random sampling in the process. Secondly, these studies seldom employed the use of standard psychological personality tests. Instead, the participants were interviewed by the researchers on structured questionnaires, which focused on the assessment of demographic data and the trajectory of participants' gambling behavior and habits. However, there was an absence of in-depth description and exploration of the personality characteristics of the participants. Thus, it is difficult, if not impossible, to understand and analyze the personality traits of the gamblers.

With these concerns in mind, we will survey on the existing literature on personality characteristics of gamblers and outline the major personality traits of Chinese gamblers in this section. Our emphasis is to highlight the similarities and differences between Chinese gamblers and Western gamblers and to present a picture of the personality of Chinese gamblers.

5.2 Common Characteristics Among Chinese Problem Gamblers

Within the literature on gambling, the following are noted as the common personality characteristics of gamblers:

(a) Impulsivity

One consistent finding of the personality characteristic of gamblers is impulsivity (Chan et al. 2016; Petry 2005; Slutske et al. 2005). In a study with a nontreatment sample of 939 young participants, Slutske and her associates (2005) found that problem gambling was significantly correlated with risk-taking and impulsivity. This finding of impulsive and risk-taking behavior is also reported by Jackson et al. (2008) in a prevalence study on 2788 eighth grade students in Victoria, Australia. The researchers identified risk-taking and antisocial behaviors as the two most important personality characteristics among male adolescent problem gamblers. One consistent finding in the literature of problem gambling is that problem gamblers are characterized by higher rates of impulsivity than non-problem gamblers (Alessi and Petry 2003; Blaszczynski et al. 1997; Carlton and Manowitz 1994; Nower et al. 2004).

Cyders (Cyders and Smith 2007; Cyders et al. 2007a, b) investigated impulsivity as a personality construct. Clinically, there are five separate, though empirically related, constructs in impulsivity. Firstly, impulsivity is significantly related to one's emotions: negative urgency is the tendency to behave rashly when one is emotionally upset, and positive urgency is the propensity to act rashly when one is experiencing a positive mood. Besides, impulsivity encompasses one's lack of planning on one's behavior and the failure to persevere on finishing one's tasks. Lastly, the fifth construct is sensation-seeking or the tendency to seek thrilling or novel stimulus. As a personality trait, impulsivity can be distinguished into functional impulsivity and dysfunctional impulsivity (Nower and Blaszczynski 2006). Functional impulsivity describes a person who makes a quick decision on his/her behavior, which is beneficial to his personal growth and long-term development. On the contrary, a person with dysfunctional impulsivity tends to make a quick decision, which results in undesirable consequences. A gambler's repeated chasing over losses is a good example of dysfunctional impulsivity.

As an integral personality trait, impulsivity has been a significant diagnostic symptom of disordered gambling (American Psychiatric Association 2013). More impulsive gamblers demonstrate more severe clinical and adjustment problems in their lives. In treatment settings, individuals exhibiting high levels of impulsivity are more likely to drop out of treatment (Leblond et al. 2003). Thus, helping gamblers to establish their self-control should be an important element in treatment.

Neurologically, individuals with disordered gambling share striking similarities with persons with substance dependence, as both disorders are characterized by a lack of self-regulation and self-control (Goldstein and Volkow 2002; Goldstein et al. 2001; Goudriaan et al. 2006). Such deficiency among problem gamblers may be due to abnormalities in the brain reward circuitry (Potenza et al. 2003). Neurological-based investigations indicate specifically that diminished dopamine receptor availability causes a chronic reward deficiency in the brain which, in turn, might contribute to vulnerability to engage excessively in self-indulging addictive behaviors (Blum et al. 1996; Chim 2011). Failure to resist impulses and a lack of self-regulation often lead to poor decision-making. For instance, a disordered gambler often demonstrates a preference for a smaller reward while discounting a major reward (Goudriaan et al. 2005). This behavioral pattern might account for their repeated chasing behavior over losses, a significant diagnostic criterion for disordered gambling (*Diagnostic and Statistical Manual, 5th Version*, American Psychiatric Association 2013). Along this argument, Nower and Blaszczynski (2006) asserted that among problem gamblers, impulsive and sensation-seeking personality is one of the many predisposing factors, which interacts with other personality variables such as cognitive beliefs, emotional states, and motivational propensities to trigger problematic gambling behaviors.

To date, there are few empirical research on impulsivity and Chinese disordered gamblers. Most of the studies reported in mainland China did not employ validated assessing instruments in personality. Many of these studies projected a negative view on problem gamblers. For instance, Li (2014) described problem gamblers as "sick and unhealthy." Viewed from Chinese moral virtues, Li (2014) pointed out the many shortcomings of problem gamblers.

In the existing literature on the personality of Chinese gamblers, only those reported outside of mainland China used validated measures. For instance, in a research study conducted on Macao casino gamblers, Chan and Ohtsuka (2013) found that problem gamblers' impulsivity was demonstrated by their lack of self-discipline and insight into their problems. Furthermore, these individuals demonstrated impaired ability to delay gratification of wants in chasing over losses. Consequently, their responses to treatment were poor. This finding supports the argument of Strayhorn (2002) who defines impulsivity as deficits in self-control, expressed as failure to delay gratification, lack of self-discipline, absence of long-term planning and forethought, risk-taking, and sensation-seeking.

On this issue, Chan and his students (Khiatani et al. 2013; Tse et al. 2012) interviewed disordered gamblers who were also members of the criminal world. Most of these individuals belonged to Chinese criminal gangs. Some had spent a long time in prisons. In the interviews, the researchers found most of these gamblers demonstrated antisocial and impulsive behaviors. They could best be described as egocentric, cunning, socially irresponsible, risk-taking, and lacked the capacity to empathize with others. These findings support the propositions of Pathway Three of the BN model.

Paradoxically, traditional Confucian teaching treasures the virtues of Ren (仁) or humility, modesty, and interpersonal harmony in one's conduct. These virtues run against the commonly reported traits of gamblers such as impulsivity and risk-taking. In our analysis on the cultural history of Chinese gambling, we trust that our traditional Chinese virtues of *Li* (propriety) and *Yi* (righteousness) proposed in Confucianism have been severely undermined by the 10-year Cultural Revolution (1966–1976) in Mainland China. Then, with economic modernization in China in the last 40 years, our traditional Chinese culture has slowly been suppressed or even overtaken by Western values such as individualism, hedonism, and consumerism. For the majority of Chinese nowadays, gambling, with its emphasis on monetary gains and sensory excitement, is a socially acceptable pastime in China. It is no longer a social vice. Gamblers are not viewed as sinners anymore, as long as they do not run into heavy losses.

(b) Negative Emotionality

One of the most consistent findings on the personality characteristics of problem gamblers is that problem gamblers are found to be more clinically depressed than non-gamblers. Ciarrocchi et al. (1991) used the Minnesota Multiphasic Personality Inventory (MMPI) (Hathaway and McKinley 1943) as the assessing instrument and found that a number of the problem gamblers demonstrated elevated scores on scale 4-Pd (psychopathic deviate) and scale 2-D (depression). Individuals with their clinical profile often indicate significant psychopathology including depression, emotional liability, and antisocial traits. However, it is not clear that the negative emotionality is the cause or the consequence of the gambling behavior. The study only implies a correlation between the two constructs only.

More recently, McCown and Chamberlain (2005) conducted a study on 387 pathological gamblers recruited from treatment facilities. Employing MMPI-2 as the assessing instrument, the researchers identified two distinct clusters that accounted for 56% of the gamblers in treatment. The first cluster was characterized by elevations on scales 1-Hs (hypochondriasis), 2-D (depression), and 3-Hy. Individuals with this profile are usually depicted as prone to emotional problems. They might have mental health complications such as depression and anxiety. In face of stress, these gamblers may gamble to escape from their personal problems. Further analysis on the demographic data of the participants indicated that women were overrepresented in this group. The second cluster, accounting for 26% of the participants, was characterized by elevations on scale 9-Ma (mania) and scale 4-Pd (psychopathic deviate), and low on scale 0-Si (social introversion). Behaviorally, this clinical profile describes gamblers with antisocial and impulsive lifestyle. These individuals lack the ability to make moral decisions appropriately. Probably out of these traits, they often gamble heavily and chase over losses. Very often, they fail to maintain a socially responsible lifestyle.

Empirical studies on neuroticism and Chinese gambling are few. Taormina (2009), in a study on problem gamblers in Macao, found that gambling behaviors were positively correlated with neuroticism. The findings indicated that the gamblers' adherence to traditional Chinese cultural values on gambling might create significant ambivalence and cognitive dissonance (a discrepancy between what one thinks and what one does) and negative emotionality. Viewed from this perspective, in another study carried out on Macao, Taormina and Chong (2015) investigated 200 Macao residents aged 18 to 67 years on their cognitive dissonance, or the inconsistency between what they believed and did in gambling. Their findings revealed that the respondents who reported high gambling behavior and strong negative beliefs about gambling often scored high in the instrument assessing cognitive dissonance. Respondents who fell into this "high cognitive dissonance group" also scored high (though not significant) in the Neuroticism-Worry measure. In other words, individuals with higher cognitive dissonance were strongly associated with more frequent gambling, which in turn contributed to their experiences of negative emotions.

Among these individuals, women gamblers were found to be more inclined to have negative emotionality. Chan and his colleagues (2012), in a qualitative investigation on female sex workers in Hong Kong, reported that female gamblers were more inclined to employ gambling as a means of emotional escape. In addition to gambling, many of these gamblers also indulged in other types of addiction. They were prone to have depression and anxiety problems. As a defense mechanism, gambling is functional as it can help the person to stay away from her personal problems. Hence, for these gamblers, negative emotions, such as depression and anxiety, precede their gambling behavior. However, these participants only represented a small portion of female population in Hong Kong. Further studies are encouraged to include female gamblers from all walks of life.

5.3 Chinese Gamblers' Collectivistic Culture and Personality

When compared to Western culture, Chinese society is largely a collectivistic culture. Schwartz (1990) explains that collectivism, as a cultural value, is characterized by an emphasis on cohesiveness among individuals. In this regard, the needs of the group take a higher priority over those of an individual's. Individuals who are ascribed to such a worldview are inclined to find the group's common values and goals as particularly salient. Moreover, they are more likely to support and help each other in the same community. They also demonstrate greater orientation toward the needs and values of in-group members than toward those in the out-group (Oyserman 1993). In a collectivist culture, the honor and concerns of one's clan and family are more important than one's own. There is a Chinese famous motto precisely describes the mentality of collectivistic culture – "One for all, and all for one (人人為我,我為人人)." As members of a collective culture, Chinese disordered gamblers dare not to voice out their gambling problems which will bring shame and disgrace to their families and to the entire community. Thus, many problem gamblers rarely disclose their gambling problems to others unless it is severe enough and intolerable (Fong and Tsuang 2007). This cultural trait may be the reason behind the relatively low rate of treatment that Chinese gamblers seek.

Secondly, when compared to Western gamblers, the families of Chinese problem gamblers are more willing to loan the gamblers money to pay off their debts (Chan 2014). They do this because they love the gamblers. Or, very often, they help them because they do not want others in the same community to know about the gambler's debts, which is regarded as a source of social disgrace in Chinese culture.

They do not want such kind of shameful event to be released to the public. Paradoxically, such monetary help might provide a "cushion support" to the gamblers and might even reinforce them to gamble more.

Thirdly, the Chinese players' choices of games reflect their collectivist mentality. Lam (2005 2007) observed that Chinese casino players love to play the game of baccarat more than electronic games. Along with this particular observation, Chan and Ohtsuka (2010), in their study on social gambling in Hong Kong and Macao, reported that Chinese people particularly favor mahjong, a type of table game commonly shared among family members and friends. There are many versions of this game (Mainland Chinese version, Guangdong version, Taiwanese version, etc.), the most popular one being the Cantonese mahjong (Guangdong version). In this table game, the players share gossips and family stories while playing the game. Very often, Chinese people play this game during festivals and holidays. In a collectivist culture, electronic gaming devices (EGM), very popular in Australia and in the United States, are never a favorite game in Macanese casinos. For the Chinese gamblers, EGM is too individualistic – the players are playing against machines, and there is no sharing and discussion among the fellow players even though they are in the same casino hall. Chinese gamblers often prefer baccarat to EGMs (Liu and Wan 2011).

Researchers have investigated the differences and the similarities of gaming behaviors of Chinese. Wan et al. (2013) compared the gaming behaviors of Mainland Chinese, Hong Kong Chinese, and Taiwanese. They found that Mainland Chinese gamblers preferred group gambling. They liked to gather around baccarat tables, yelled at each other and cheered over their winnings during the games. Smoking was common among Mainland Chinese gamblers. Hong Kong gamblers were less compliant to dealers' guidance and frequently complained during the games. Taiwanese gamblers' characteristics fell between their two counterparts. Lastly, in a collectivist culture, sharing the game and proceeds are significant parts of gaming. Hence, it is very common that Chinese gamblers love to give winning money to their relatives after they have won the grand prize in lottery games (Chan 2012).

5.4 Locus of Control and Superstitious Behavior of Chinese Gamblers

Locus of control is the degree to which people believe that they have control over the outcome of events in their lives (Rotter 1966). A person's locus of control is conceptualized as internal (a belief that one is able to effect changes on one's life) or external (a belief that forces or factors outside of the individual are responsible for events one is experiencing). In the area of gambling, a person with an internal locus of control is more likely to have illusion of control, which can be defined as "the belief that one may have a greater probability of obtaining an outcome than would be expected by chance" (Petry 2005, p. 210). Individuals with a high internal locus of control believe events in their lives are the consequences of their actions. Research on lottery players indicated that the frequency of lottery play was associated with increased internal locus of control and high desires for control (Miyazaki et al. 2001). Employing the South Oaks Gambling Screen (Lesieur and Blume 1987) as the assessment tool, Moore and Ohtsuka (2001), in a sample of 1000 adolescents and young adults, found that illusion of control and internal locus of control both predicted gambling frequency and problem gambling behavior.

Conversely, a high level of external locus of control might indicate that the person ascribes circumstances more to luck and superstitious beliefs. On this regard, researchers have found that gamblers are frequently found to be superstitious (Ohtsuka and Chan 2010). Most of the participants in a sample of Chinese mahjong players scored high on the scale of superstitious beliefs (Chan and Ohtsuka 2009). One interesting finding in this study was that majority of the participants, including the non-gamblers, held Chinese superstitious beliefs. The research indicated that ethnic Chinese ascribed life events to superstitious beliefs. This mentality could be related to the culture they were brought up in (especially those middle-aged Chinese people, who grew up from an agricultural society where superstitious beliefs were predominant).

For the majority of Chinese individuals, "luck" is closely related to fate. Chinese people think a lucky person should have obtained blessing from the gods and his/her ancestors (Fong 2014). By manipulating the external sources of luck (e.g., wearing trinkets, donning red underwear, practicing particular rituals, practicing Feng Shui, and giving luck talks during traditional Chinese festivals), the gamblers can enhance their luck in gambling (Ohtsuka and Chan 2010; Mak and Ng 2005; Fong 2000). Simply put, Chinese gamblers believe that one's fate or *ming* (命) is never static (though it is mostly predetermined) – one can change one's fate by actively engaging in superstitious acts. Some of these acts are irrational (e.g., going to the toilet after a series of losses on the mahjong table, wearing specific ornament or clothing that brings good luck), changing the contextual objects in one's room or *Feng Shui*, (moving to a new baccarat table or putting specific colors or paintings on the wall of the casino). Through these specific strategies, gamblers can achieve better self-efficacy in winning and keep on gambling despite repeated losses.

In Chinese culture, luck and fate are believed to be predestined by supernatural powers. Thus, Chinese gamblers often test their luck by gambling as one famous Chinese proverb says, "If you don't bet, you don't know how lucky you are." Thus, if one wins in a gambling situation, it reflects one's good luck and blessing by supernatural forces.

More recently, Lim and Rogers (2017) investigated the correlation between luck and gambling problems among 333 Chinese gamblers from Hong Kong, Macao, Mainland China, Singapore, and the United Kingdom. The research aimed to investigate the relationship between external sources of luck and the participants' problem gambling. Fifty-three (15.4%) of 333 participants were considered as probable problem gamblers, assessed by the Problem Gambling Severity Index (PGSI) (Ferris and Wayne 2001). Participants who held stronger beliefs in external sources of luck (i.e., luck could be "controlled" by them) reported significantly more cognitive biases (e.g., illusion of control, interpretive biases, and perceived control). Besides, individuals demonstrating more cognitive biases were associated with significantly more gambling problems. From a cultural viewpoint, the authors argue that Chinese gamblers' beliefs in "adjustable" luck are significantly related to their illusions of control. Put in more succinct terms, Chinese individuals believe that fate or *ming* is the major determinant of our lives. Fate determines how long we live, what kinds of career we have, and, in gambling, how much we win in a gambling situation. However, our fate is somewhat adjustable through various factors such as luck, *Feng Shui*, and/or one's charitable work and studies.

5.5 The Cultural-Based Model for Chinese Superstitious Beliefs in Gambling

In our analysis, we hypothesize a theoretical model of superstitious behavior in gambling (see Fig. 5.1) to explain Chinese gambling from a cultural perspective:

1. Firstly, most ethnic Chinese believe in a traditional hierarchical belief system that determines all the events in one's life. These are fate (ranked number one), luck (second), *Feng Shui*, or contextual factors of one's living or work environment (third), charities and inner virtues (fourth), and engaging in useful studies (fifth). In Chinese words, these are 一命、二運、三風水、四積陰德、五讀書.
2. Fate (命) is the fundamental element of everything that happens in our lives. Fate determines whether we are rich or poor, educated or illiterate, sleeping in a

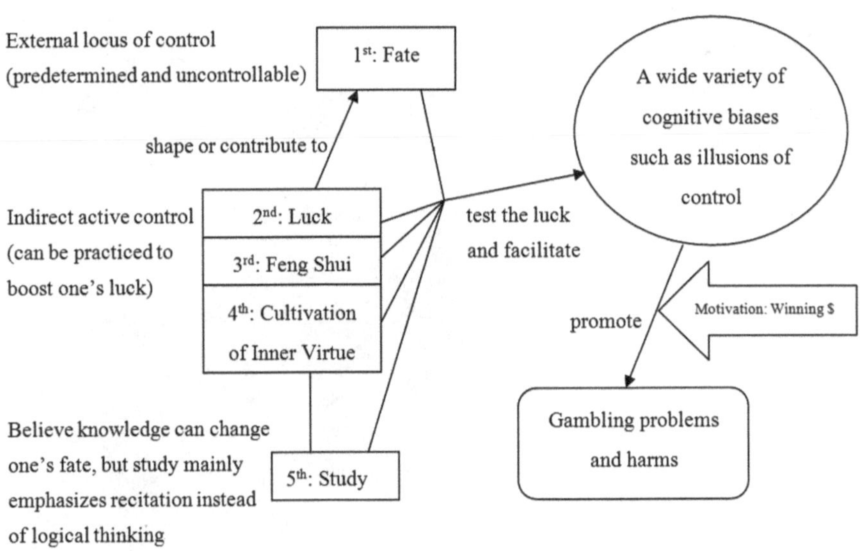

Fig. 5.1 A cultural-based model of Chinese superstitious beliefs in gambling

luxurious apartment, or living on the street as beggars. Our fate is basically set in stone the minute we are born. Thus, Chinese people love to observe the stars and interstellar phenomena at the time of birth. Even nowadays in China, some Chinese parents would purposefully ask doctors to perform special medical procedures to delay or hasten the delivery of a child so that the child is born on the exact "lucky" minute. In addition to the hour of delivery, other factors that contribute to our fate are the good deeds performed by our parents and grandparents and even our behaviors in our previous lives (as many Chinese believe in reincarnation). Though our fate determines the major events that happen in our lives, it is believed to be never static. Chinese believe there are other factors that can shape our fate, at least to a certain extent. These factors are listed as follows.

3. Luck (運), *Feng Shui* (風水), charities, and inner virtues (積陰德) are factors that can influence our fate. People can boost their luck (in Chinese term, "催運") by actively engaging in certain behaviors (Fong 2000; Mak and Ng 2005; Chang et al. 2009). These behaviors include donating money to charities, rearranging one's furniture in one's living environment, wearing special clothes, and praying to gods. In addition, engaging oneself in useful studies (讀書) is the last resort that people can change their fate. In this view, a person born with a poor fate can be successful if he/she actively pursues further studies. Thus, many Chinese gamblers spend hours studying past records of a particular soccer team before they bet on it, while many Hong Kong people trace the past records of Mark Six before they bet on it (Fig. 5.2).
4. Figure 5.1 summarizes our proposed cultural-based model of Chinese superstitious beliefs in gambling.

Fig. 5.2 A middle-aged man was studying past records of horse racing in a fast-food restaurant on a racing day. (Photo by Li Wai Lim taken on August 25, 2017)

The hypothesized cultural-based model can explain the superstitious beliefs and behaviors of Chinese gamblers. From this cultural perspective, Chinese people, when compared to Westerners, are more liable to accept beliefs that enhance their control on gambling. Such illusion of control maintains their persistence on gambling despite their repeated losses.

5.6 Implication of the Five-Factor Model (FFM) on Future Research on Chinese Problem Gamblers

Costa and McCrae's Five-Factor Model (1992) measures the five dimensions of personality traits, namely, extraversion (E), agreeableness (A), conscientiousness (C), neuroticism (N), and openness to experience (E).

A number of researchers have employed the model to investigate personality traits of problem gamblers. Bagby et al. (2007), in comparing samples of pathological gamblers and controls, found that samples of pathological gamblers had significantly higher N, lower C, and lower "trust" (one of the facets of A). Similar findings were reported by Myrseth et al. (2009) and Karre et al. (2009). More recently, MacLaren et al. (2011) recruited 369 undergraduate students (284 females and 85 males). A collection of inventories was used including the Shorter PROMIS Questionnaire Gambling Scale (SPQ) (Lefever 1988; Stephenson et al. 1995) and the NEO PI-R (Costa and McCrae 1976, 1992). Statistical analysis indicated that the participants demonstrated levels of high impulsiveness (facet of N), low straightforwardness (facet of A), low dutifulness (facet of C), and low self-discipline (facet of C). Put in more layman's terms, problem gamblers were found more likely to be impulsive and have troubles carrying out social duties and responsibilities.

To date, no research has been carried out on the Five-Factor Model in China. Clinical experiences working with problem gamblers indicated that Chinese gamblers are characterized by high level of impulsiveness and low level of self-discipline (Chan 2012). Their impulsiveness is often demonstrated by their repeated chasing after losses and an inability to delay gratification (Chan and Ohtsuka 2013). Our future challenge is to design an empirically validated translation of FFM and carry out related studies among the gamblers in Chinese communities.

5.7 Chapter Summary

This chapter discusses the personality characteristics of Chinese gamblers. Chinese gamblers share a number of similarities and differences with the Western gamblers. Firstly, most Chinese gamblers are impulsive and sensation-seeking. They are more likely to experience negative emotions, which may be the consequences of their habitual gambling. Many Chinese female gamblers are more prone to have negative emotionality. For them, gambling is a form of emotional escape. Lastly, many Chinese gamblers share a number of antisocial traits such as irresponsibility in life, lack of empathy for others, and lack of self-control with Wester gamblers. Some might even commit crimes to finance their gambling.

On the other hand, there are significant differences in the area of personality between Chinese gamblers and Western gamblers. Chinese gamblers hold more superstitious beliefs than Western gamblers. Good examples of such superstitions are wearing red underwear during gambling. These superstitious beliefs provide the gamblers an illusionary control over gambling outcomes. Furthermore, as members in a collective culture where one finds one's meanings and purposes, Chinese gamblers enjoy games which they can share and compete with each other. Thus, table games such as mahjong and baccarat are often more preferred than individualized game like electronic gaming device (EGM). Lastly, "saving face" is an important issue in the Chinese collective culture. Thus, when compared to Western gamblers, Chinese casino players like to show off their winnings and yell at each other at the baccarat tables (Lam 2007). When they win a larger amount of money, they love to give a considerable amount to their friends and family. The importance of "saving face" can also explain the gamblers' refusal to admit their problems in front of their families.

The analysis on Chinese gamblers' unique personality style is a difficult task, in lieu of the diversity of problem gamblers' development background, motivations, and genetic dispositions (Blaszczynski and Nower 2002). The cultural-based model of Chinese superstitious beliefs in gambling we propose in this chapter is hypothesized based on our prolonged observations, clinical experience, and generalizations on our previous research studies regarding Chinese gamblers. Further studies are definitely required to validate the model. To conclude, our analysis casts doubt on Alan Lang's hypothesis on addictive personality syndrome. We thus concur with Chan et al. (2016) assertion that as "problem gamblers often come from diverse backgrounds with different motivations for gambling, there should not be one single type of addictive personality (p.71)."

References

Alessi, S. M., & Petry, N. M. (2003). Pathological gambling severity is associated with impulsivity in a delay discounting procedure. *Behavioural Processes, 64*(3), 345–354.

American Psychiatric Association. (2013). *Diagnostic and statistical manual of mental disorders* (5th ed.). Washington, DC: Author.

Bagby, R. M., Vachon, D. D., Bulmash, E., Toneatto, T., Quilty, L. C., & Costa, P. T. (2007). Pathological gambling and the five factor model of personality. *Personality and Individual Differences, 43*, 873–880.

Blaszczynski, A., & Nower, L. (2002). A pathways model of problem and pathological gambling. *British Journal of Addiction, 97*, 487–499.

Blaszczynski, A., & Tempel, K. (2008). *Cognitive foundations of pathological gambling*. Finding Common Ground, the 18th annual conference for the National Association for Gambling Studies. Australia: National Association for Gambling Studies.

Blaszczynski, A., Steel, Z., & McConaghy, N. (1997). Impulsivity in pathological gambling: The antisocial impulsivist. *British Journal of Addiction, 92*(1), 75–87.

Blum, K., Sheridan, P. J., Wood, R. C., Braverman, E. R., Chen, T. J., Cull, J. G., & Comings, D. E. (1996). The D2 dopamine receptor gene as a determinant of reward deficiency syndrome. *Journal of the Royal Society of Medicine, 89*, 396–400.

Carlton, P. L., & Manowitz, P. (1994). Factors determining the severity of pathological gamblers in males. *Journal of Gambling Studies, 10*(2), 147–157.

Chan, C. C. (2012). The psychology of problem gambling and poverty. In *Proceedings of the international conference "Joining hands to identify new roads for poverty alleviation"* (pp. 107–111). Macao SAR, China.

Chan, C. C. (2014, November). The psychology of gambling and gambling treatment. A keynote address at the 2nd Macau Medical Association Forum-MMAF, Macao SAR, China.

Chan, C. C., & Ohtsuka, K. (2009, May). *Superstitions among mahjong players in Macau: A cultural perspective on a popular Chinese gambling game played at home*. Paper presented at the 14th international conference on Gambling and Risk-Taking, Lake Tahoe, Nevada, USA.

Chan, C. C., & Ohtsuka, K. (2010, June). *A study on the typology of Chinese gamblers in Hong Kong*. Paper presented at the Diversity in Health 2010 conference, Melbourne, Australia.

Chan, C. C., & Ohtsuka, K. (2013). The clinical and social construction of the *Paichais* of Macau. *The Asian Journal of Gambling Issues and Public Health, 3*(6), 1–11. Retrieved from https: https://doi.org/10.1186/2195-3007-3-6.

Chan, C. Y., Yick, K. S. C., Khiatani, P. V., Tse, T. H. M., & Chan, C. C. (2012, November). Problem gambling among female sex workers in Hong Kong. Paper presented at the 22nd National Association for Gambling Studies annual conference, Launceston, Australia.

Chan, C. C., Li, W. L., & Leung, C. I. (2016). *Problem gambling in Hong Kong and Macao: Etiology, prevalence and treatment*. Singapore: Springer.

Chang, P. T., Lee, J. H., Hung, K. C., Tsui, J. T., & Perng, C. (2009). Applying fuzzy weighted average approach to evaluate office layouts with Feng-Shui consideration. *Mathematical and Computer Modelling, 50*(9–10), 1514–1537. https://doi.org/10.1016/j.mcm.2008.07.038.

Chen, H. P. (2012). *Internet Survey among Chinese Lottery Buyers' Behaviors*. Lottery Research Center of China, Beijing Normal University. (陳海平 (2012). 中國彩民行為網絡調查. 北京師範大學中國彩票事業研究中心). Retrieved from http://www.71.cn/2012/0422/665711.shtml

Cheng, W. K. (2006). *From Pathological Gambling to Help Seeking: Cases of Female Pathological Gamblers in Hong Kong.* Unpublished master thesis. Hong Kong: University of Hong Kong.

Chim, D. (2011). Gambling addiction in Asia: Need for a medical perspective? *Asian Journal of Gambling Issues and Public Health, 2*(1), 68–74.

Ciarrocchi, J. W., Kirschner, N. M., & Falik, F. (1991). Personality dimensions of male pathological gamblers, alcoholics, and dually addicted gamblers. *Journal of Gambling Studies, 7*(2), 133–141. https://doi.org/10.1007/BF01014528.

Costa, P. T., & McCrae, R. R. (1976). Age differences in personality structure: A cluster analytic approach. *Journal of Gerontology, 31*(5), 564–570. https://doi.org/10.1093/geronj/31.5.564 PMID 950450.

Costa, P. T., & McCrae, R. R. (1992). *Revised NEO personality inventory (NEO-PI-R) and NEO dive-factor inventory (NEO-FFI) professional manual*. Odessa: Psychological Assessment Resources.

Cyders, M. A., & Smith, G. T. (2007). Mood-based rash action and its components: Positive and negative urgency and their relations with other impulsivity-like constructs. *Personality and Individual Differences, 43*, 839–850.

Cyders, M. A., Smith, G. T., Spillane, N. S., Fischer, S., Annu, A. M., & Peterson, C. (2007a). Integration of impulsivity and positive mood to predict risky behavior: Development and validation of a measure of positive urgency. *Psychological Assessment, 19*, 107–118.

Cyders, M. A., Flory, K., Rainer, S., & Smith, G. T. (2007b). *Prospective study of the integration of mood and impulsivity to predict increases in maladaptive action during the first year of college.* Paper presented at the annual meeting of the Research Society on Alcoholism, Chicago, IL.

Ferris, J., & Wynne, H. (2001). *The Canadian problem gambling index: User's manual.* Toronto: Canadian Centre on Substance Abuse.

Fong, M. (2000). 'Luck talk' in celebrating the Chinese new year. *Journal of Pragmatics, 32*(2), 219–237.

Fong, T. (2014, July 10). *Asian gambling addiction: more than just chance.* Sam Louie MA, LMHC Minority Report. Retrieved from http://www.ncbi.nlm.nih.gov/pmc/articles/PMC3004737

Fong, T. W., & Tsuang, J. (2007). Asian-Americans, addictions, and barriers to treatment. *Psychiatry, 11*, 51–59.

Goldstein, R. Z., & Volkow, N. D. (2002). Drug addiction and its underlying neurobiological basis: Neuroimaging evidence for the involvement of the frontal cortex. *American Journal of Psychiatry, 159*(10), 1642–1652.

Goldstein, R. Z., Volkow, N. D., Wang, G. J., Fowler, J. S., & Rajaram, S. (2001). Addiction changes orbitofrontal gyrus function: Involvement in response inhibition. *Neuroreport, 12*(11), 2595–2599.

Goudriaan, A. E., Oosterlaan, J., de Beurs, E., & Van Den Brink, W. (2005). Decision making in pathological gambling: A comparison between pathological gamblers, alcohol dependents, persons with Tourette syndrome, and normal controls. *Cognitive Brain Research, 23*(1), 137–151.

Goudriaan, A. E., Oosterlaan, J., de Beurs, E., & Van Den Brink, W. (2006). Neurocognitive functions in pathological gambling: A comparison with alcohol dependence, Tourette syndrome and normal controls. *Addiction, 101*(4), 534–547.

Hathaway, S. R., & McKinley, J. C. (1943). *Manual for the Minnesota multiphasic personality inventory*. New York: Psychological Corporation.

Jackson, A. C., Dowling, N., Thomas, S. A., Bond, L., & Patton, G. (2008). Adolescent gambling behavior and attitudes: A prevalence study and correlates in an Australian population. *International Journal on Mental Health Addiction, 6*, 325–352.

Karre, P. R., Mottus, R., & Konstabel, K. (2009). Pathological gambling in Estonia: Relationships with personality, self-esteem, emotional states and cognitive ability. *Journal of Gambling Studies, 25*, 377–390.

Khiatani, P. V., Yick, K. S. C., Chan, C. Y., Tse, T. H. M., & Chan, C. C. (2013, December). *The quasi-legitimate "third place": A qualitative investigation into the culture and context of gambling houses in Hong Kong.* Paper presented at the 2nd Asia Pacific conference on Gambling & Commercial Gaming Research, Kaohsiung, Taiwan.

Lam, D. (2005). Slot or table? A Chinese perspective. *UNLV Gaming Research & Review Journal, 9*(2), 69–72.

Lam, D. (2007). An observation study of Chinese baccarat players. *UNLV Gaming Research & Research & Review Journal, 11*, 63–73.

Lang, A. R. (1983). Addictive personality: A viable construct. In P. K. Levison, D. R. Gerstein, & D. R. Maloff (Eds.), *Commonalities in substance abuse and habitual behavior* (pp. 157–236). Lexington, MA: Lexington Books.

Leblond, J., Ladouceur, R., & Blaszczynski, A. (2003). Which pathological gamblers will complete treatment? *British Journal of Clinical Psychology, 42*(2), 205–209.

Lefever, R. (1988). *How to identify addictive behavior*. London: PROMIS Publishing.

Lesieur, H. R., & Blume, S. B. (1987). The south oaks gambling screen (SOGS): A new instrument for the identification of pathological gamblers. *American Journal of Psychiatry, 144*, 1184–1188.

Li, G. (2014). Research on the sales fairness of Chinese lottery industry. *Journal of Shanghai Normal University (Philosophy & Social Sciences Edition), 43*(4), 33–45. https://doi.org/10.13852/J.CNKI.JSHNU.2014.04.004.

Lim, M. S. M., & Rogers, R. D. (2017). Chinese beliefs in luck are linked to gambling problems via strengthened cognitive biases: A mediation test. *Journal of Gambling Studies, 33*(4), 1325–1336. https://doi.org/10.1007/s10899-017-9690-6.

Liu, X., & Wan, Y. K. P. (2011). An examination of factors that discourage slot play in Macau's casinos. *International Journal of Hospitality Management, 30*(1), 167–177.

MacLaren, V. V., Best, L. S., Dixon, M. J., & Harrigan, K. A. (2011). Problem gambling and the five factor model in university students. *Personality and Individual Differences, 50*, 335–338.

Mak, M. Y., & Ng, S. T. (2005). The art and science of Feng Shui – A study on architects' perception. *Building and Environment, 40*(3), 427–434. https://doi.org/10.1016/j.buildenv.2004.07.016.

McCown, W., & Chamberlain, L. (2005). *Gambling disorders: Experimental and empirical research*. Victoria: Trafford.

Miyazaki, A. D., Brumbaugh, A. M., & Sprott, D. E. (2001). Promoting and countering consumer misconceptions of random events: The case of perceived control and state-sponsored lotteries. *Journal of Public Policy & Marketing, 20*(2), 254–267. https://doi.org/10.1509/jppm.20.2.

Moore, S., & Ohtsuka, K. (2001). Youth gambling in Melbourne's west: Changes between 1996 and 1998 for Anglo-European background and Asian background school-based youth. *International Gambling Studies, 1*, 87–101.

Myrseth, H. (2011). *Pathological Gambling: Treatment and Personality Factors*. Unpublished doctoral thesis. Norway: University of Bergen.

Myrseth, H., Pallesen, P., Molde, H., Johnsen, B. H., & Lorvik, I. M. (2009). Personality factors as predictors of pathological gambling. *Personality and Individual Differences, 47*, 933–937.

Nower, L., & Blaszczynski, A. (2006). Impulsivity and pathological gambling: A descriptive model. *International Gambling Studies, 6*(1), 61–75. https://doi.org/10.1080/14459790600644192.

Nower, L., Derevensky, J., & Gupta, R. (2004). The relationship of impulsivity, sensation seeking, coping and substance use in youth gamblers. *Psychology of Addictive Behaviors, 18*(1), 49–55.

Ohtsuka, K., & Chan, C. C. (2010). Donning red underwear to play mahjong: Superstitious beliefs and problem gambling among Chinese mahjong players in Macau. *Gambling Research, 22*(3), 18–33.

Oyserman, D. (1993). The lens of personhood: Viewing the self, others, and conflict in a multicultural society. *Journal of Personality and Social Psychology, 65*, 993–1009.

Pervin, L. A., Cervone, D., & John, O. P. (2005). *Personality: Theory and research* (9th ed.). Hoboken: Wiley.

Petry, N. M. (2005). *Pathological gambling: Etiology, comorbidity, and treatment*. Washington, DC: American Psychological Association.

Potenza, M. N., Steinberg, M. A., Skudlarski, P., Fulbright, R. K., Lacadie, C. M., Wilber, M. K., Fulbright, R. K., Lacadie, C. M., Wilber, M. K., Rounsaville, B. J., Gore, J. C., & Wexler, B. E. (2003). Gambling urges in pathological gambling: A functional magnetic resonance imaging study. *Archives of General Psychiatry, 60*(8), 828–836.

Rotter, J. B. (1966). Generalized expectancies for internal versus external control of reinforcement. *Psychological Monographs: General & Applied, 80*(1), 1–28.

Schwartz, S. H. (1990). Individualism–collectivism: Critique and proposed refinements. *Journal of Cross-Cultural Psychology, 21*, 139–157.

Slutske, W. S., Caspi, A., Moffitt, T. E., & Poulton, R. (2005). Personality and problem gambling. *Archives of General Psychiatry, 62*, 769–775.

Stephenson, G. M., Maggi, P., Lefever, R. M. H., & Morojele, N. K. (1995). Excessive behaviors: An archival study of behavioral tendencies reported by 471 patients admitted to an addiction treatment centre. *Addiction Research, 3*, 245–265.

Strayhorn, J. M. (2002). Self-control: Theory and research. *Journal of the American Academy of Child and Adolescent Psychiatry, 41*, 7–16.

Taormina, R. J. (2009). Social and personality correlates of gambling attitudes and behavior among Chinese residents of Macau. *Journal of Social and Personal Relationships, 26*(8), 1047–1071. https://doi.org/10.1177/0265407509347935.

Taormina, R. J., & Chong, B. K. H. (2015). Cognitive dissonance among Chinese gamblers: Cultural beliefs versus gambling behavior. *IAFOR Journal of Psychology & the Behavioral Sciences, 1*(1). https://doi.org/10.22492/ijpbs.1.1.03.

The Hong Kong Polytechnic University. (2002). *Report on a Study of Hong Kong People's Participation in Gambling Activities*. Hong Kong: The Hong Kong Polytechnic University. Retrieved from http://www.hab.gov.hk/file_manager/en/documents/whats_new/gambling/report-eng.pdf

The Hong Kong Polytechnic University. (2011). *The Study on Hong Kong People's Participation in Gaming Activities*. Hong Kong: The Hong Kong Polytechnic University Retrieved from http://www.hab.gov.hk/file_manager/en/documents/policy_responsibilities/others/gaming_report_2011.pdf.

The Hong Kong Polytechnic University. (2017). *Report on the study of Hong Kong people's participation in gambling activities in 2016*. Hong Kong: The Hong Kong Polytechnic University. Retrieved from https://www.hab.gov.hk/file_manager/en/documents/policy_responsibilities/others/gambling_report_2016.pdf

The University of Hong Kong. (2005). *Report on a study of Hong Kong people's participation in gambling activities*. Hong Kong: The University of Hong Kong. Retrieved from http://www.hab.gov.hk/file_manager/en/documents/whats_new/gambling/KeyStat_200514_e.pdf

Tse, T. H. M., Khiatani, P. V., Yick, K. S. C., Chan, C. Y., & Chan, C. C. (2012, November). *More than a simple game of "cops and robbers": What marks the differences between law-enforcement personnel and individuals with a criminal background with gambling problems?* Paper presented at the 22nd National Association for Gambling Studies Annual Conference, Launceston, Australia.

Wan, Y. K. P., Kim, S., & Elliot, S. (2013). Behavioral differences in patterns of gambling among Chinese subcultures as perceived by Macao casino staff. *Cornell Hospitality Quarterly, 54*(4), 358–369.

Wong, I. L. K. (2010). Gambling behavior among underage adolescents in Hong Kong. *Asian Journal of Gambling Issues and Public Health, 1*(1), 47–60.

Wong, D. F. K., Chung, C. L. P., Wu, J., Tang, J. Y. C., & Lau, P. T. C. (2015). A preliminary study of an integrated and culturally attuned cognitive behavioral group treatment for Chinese problem gamblers in Hong Kong. *Journal of Gambling Studies, 31*(3), 1015–1027. https://doi.org/10.1007/s10899-014-9457-2.

Chapter 6
Psychological Treatments for Chinese Disordered Gamblers

Psychological treatments for disordered gambling have been a major concern in clinical psychology (Chan 2014; Chan et al. 2016). In terms of clinical efficacy, reported successful treatments include psychoanalytic intervention (Bergler 1957; Clarkson 2015; Rosenthal and Rugle 1994), behavioral therapy (Kraft 1970; Gurney 1968; Seager et al. 1966), aversion therapy (Barker and Miller 1966), imaginal desensitization (ID) (Blaszczynski and Nower 2014), self-exclusion program (Huang 2011), cognitive restructuring (Korn and Shaffer 2004), mindfulness therapy (Chen et al. 2014), and participation in meetings in Gamblers Anonymous (GA) (Ferentzy et al. 2006, 2009, 2010, and 2014). Some researchers have combined different treatment modalities into their therapeutic programs. For instance, Sharpe and Tarrier (1992) designed a treatment package that included relaxation, imaginal and in vivo exposure, and cognitive restructuring. In a similar vein, Grant et al. (2009) carried out a randomized trial study to compare groups that received ID plus motivational interviewing (MI) and Gamblers Anonymous (GA) among 68 pathological gamblers (25 males, 43 females). Both groups of investigators found the combined packages to be more effective than programs that were designed based on a single treatment modality. In reviewing the literature on the psychological treatments of disordered gambling, international gambling experts Professor Blaszczynski and Professor Nower concluded:

> "There is general consensus that cognitive-behavioural therapy (CBT) represents the current 'gold' or 'best practice' standard, regardless of whether it administered in-group, individual or self-help bibliotherapy format, alone or in combination with motivational enhancement therapy (MET) and mindfulness. (p. 204)." In other words, in the treatment of disordered gambling, all roads lead not to Rome but to cognitive-behavioral therapy.

C. C. Chan et al., *The Psychology of Chinese Gambling*,
https://doi.org/10.1007/978-981-13-3486-3_6

6.1 Evidence of Cognitive-Behavioral Therapy on Treating Chinese Problem Gamblers

In essence, cognitive-behavioral therapy (CBT) consists of two fundamental theoretical components: cognitive formulations of the person and behavioral modification of the corresponding behavioral patterns. Within the cognitive elements, CBT targets at helping the client identify his/her irrational thinking and cognitive biases. The key principle is assisting the person to develop an insight into his/her gambling problems. Therapeutic techniques include psycho-education, problem solving, and cognitive restructuring that aim to modify distorted thinking and biases and correct maladaptive self-statements. Behaviorally, CBT applies learning principles in modifying the gambler's behavioral patterns and habits, as well as helping the patient develop appropriate coping skills. Toward these goals, commonly employed behavioral techniques are aversion therapy, stimulus substitution procedures (substitution of gambling behaviors with healthy behaviors), financial planning and limit-setting, stimulus control, imaginal desensitization, in vivo exposure and response prevention, and assertiveness and refusal skills training. Notwithstanding the success of CBT in Western countries, to date, only a few randomized control trials (RCTs) have been performed in Chinese communities. Wong and his colleagues (2015) performed a RCT on the effectiveness of a CBT program for Chinese problem gamblers in Hong Kong. The researchers named the program a "culturally attuned" program, though it apparently adapted the treatment program from Petry's (2005). Elements of this 10-week program included motivational enhancement, identification of triggers for gambling, understanding of the cognitive biases in gambling, learning of behavioral and cognitive strategies for change, and relapse prevention. Thirty-eight problem gamblers, all males, were randomly assigned to a treatment group ($N = 18$) and a control group ($N = 20$). The control group participants received another set of "routine individual counseling" which included debt counseling, grief counseling for loss, family and marital counseling, and crises intervention. Posttreatment findings indicated that the treatment group performed better as they reduced their gambling behaviors significantly. The limitation of this study is that the authors failed to explain the details of the treatment given to the control group. It appears that the researchers were comparing the effects of CBT and non-CBT counseling among Chinese problem gamblers. Moreover, perhaps more importantly, there are limited details on how the "culturally attuned" program was constructed. A good "culturally attuned" program would consider the specific needs and perspectives of the ethnic community. Another limitation falls on the participants recruited, who were males only, reducing the generalizability of this study.

Considering the shortcomings of CBT which puts less emphasis on the emotional components (e.g., depressed mood) of problem gamblers, a more recent study done by Zhuang et al. (2018) in Hong Kong designed a cognitive-behavioral intervention (CBI) which included the understanding and the coping of negative emotions among problem gamblers. They successfully recruited 84 male participants. Forty-two of them were allocated to the eight-session CBI group treatment, while another half was involved in a non-therapeutic eight-session social activity group. Posttreatment results indicated that participants who took part in CBI treatment reported significantly lower levels in gambling severity, reduced negative emotions (measured by their stress levels), decreased erroneous cognition (i.e., interpretive bias in gambling), and money spent on gambling. Effects could be sustained up to 6-month follow-up. Zhuang's study added an emotional regulation component to CBT, which is effective in treating Chinese problem gamblers. Nevertheless, their study merely recruited male problem gamblers. Participants were also only allowed to choose between the treatment group and the social activity group.

6.2 Clinical Issues in Helping the Chinese Disordered Gamblers

With the above concerns in mind, the present chapter thus intends to fill in the research gap by investigating the following issues and perspectives in helping the Chinese disordered gamblers:

(a) Understanding the particular needs and elements of ethnic Chinese culture that are clinically crucial in the development and treatment of disordered gambling
(b) Development of an appropriate and culturally attuned treatment program for the Chinese community

Several international writers have proposed programs on treating Chinese problem gamblers (Loo et al. 2008; Oei and Raylu, 2007). In Hong Kong and Macao, Chan and his students (Chan 2014; Chan et al. 2016) have outlined a number of cultural characteristics of the ethnic Chinese community that are prominent in the consideration and design of a treatment package. These are:

(a) **Chinese collectivist culture and family structure**

As a collectivist culture built upon Confucian philosophy (Lam 2014), Chinese culture emphasizes the family unit as the fundamental cornerstone of a person's heritage and identity (Chan 2014). The family does not only give a person his/her last name (e.g., Chan, Wong, or Li); it renders the person a position with corresponding roles and responsibilities in the community. For instance, the eldest son of the family is expected to take up the role of a patriarch when the father passes away. In Chinese community, a strong male (masculine) figure is vital and functionally instrumental in maintaining integrity and stability within the family and society as a whole. At the bottom of this moral and social framework lies the Confucian philosophy which defines one's social identity ontologically. As we have mentioned in Chapter 1, Chinese virtues such as *Li* or propriety, *Yi* or righteousness, *Lim* or honesty and integrity, and *Chi or* shamefulness promote or even dictate social relationships and behaviors in the community. The virtue of *Chi* or shamefulness is crucial in our understanding of psychological treatment for gamblers. The concept of shamefulness means one should not bring disgrace on oneself and his/her family. Out of this concern, problem gambling is often viewed as a stigma of shame in Chinese society (Oei and Raylu 2007). In this regard, the Chinese sense of righteousness rests more on a sense of shame rather than a sense of guilt (Chan 2014). In the community, a good and respectable person is one who brings good fortune and honor to one's family. By the same token, the worst thing a son can do is to bring shame and disgrace upon the family and the clan. "Saving face" in the Chinese community is more important than one's mental health. This perspective explains why Chinese disordered gamblers often deny their own problems (i.e., failed to accept their compulsive gambling has become a problem) and do not seek professional help.

Besides, Chinese society is largely engineered and structured on a patriarchal family hierarchy (Chan 2014). In the community, especially small rural communities, the father or the grandfather is the leader and the head of the family. He is given, by mandate of his identity, the authority to decide all major familial decisions. Very often, Chinese traditions depict the father figure as an audacious and moral character. As such, he is never expected to show his weaknesses, shortcomings, or even negative emotions in front of his family. "Saving face" is a pertinent issue, an aspect of *Chi* or shamefulness. Thus, family therapy, in which all family members should participate, is often not a preferred treatment among Chinese problem gamblers.

Hence, in Chinese culture, a good treatment should help the male gamblers develop self-control on his gambling while moistening his dignity (saving their faces) in family. The treatment should take into account the issues of embarrassment and shame commonly felt among Chinese problem gamblers (Lin 2002). Out of this concern, family members should not be invited to either a clinical counseling session or GA meeting. In our experiences of working with male disordered gamblers, they were usually very quiet during Gamblers Anonymous meetings if their family members were in the meeting room (Li et al. 2016a, b). We speculate that they would not want their family to see their weaknesses and problems. However, outside of the treatment session, family support is very important in the gamblers' rehabilitation processes. In our treatment programs, we always arrange and support family activities for the gamblers on Sundays. One event we always arrange is soccer game on Sunday, for which all family members are invited. Another typical event is going to church together every Sunday morning.

Furthermore, the care and support of families and communities is vital in motivating disordered gamblers to continue treatment. Bearing this in mind, it is appropriate to include sessions of motivational interviewing (Prochascha and DiClementi 1992) at the first two sessions of the treatment. Petry (2005) proposes a number of motivational interviewing techniques. One commonly used strategy is to ask the gambler to list out the benefits and gains together with the difficulties and problems associated with gambling. In this exercise, the client is asked to list the possibilities he/she could have if not for his/her preoccupation with gambling. These "what if?" strategies aim at helping the client develop his motivation for change. Recent empirical research indicated that a treatment combining MI and CBT was effective in alleviating problem gambling in either an individual or a group format (Oei et al. 2010). Combined brief MI with CBT also significantly decreased drop-out rates than utilizing CBT alone (Milton et al. 2002; Wulfert et al. 2006). During sessions of motivational enhancement, the therapist can help the gambler identify areas and aspects that he/she feels guilty about toward his/her family. They are further asked to make promises to themselves and to their families concerning their gambling problems. It would also be helpful for the patient to sign a behavioral contract. A typical behavioral contract is as follows:

> I ________ promise my family and the therapist, Dr. Chan, that I would stop gambling starting today (Date). I understand problem gambling has impacted my family. (The patient can make a few examples here.) If I succeed in controlling my gambling habits, my family will (List a few activities the family can do together). If I fail, my family will.......... (Good example is not talking to him for 3 weeks.)

Signatures

____________	________________	______________
Patient	Family member	Therapist

The behavioral contract can be adjusted and even changed during the course of the therapy sessions. The crucial point is that the family is involved in the treatment process though they would not be physically present in the counseling room. One particular therapy focusing on relieving guilt and shame toward the family is Naikan therapy (Chervenkova 2014) from Japan. Naikan therapy aims at helping the gambler to develop insight into their problems. Through this process, the patients learn to accept themselves and their families.

(b) **The efficacy of certain treatment techniques among Chinese patients**

In our experiences of working with Chinese gamblers, we find that most disordered gamblers have problems with intervention strategies and tasks that require cognitive imaginary and role play. This is evident in the therapeutic technique of imaginal desensitization. This approach has been considered as an effective approach in treating disordered gamblers (Blaszczynski and Nower 2014). In this approach, the gambler will be asked to covertly imagine certain gambling situations and, during the process, the gambler learns to refrain from gambling. The goal is to help the gambler to learn self-control through the process of imagination. A typical guided imaginary scenario is given as follows:

"Joe, please close your eyes and imagine a typical gambling day in your life. You always go to the Hong Kong Jockey Club near your home. And today, as usual, you go in to bet on the British soccer games. Anxious and afraid, you enter the side gate of the Jockey Club. You walk towards the betting office. You are afraid to meet your friends who might tell your wife about your gambling. You only have $1000 in your pocket and your family needs the money to pay bills. Hesitated for a while, you take out the betting ticket and hand it to the cashier with your money. Stop. Think about your family. Think about what will happen when you lose all your money. They have to borrow money from relatives. So, you stop, take the money and leave the place."

Through this process, the gambler is led to develop self-control through the imaginary process. The focus of the therapy is that the gambler can learn coping skills through cognitive training. Notwithstanding the success of the therapy in Western countries (Blaszcznski and Nower 2014), we find very few Chinese gamblers can benefit from this approach (Chan 2014). One reason may be that ethnic Chinese are trained, since childhood, to follow orders, concrete rules, and regulations. This echoes with what we have stated in the previous chapter that the education Chinese people receive puts emphasis on recitation, instead of logical thinking and creativity. Thus, creative thinking is often discouraged or even overlooked in school systems. As adults, Chinese individuals like to work according to established standards and specific rules. Traditionally, Chinese people are compliant to rules set by authority or supreme powers. Thus, in the therapeutic context, Chinese clients often prefer behavioral rules and instructions. In the first author's experiences of working with Chinese clients, they like to ask questions like "What should I do to help myself?" or "What actions should I take if I cannot pay off my gambling debts?". In other words, successful therapy with Chinese disordered gamblers should rest more on concrete behavioral therapeutic strategies than cognitive imaginative procedures.

(c) **Medicalization of psychological problems**

For the majority of ethnic Chinese, seeking psychological consultation on personal problems is not a socially appropriate means to solve personal problems. One reason is that Chinese families are reluctant to disclose their problems, especially the subject of gambling which is considered as a social disgrace to the whole family. Many family members of disordered gamblers often cover up their problems. They would usually pay off the gambling debts of the gamblers. In these occasions, they might, rather unintentionally, reinforce their gambling and become enablers of their excessive gambling behaviors. Thus, some disordered gamblers will only come when they are heavily in debt or when they are forced by their families to come. The situations are usually very worse when they come to the counseling session or GA meeting.

Moreover, in our experiences of working with these gamblers (Chan 2014; Chan et al. 2016), they often underreport the severity of their problems or somatic complaints (e.g., loss of appetite, fatigue, and/or insomnia), which are often physical symptoms of depression and anxiety resulting from the stresses and monetary losses of excessive gambling. Some of them may report having these problems prior to their development of gambling. These clients display the characteristics of emotional-vulnerable problem gamblers (Pathway 2 of the Blaszczynski and Nower Model, 2002). In these cases, the treatment specialists need to pay particular concern to their somatic problems with an accepting tone rather than challenging them (Sue 1997). From a psychodynamic viewpoint, these somatic complaints are the manifestation of their underlying concerns, difficulties, and yearnings. Thus, while these problems can be treated with CBT and pharmacological intervention, the therapists need to explore the clients' underlying problems (i.e., their gambling problems). Helping the client achieve insight and personal growth should be on the priority list of the treatment package.

In Chinese culture, medical treatment is often the more preferred choice of treatment for psychological problems. Chinese individuals often see disordered gambling as a biologically based disorder. As such, they are more likely to seek medical treatment rather than psychotherapy. For them, counseling, or many Chinese name it "talk therapy," carries little therapeutic effects. They expect a quick-fix or even immediate treatment effects for all their problems. Thus, it is rather difficult for them to participate in psychodynamic therapy that lasts more than half a year or even several years. Research has indicated that, for the majority of Chinese clients, the time necessary for therapeutic effect significantly affects their treatment adherence and willingness to continue the particular treatment modality (Iwamasa et al. 2006). In other words, they would often prefer a short treatment package that is geared toward the elimination of basic symptoms to a long-term plan for personal growth.

Based on our analyses and experiences of working with Chinese disordered gamblers, we put forward a list of recommendations in the design of a successful treatment:

(a) The treatment should be of a short-term basis (e.g., psychodynamic therapy is not recommended). The best treatment is an 8-week program.
(b) Treatment that employs therapeutic techniques such as hypnosis, guided imagery, and imaginal desensitization should be avoided.
(c) Instead, therapeutic techniques that can elicit positive outcomes within a relatively short period of time should be given priority. Thus, cognitive-behavioral therapy based on learning principles should form the foundations of the treatment package.
(d) Family therapy in which all family members are invited to the treatment sessions is not recommended.
(e) Motivating the clients is important. Motivational enhancement therapy (MET) should be given at the early sessions of the treatment package.
(f) Family support is important. This is one of the prominent motivators for the client's successful completion of the treatment program.
(g) Gamblers receiving individual therapy should be encouraged to attend Gamblers' Anonymous (GA) meetings as an adjunct treatment. As Chinese individuals are more reluctant to disclose their gambling problems (which are a source of social disgrace) to treatment specialists, the mutual support and self-help nature of GA can be of great help. In these meetings, the clients can learn from the successful experiences of fellow gamblers.

6.3 A Proposed Multimodal Treatment Model for Chinese Problem Gamblers

We now propose a special treatment package for Chinese disordered gamblers. The underlying principles are based on the recommendations we have highlighted. In essence, the treatment rests on motivational enhancement, psycho-education, developing self-control, assertiveness training, cognitive-behavioral therapy, positive psychology, and a revised version of the American 12-step approach to problem gambling (Ferentzy et al. 2006, 2009, 2010, 2014). The content of the 12-step approach needs to be adjusted as the original version is built on Christian counseling approach, with which some Chinese problem gamblers, especially non-Christians, find confrontational (Fong and Tsuang 2007). Since 2011, Chan and his students have carried out a series of research projects in the GAs of Hong Kong (Chan and Ohtsuka 2011; Yeung et al.2014). An earlier version of the proposed program named as *multimodal treatment approach* has been successfully implemented in a pilot study with members of a GA in Hong Kong (2016a, b). Problem gamblers who participated in the multimodal treatment (group CBT + GA) scored significantly lower in the Yale-Brown Obsessive Compulsive Scale Modified for Pathological Gambling (PG-YBOCS) (Pallanti et al. 2005) than those who took part in GA alone. In addition, participants who attended the multimodal treatment had a higher treatment adherence than their counterparts. A detailed presentation of the program is attached in the following section.

6.3.1 *Multimodal Treatment Approach*

The proposed treatment program consists of eight sessions of group CBT, followed by subsequent enrolment in GA which adopts a modified 12-step approach specially attuned to Chinese disordered gamblers. The eight-session group CBT is scheduled as follows:

Sessions 1 and 2: Motivational interview (MI)
Session 3: Psycho-education on concepts of disordered gambling, impulse control, chasing behavior, and the impacts of one's gambling disorders on the family
Session 4: Behavioral coping strategies to reduce gambling urge
Session 5: Refusal skills and assertive training
Session 6: Cognitive restructuring
Session 7: Positive psychology on positive living
Session 8: Relapse prevention

Considering the collectivistic nature of Chinese culture, the present proposed treatment program puts more emphasis on the behavioral component than on cognitive session. Besides, motivational interview (MI) is presented to the participant in the initial two sessions. At the later part of the program, we introduce the concepts and lifestyle of positive psychology to our participants. The aim is to promote emotional, social, and psychological well-being. In particular, we will follow Professor Seligman's PERMA model as a means to achieve personal happiness (Park et al. 2004). In this model, disordered gamblers learn to join in activities that give them positive emotions (P), engaging in personal and socially appropriate challenges (E), seeking reinforcing social relationships (R), developing meaningful purposes in life (M), and obtaining achievement in work, studies, and services in the community (A).

In addition to individualized therapy, the gamblers are encouraged to actively participate meetings in a GA group. Chan and his students have developed a culturally attuned 12-step GA recovery program (Yeung et al. 2014) particularly for Chinese problem gamblers who do not believe in Christian values and faith, which structures the basis of the traditional 12-step program. The 12 major themes of the meetings are as follows:

Step 1: Understanding and admitting one's gambling problems honestly
Step 2: Making promises to quit gambling in front of all group members
Step 3: Moving forward in life by opening one's heart to others and be ready to change one's lifestyle
Step 4: Reviewing relationships and taking up responsibilities in life
Step 5: Overcoming problems in life
Step 6: Setting goals and getting ready to change
Step 7: Restructuring one's thought patterns and modifying one's behavioral patterns
Step 8: Documenting previous harms to others and reflecting on one's responsibilities in the process
Step 9: Repairing or compensating to others and effective planning for the future
Step 10: Monitoring progress in one's path to social rehabilitation
Step 11: Building ego strength to overcome gambling urges. Relapse prevention.
Step 12: Helping others when the gambler has overcome gambling problems

Traditional GA is a Christian-based recovery program (Ferentzy et al. 2014). The first meeting of GA was held in Los Angeles, California, on September 13, 1957. Since GA was developed in Western countries, it might not be suitable for ethnic Chinese individuals. Therefore, adjustment in the program structure has to be made. Our modified version of 12-step recovery program in GA serves to fulfill this purpose.

Figure 6.1 displays the cover of the book, "*Handbook for Gamblers Anonymous' Mutual Help Groups – 12 Steps to Gambling Recovery*," written by the first author of this book and his students. The manual can be downloaded free at http://www.caritas.org.mo/en/publication/other-publications

Fig. 6.1 Book cover of "*Handbook for Gamblers Anonymous' Mutual Help Groups - 12 Steps to Gambling Recovery*". (Source: Ng et al. (2015). Permission to reprint granted by the authors. This book is written in Chinese)

6.4 Interventions of Disordered Gambling Among Chinese Immigrants in Western Countries

Last but not the least, gambling is a popular pastime among Chinese immigrants in Western countries. Among the many Chinese games, mahjong is one of the most popular gambling activities. Drawing samples from the Chinese communities in Australia, Zheng et al. (2010) reported that 3.8% of their Chinese Australian samples were problem gamblers, much higher than 0.8% problem gambling rate in the NSW general population (Nielsen 2006). During holidays and festivals, Chinese immigrants enjoy visiting other each in their new homes. During these gatherings, mahjong, together with good traditional Chinese dining, is often the favorite pastime. In the United States, Kim (2012) argued that higher gambling availability has helped increase gambling activities among Asian immigrants who come from gambling-permissive cultures. Unlike Western gamblers, Chinese disordered gamblers seldom seek help actively unless they have "hit the bottom." Possible reasons for the low treatment rate include stigma and shame, preference of solving the problems by themselves, language barriers, and the deficiency in the knowledge of disordered gambling as a kind of mental disorder (Chan et al. 2016). For the Chinese gamblers, face-to-face counseling may not be the best option as they often feel embarrassed to disclose their gambling problems to treatment providers. And, they are most reluctant to seek professional help from strangers (Blaszczynski et al. 1998; Fong and Tsuang 2007; Kim and Keefe 2010; Papineau 2005).

Thus, short-term interventions such as online CBT and telephone-delivered counseling may be viable alternative treatment. Parhami et al. (2012) carried out a pilot study of telephone-delivered intervention for eight Chinese American disordered gamblers. The treatment consisted of six 1-h telephone-delivered sessions structured on principles of MI and CBT. Results of this study indicated that most of the participants decreased their gambling behaviors. They also reported an improvement in overall life satisfaction. However, the study findings in this study might not be generalizable to other settings due to its small sample size and low enrollment rate (only 8 people enrolled in the study out of 140 people made inquiries about the treatment program). Further investigation is warranted to examine the effectiveness of this treatment program.

6.5 Conclusion

This chapter attempts to present a treatment model for the Chinese disordered gambler. We have outlined a number of principles in the designing of the program. Our proposed program is based on the individual cognitive-behavioral therapy with an adjunct support of the weekly participation in a GA. Hence, we basically agree with Professor Blaszczynski and Professor Nower that in the treatment of disordered gamblers, all roads, though sometimes with a few detours in the Chinese communities, lead not to Rome but to cognitive-behavioral therapy.

References

Barker, J. C., & Miller, M. (1966). Aversion therapy for compulsive gambling. *Lancet, 1*, 491–492.

Bergler, E. (1957). *Psychology of gambling*. New York: Hill and Wang.

Blaszczynski, A., & Nower, L. (2014). Cognitive-behavioral therapy: Translating research into clinical practice. In D. Richard, A. Blaszczynski, & L. Nower (Eds.), *The Wiley-Blackwell handbook of disordered gambling* (pp. 204–224). New York: Wiley.

Blaszczynski, A., Huynh, S., Dumlao, V. J., & Farrell, E. (1998). Problem gambling within a Chinese speaking community. *Journal of Gambling Studies, 14*, 359–380. https://doi.org/10.1023/A:1023073026236.

Chan, C. C. (2014, November). *The Psychology of gambling and gambling treatment*. A keynote address at the 2nd Macau Medical Association Forum-MMAF, Macao SAR, China.

Chan, C. C., & Ohtsuka, K. (2011). Pathways to development of problem gambling among Chinese gamblers in Hong Kong: Validation of the Blaszczynski and Nower (2002) model. *The Asian Journal of Gambling Issues and Public Health, 2*, 17–28.

Chan, C. C., Li, W. L., & Leung, C. I. (2016). *Problem gambling in Hong Kong and Macao: Etiology, prevalence and treatment*. Singapore: Springer.

Chen, P., Jindani, F., Perry, J., & Turner, N. L. (2014). Mindfulness and problem gambling treatment. *Journal of Gambling Issues and Public Health, 4*(2), 1–17.

Chervenkova, V. (2014). Rites of incubation in the modern world: The symbolic experience of death-rebirth-reconnection in Naikan Therapy. *World Cultural Psychiatry Research Review, 9*(3), 123–131.

Clarkson, T. (2015, May). *Psychodynamic psychotherapy as a short term treatment for problem gambling*. Paper presented at the 4th Asian Problem Gambling and Addiction Conference, 2015, Hong Kong.

Ferentzy, P., Skinner, W., & Antze, P. (2006). Recovery in gamblers anonymous. *Journal of Gambling Issues*, (*17*), 6–12.

Ferentzy, P., Skinner, W., & Antze, P. (2009). Gamblers Anonymous and the twelve steps: How in an informal society has altered a recovery process according to the special needs of problem gamblers. *Journal of Gambling Issues, 23*, 42–65.

Ferentzy, P., Skinner, W., & Antze, P. (2010). Changing spousal roles and their effects on Gamblers Anonymous: GamAnon, social support, wives and husbands. *Journal of gambling studies, 26*, 487–501.

Ferentzy, P., Skinner, W., & Antze, P. (2014). Understanding Gamblers Anonymous—A practitioner's guide. In D. S. C. Richard, A. Blaszczynski, & L. Nower (Eds.), *The Wiley-Blackwell handbook of disordered gambling* (pp. 251–262). New York: Wiley.

Fong, T. W., & Tsuang, J. (2007). Asian-Americans, addictions, and barriers to treatment. *Psychiatry, 4*, 54–58.

Grant, J. E., Donahue, C. B., Odlaug, B. L., Kim, S. W., Miller, M. J., & Petry, N. M. (2009). Imaginal desensitization plus motivational interviewing for pathological gambling: Randomized controlled trial. *The British Journal of Psychiatry, 195*(3), 266–267.

Gurney, A. B. (1968). Gurney treatment of a compulsive horse-gambler by aversion therapy. *British Journal of Psychiatry, 114*, 329–333.

Huang, G. H. (2011). Responsible gambling policies and practices in Macao: A critical review. *Asian Journal of Gambling Issues and Public Health, 2*(1), 49–60.

Iwamasa, G. Y., Hsia, C., & Hinton, D. (2006). Cognitive behavioral therapy with Asian Americans and Asian populations. In P. A. Hays & G. Iwamasa (Eds.), *Culturally responsive cognitive-behavioral therapy: Assessment, practice, and supervision* (pp. 117–140). Washington, DC: American Psychological Association.

Kim, W. (2012). Acculturation and gambling in Asian Americans: when culture meets availability. *International Gambling Studies, 12*(1), 69–88. https://doi.org/10.1080/14459795.2011.616908.

Kim, W., & Keefe, R. H. (2010). Barriers to health-care setting among Asian Americans. *Social Work in Public Health, 25*, 286–295. https://doi.org/10.1080/19371910903240704.

Korn, D. A., & Shaffer, H. J. (2004). *Massachusetts department of public health's practice guidelines for treating gambling-related problems: An evidence-based treatment guide for clinicians*. Boston, MA: Massachusetts Council on Compulsive Gambling.

Kraft, T. (1970). A short note on forty patients treated by systematic desensitization. *Behavior Research and Therapy, 8*, 219–220.

Lam, D. (2014). *Chopsticks and gambling*. New Brunswick: Transaction Publishers.

Li, W. L., Chan, W. C., & Chan, C. C. (2016a, September). *Adding Cognitive-Behavioral Therapy (CBT) to Gamblers Anonymous (GA) in relapse prevention for Chinese problem gamblers: A Pilot Study Using Within-subject design.* Poster presented at 2nd Singapore international public health conference, and 11th Singapore Public Health & Occupational Medicine conference, Singapore.

Li, W. L., Chan, C. C., & Chan, W. C. (2016b, December). *Combining Group Cognitive-Behavioral Therapy (CBT) with Gamblers Anonymous (GA): A pilot study on Hong Kong Chinese problem gamblers*. Paper presented at the Asia Mental Health conference 2016, Hong Kong, China.

Lin, Y. N. (2002). The application of cognitive-behavioral therapy to counseling Chinese. *American Journal of Psychotherapy, 56*(1), 46–58.

Loo, J. M. Y., Raylu, N., & Oei, T. P. S. (2008). Gambling among the Chinese: A comprehensive review. *Clinical Psychology Review, 28*(7), 1152–1166.

Milton, S., Crino, R., Hunt, C., & Prosser, E. (2002). The effect of compliance improving interventions on the cognitive-behavioral treatment of pathological gambling. *Journal of Gambling Studies, 18*(2), 207–229.

Ng, S. C., Wu, H. F., Wong, M. F., Yeung, W., Shek, Y. L., & Chan, C. C. (2015). *Handbook for gamblers anonymous' mutual help groups – 12 steps to gambling recovery*. Mother Mary Social Studies Centre, Caritas, Macao. ISBN 978-99965-745-4-2.

Nielsen, A. C. (2006). *Prevalence of gambling and problem gambling in NSW – A community survey 2006*. NSW Office of Liquor, Gaming and Racing, Department of the Arts, Sport and Recreation.

Oei, T. P. S., & Raylu, N. (2007). *Gambling and problem gambling among the Chinese*. Brisbane: Behaviour Research and Therapy Centre.

Oei, T. P. S., Raylu, N., & Casey, L. M. (2010). Effectiveness of group and individual formats of a combined motivational interviewing and cognitive behavioral treatment program for problem gambling: A randomized controlled trial. *Behavioral and Cognitive Psychotherapy, 38*, 233–238. https://doi.org/10.1017/S1352465809990701.

Pallanti, S., DeCaria, C. M., Grant, J. E., Urpe, M., & Hollander, E. (2005). Reliability and validity of the pathological gambling adaptation of the Yale-Brown Obsessive-Compulsive Scale (PG-YBOCS). *Journal of Gambling Studies, 21*(4), 431–443.

Papineau, E. (2005). Pathological gambling in Montreal's Chinese community: An anthropological perspective. *Journal of Gambling Studies, 21*, 157–178. https://doi.org/10.1007/s10899-005-3030-y.

Parhami, I., Davtian, M., Hanna, K., Calix, I., & Fong, T. W. (2012). The implementation of a telephone-delivered intervention for Asian American disordered gamblers: A pilot study. *Asian American Journal of Psychology, 3*(3), 145–159. https://doi.org/10.1037/a0029799.

Park, N., Peterson, C., & Seligman, M. E. P. (2004). Strengths of character and well-being. *Journal of Social and Clinical Psychology, 23*(5), 603–619.

Petry, N. M. (2005). *Pathological gambling: Etiology, comorbidity, and treatment*. Washington, DC: American Psychological Association.

Prochaska, J. O., & DiClemente, C. C. (1992). Stages of change in modification of problem behaviours. *Progress in Behaviour Modification, 28*, 183–218.

Rosenthal, R. J., & Rugle, L. J. (1994). A psychodynamic approach to the treatment of pathological gambling: Part I: Achieving abstinence. *Journal of Gambling Studies, 10*, 21–42.

Seager, C. P., Pokorny, M. R., & Black, D. (1966). Aversion therapy for compulsive gamblers. *The Lancet, 1*, 546.

Sharpe, L., & Tarrier, N. (1992). A cognitive-behavioral treatment approach for problem gambling. *Journal of Cognitive Psychotherapy, 6*, 193–203.

Sue, D. (1997). Counseling strategies for Chinese Americans. In C. C. Lee (Ed.), *Multicultural issues in counseling: New approaches to diversity* (2nd ed., pp. 173–187). Alexandria, VA: American Counseling Association.

Wong, D. F. K., Chung, C. L. P., Wu, J., Tang, J. Y. C., & Lau, P. T. C. (2015). A preliminary study of an integrated and culturally attuned cognitive behavioral group treatment for Chinese problem gamblers in Hong Kong. *Journal of Gambling Studies, 31*(3), 1015–1027. https://doi.org/10.1007/s10899-014-9457-2.

Wulfert, E., Blanchard, B. E., Freidenberg, B. M., & Martell, R. (2006). Retaining pathological gamblers in cognitive behavior therapy through motivational enhancement: A pilot study. *Behavior Modification, 30*(3), 315–340.

Yeung, W., Wu, H. F., Wong, M. F., Ho, W. N., & Chan, C. C. (2014, July). *Introduction to gamblers anonymous: A Twelve-step workbook (modified version)*. Paper presented at the International Conference on Gaming, Leisure and Entertainment, 2014, Macao. (楊穎、胡海峰、黃妙芬、何泳楠及陳智川 (2014年7月). 十二步匿名戒賭互助小組工作手冊*(特別版)*之簡介. 博彩•休閒•娛樂國際學術研討會,澳門,中國)

Zheng, W. Y., Walker, M., & Blaszczynski, A. (2010). Mahjong gambling in the Chinese-Australian community in Sydney: A prevalence study. *Journal of Gambling Studies, 26*, 441–454. https://doi.org/10.1007/s10899-009-9159-3.

Zhuang, X. Y., Wong, D. F. K., Ng, T. K., Jackson, A. C., Dowling, N. A., & Lo, H. H. M. (2018). Evaluating the effectiveness of an integrated cognitive behavioural intervention (CBI) model for male problem gamblers in Hong Kong: A matched-pair comparison design. *Journal of Gambling Studies*. https://doi.org/10.1007/s10899-018-9747-1.

Chapter 7
The Future of Chinese Gambling: A Cultural Conclusion

In anticipating the future of gambling in Hong Kong and Macao, two self-administrative regions (SARs) in the People's Republic of China, Chan et al. (2016) wrote: "-----We have witnessed gambling in Macao changing and evolving from a city of sin in the past to today's city of dreams. We do look forward to seeing the transformation of Macao from a city of gambling to a metropolitan city of global tourism and leisure destination-------- An Asian icon of gaming and prosperity. And as long as commercial gambling is carried out responsibly and morally, it will, definitely, offer hopes and dreams of a better livelihood for the 640,000 residents in this small enclave in the southern part of China." While the authors are optimistic that regulated commercial gambling can bring prosperity and hope for the people of Macao, their studies only focus on gambling in Hong Kong and Macao. What is the future of gambling in Mainland China, then? As we have outlined the historical development of gambling in China in Chap. 1, we understand that contemporary illegal gambling is a serious problem in this country with a population of 1.4 billion. How would the Chinese government tackle this legal and moral problem? How the concepts of responsible gambling are received in China? With the rapid expansion and proliferation of casino gambling across Asia, will the PRC government, a political regime built upon solid socialist principles of Marxism-Leninism, legalize commercial gambling? In other words, will casino resorts be built in China? This last chapter in our studies intends to give answers to these questions. To begin with, we will start with a discussion on the problem of illegal gambling in China.

7.1 Illegal Gambling in China

We will begin with taking a look at the illegal gambling problem in Hong Kong, a Special Administrative Region (SAR) in China. According to the Hong Kong Jockey Club (2016), illegal gambling in Hong Kong amounted to HKD 12 billion per year. Recently, Wong and Tessler (2017) carried out a street intercept survey ($N = 600$),

C. C. Chan et al., *The Psychology of Chinese Gambling*,
https://doi.org/10.1007/978-981-13-3486-3_7

during which the participants were asked about their gambling histories. Among the participants, 103 of interviewees admitted having gambled illegally in the previous year. Fifty-six percent of the illegal gamblers (IG) scored 3 or above in the Problem Gambling Severity Index (Ferris and Wynne 2001). Most of the IG were males, aged 30–49, and blue collars and bet three times or more per week. Soccer betting and horse racing were their most favorite games provided by the illegal bookmakers. Sixty-nine percent of IG participated in illegal gambling because of its attractive odds, while 46% and 42% of them attributed their reasons to ease of placing bets and convenience to bet anytime.

The prevalence of IG in Hong Kong was estimated to range from 0.2% to 0.4% with soccer betting being the most popular gambling activity (Wong and Chu 2017). Detailed analysis of the interviewees' responses indicated that 42.3% of the IG had irrational beliefs of easy win in illegal gambling. The most vulnerable group was middle-aged males. When compared with the research participants who gamble legally, incidences of disordered gambling, crime, financial crisis, relationship difficulties, and psychiatric problems are comparatively higher among illegal gamblers (Chan 2014).

Illegal gambling is a serious problem in Mainland China. In 2015, Hong Kong police uncovered a cross-border gambling ring, based in Guangdong province, which took in bets from customers in Hong Kong (MacLeod 2015). Through Internet connections, the company had their main server in Taiwan. The organization designed a well-structured operation that looked into the needs and motives of the gamblers. For instance, they provided technical support to assist the customers in Hong Kong, Macao, and Thailand to gamble online. The gambling ring had over 500 illegal gambling websites and 1 million registered gamblers.

Another type of illegal gambling is "Underground Mark Six." Mark Six is a popular lottery game sanctioned by the Hong Kong Jockey Club. In this lottery, players select 6 numbers out of a total of 49 numbers. The game runs three times a week, and the actual live drawing is often televised by local television stations. Illegal game operators designed a number of ingenious operations in their game. Firstly, they take in bets from players in Mainland China who select 6 numbers from a list of 49 numbers. However, instead of placing the bets through the Hong Kong Jockey Club, they become the banker of the game. The players will receive the same payout if they win the game. The game is attractive to the people in China as they can watch the actual drawing from Hong Kong televised programs.

Police reports in Mainland China can provide a glimpse of the seriousness of illegal gambling in China. For instance, police in Jiangsu province (江蘇省) busted a syndicate of illegal online soccer betting during the World Cup 2006. Fifty-six people were arrested. The total amount of bets was RMB 345 million (Wang 2007). The second author of this book once discussed with a friend from Shanwei (汕尾), a small beautiful city along the sea coast in eastern Guangdong province, on this issue. He estimated that the actual turnovers of underground gambling (illegal Mark Six and offshore online soccer betting) could be as much as RMB 100 million per month. The betting amount is shocking as Shanwei is a small fishing village where most of the young adults have left and are currently working in other big cities in

China. Illegal online soccer operators often set up Internet sites for their businesses. There are about 330 Chinese gambling websites. Most of these servers are set up in Taiwan, Hong Kong, Southeast Asia, and even the United States.

Online gambling started in Mainland China in 1995. The games are under the supervision of various government agencies. Online soccer betting is very popular in major cities like Guangzhou, Chengdu, Shanghai, Tianjin, and Dalian where famous soccer teams in the Chinese Premier League are located. In these games, the players can wager on the results of first half/second half of the games, the total number of goals, and even the number of yellow cards, red cards, and penalty kicks of the matches.

Zhao and Zhang (2009) outlined a number of reasons behind the successes of illegal online gambling. Firstly, the gaming operators have designed a complex and ingenious logistic system to facilitate the gamblers. A diagram of offshore online soccer betting is depicted in Fig. 7.1. Before the gambler can place a bet, the gaming operator first arranges an intermediary or third party to assess the gambler's financial and family background. After that, the potential gambler has to deposit RMB 50,000 to 100,000 to open an account before he/she can be qualified as a formal gambler. In a more succinct way, the system recruits the players into a club of gambling. It is difficult for the central government to scrutinize these accounts as the majority of accounts are handled by complex computers in overseas companies.

In October 2016, a number of Hong Kong soccer players, ex-players, and an assisted coach were arrested and charged of bribery to fix several soccer matches in Hong Kong Premier League. The bribe was believed to come from criminal gangs in Mainland China. In fact, it is not uncommon that illegal gambling enterprises in Mainland China try to control results of soccer matches in Chinese societies through their online gambling networks.

Bribery is usually involved across all layers of the Chinese Football Association Super League (CSL), from managing officials to soccer players (see Fig. 7.2). Illegal gambling enterprises manipulate outcomes of soccer matches and simultaneously heavily bet the "expected results" on other online gambling sites to earn a lot of money (Wang and Antonopoulos 2016).

Moreover, the political system of China might contribute, to a certain extent, to the severity of the problem. In essence, China's political and economic system is largely run by only a handful of people in power. In Chinese terminology, it is a

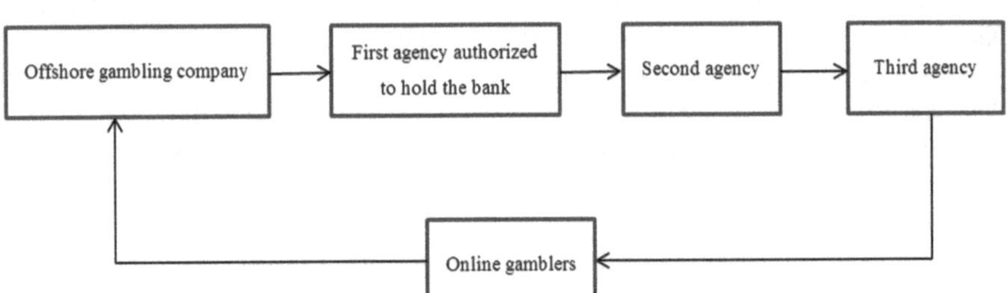

Fig. 7.1 Flow of offshore online soccer betting in Mainland China

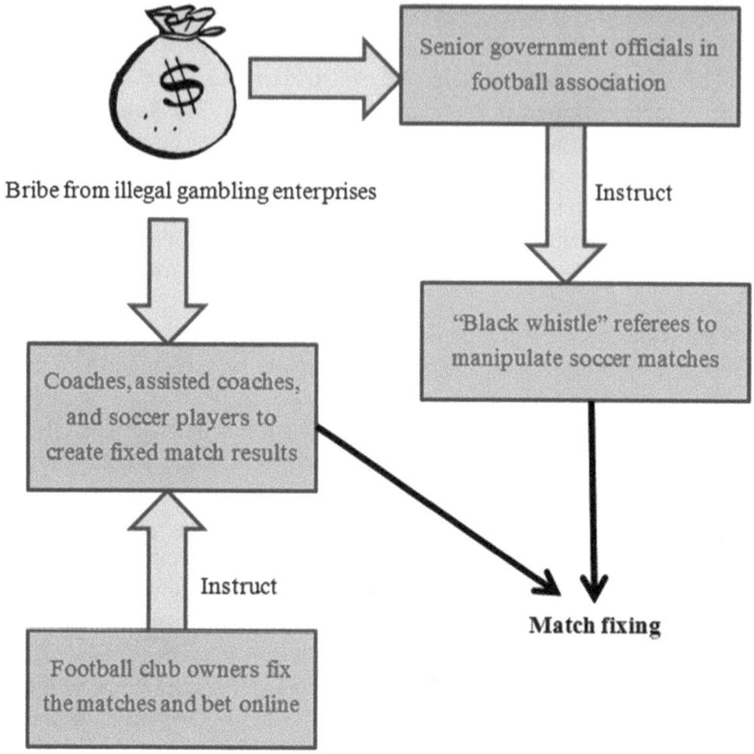

Fig. 7.2 Flow of corruption to create match fixing inside soccer field in Mainland China

system of "rule of man" (人治). Rule of man is the opposite of rule of law (法治), different from the foundation of Western democracy. In a system of rule of man, major decisions in business and politics are often social contracts, or in Chinese, made based on "*guanxi* (關係)." Under such a prevailing yet unspoken framework, a good relationship network is the golden rule to success and survival for any business (Xin and Pearce 1996). In illegal gambling, relationship network is the root of the business. Through communal relationships, potential customers persuade gamblers to bet and resolve gambling debts (Wang 2014).

Recently, there are police reports on crimes of illegal gambling. For example, Xie Caiping (謝才萍) ran a major gambling business in Chongqing (重慶) for many years before she was arrested and sentenced to jail for 18 years in 2009. It was found that Wen Qiang (文強), her husband's elder brother who served as the deputy police chief in Chongqing at that time, provided Xie protection to her gambling business (Xinhua 2009). Moreover, Xie had ties with local gangs which provided additional protection and helped collect gambling debts. Xie and her employees were disordered gamblers who managed over 20 gambling stalls. They bribed local police to establish a political-criminal network. Wen was found guilty of protecting gangs and managing illegal gambling organizations, as well as corruption charges. He was sentenced to death on July 7, 2010, in Chongqing (Tian and Zheng 2009).

A great number of gamblers, especially government officials and high-rolling gamblers, prefer gambling in Macao. Very often, these gamblers obtain their gambling money from illegal sources such as corruption. These high rollers, often recruited by junket operators in Macao, gamble in VIP rooms in Macao casinos (Pontell et al. 2014). Figure 7.3 demonstrates the flow of high-rolling Mainland Chinese gambling in VIP rooms of Macao casinos.

In summary, China-Macao gambling network is mostly run by junket operators who have extensive relationship networks. These operators usually maintain a close connection with government officials and police forces (Wang and Antonopoulos 2016). Despite the efforts the PRC government spent on policing illegal gambling enterprises in the past decade, illegal gambling is still widespread, especially among major cities of China.

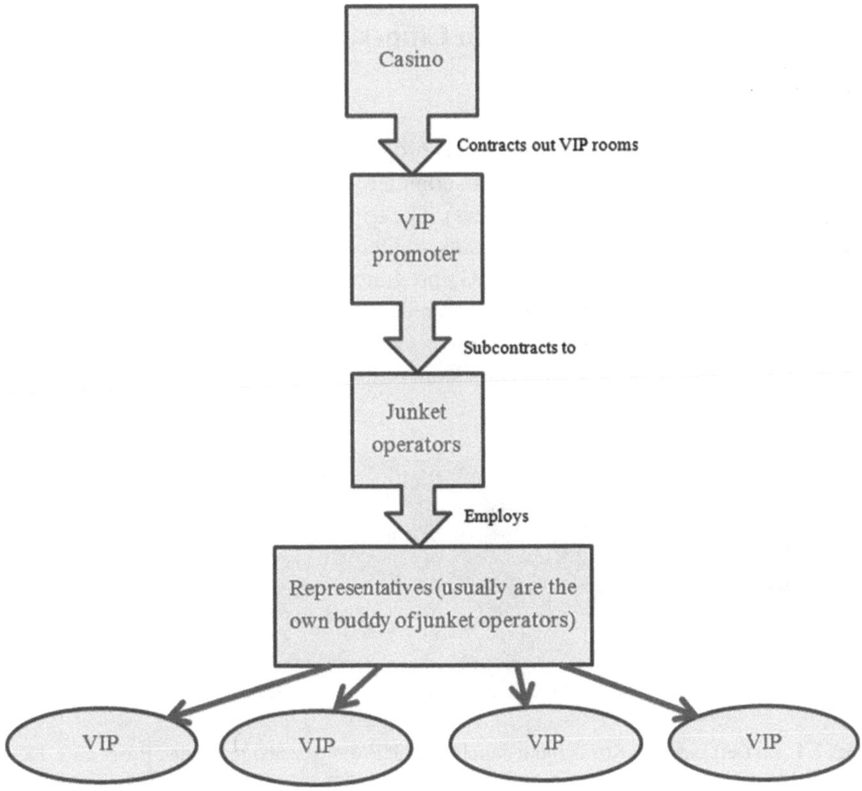

Fig. 7.3 Flow of high-rolling Chinese customers gambling in Macao casinos

7.2 Chinese People Gambling in Territories Outside of Mainland China

In recent years, a number of casino resorts were built in Myanmar, Vietnam, and Laos. Many of these casinos intend to attract players from Mainland China. Two examples of mega casino resorts built in the regions with close proximity to the border of Mainland China are Kings Romans Casino located at "Golden Triangle" (金三角, a region shared by border tripoint of Thailand, Laos, and Myanmar) inside the territory of Laos (Figs. 7.4a, b) and 12 casinos in Mongla (勐拉, also known as Little Mongla), capital of the fourth special administrative zone in Shan State (撣邦) in north-eastern Myanmar (a region very close to Yunnan (雲南), southwestern part of Mainland China). In the casinos at Laos, RMB is a popular currency there. Chinese tourists love to go there also because there is no language barrier as Mandarin is the second official language in this area (Sims 2017). As Chinese-funded enterprises continue to invest in this territory, international media commonly regard this region as an enclave of Chinese gamblers (Fawthrop 2010).

7.3 Responsible Gambling in Chinese Communities: Can It Work?

A successful responsible gambling (RG) program should include a close cooperation among three main stakeholders in commercial gaming: the government, gaming operators, and customers (gamblers). The tripartite model of RG (Blaszczynski et al. 2011) explains the roles of key stakeholders in Fig. 7.5.

A good responsible gambling (RG) program includes measures on consumer protection, harm minimization, and harm reduction. The most commonly employed RG strategies are informed choices for players, self-exclusion, third-party exclusion, casino visit limits, self-exclusion from online betting, removal of ATMs inside

Fig. 7.4 (**a**) (left picture): Royal Jinlun hotel (景蘭酒店) and casino in Golden Boten City, Laos (casino has been shut down since 2011 due to violence and murder related to gambling and debt); (**b**) (right picture): Kings Romans Casino on the bank of Mekong River (湄公河), "Golden Triangle," Laos. (Source: Sims (2017). Permission to reprint granted by the authors)

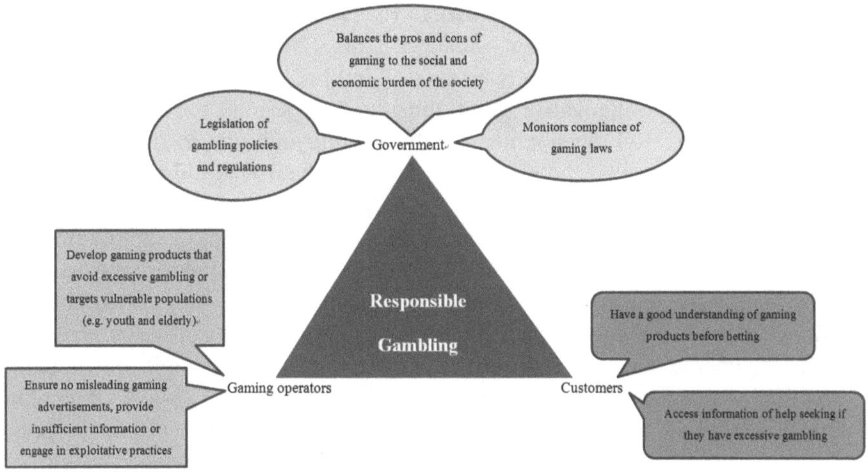

Fig. 7.5 Tripartite model of responsible gambling: The roles of key stakeholders. (Source: Blaszczynski et al. (2011))

Table 7.1 Data on Casino Exclusion Applications

Items	[a]2012	2013	2014	2015	2016	2017
Self-exclusion	27	252	262	328	326	316
Third-party exclusion	3	24	18	27	25	60
Total	30	276	280	355	351	376

Source: The Gaming Inspection and Coordination Bureau (2018)
[a]Data were available since November 1, 2012

casinos, wagering with affordable limits, and ways to access help line and help services (The Gaming Inspection and Coordination Bureau 2018; National Council on Problem Gambling 2018).

Table 7.1 (The Gaming Inspection and Coordination Bureau 2018) displays data on casino exclusion applications in Macao from November 2012 to 2017. The statistics showed a steady increase in the number of self-exclusion from 2013 to 2015. But after 2015, the number of self-exclusion cases remained stable in the next 2 years. In contrast, the number of third-party exclusion stayed more or less the same during 2013 to 2016. However, there was a sharp rise in 2017. Summing up the two set of data, it is fair to conclude that the total number of casino exclusion applications demonstrated a gradual increase in the previous 5 years. Nevertheless, the figures did not show a distinction between local residents and foreigners. Furthermore, unlike the casinos in most Western countries, Macao gaming laws do not have any provisions for automatic exclusions for disordered gamblers.

Providing information on responsible gambling is an important means to help disordered gamblers. At the time of writing, 32 out of 41 Macao casinos have set up "responsible gambling information kiosks" for players to submit self-exclusion applications (The Gaming Inspection and Coordination Bureau 2018).

Notwithstanding these measures, the overall RG program in Macao is still far from satisfaction from an international standard. Hing (2010) proposed a five-stage model of corporate citizenship in responsible gambling. The stages are elementary stage, engaged stage, innovative stage, integrated stage, and transforming stage. Through observing RG development in the gaming industry in Australia, Hing argued that it commenced the elementary stage in the 1990s, during which very few casinos implemented RG programs in helping gamblers. The engaged stage came in the 1990s, where strategies and measures of RG such as gaming information for the patrons and counseling services programs were installed in most casino resorts. With more legislation and research in gaming in the early 2000s, the RG programs in most casinos reached the transforming stage, when the government and gaming operators agreed on a shift of policies from harm minimization to harm prevention. These RG strategies include extension of shutdown periods of gaming rooms, lowering the amount of cash (up to AUD$20) inserted into electronic gaming machines (EGMs) at any one time, as well as limiting cash withdrawals from ATMs to AUD $250.

Reflecting on the Australian experiences, the RG development in gaming in Macao can be classified as reaching stage 2 (engaged stage), as a number of casinos have voluntarily participated in RG programs. Measures such as putting up signage publicizing the harm of problem gambling and self-exclusion provisions for problem gamblers were installed in most casinos. However, compared to the gaming experiences in Australia and the United States, there is much room for improvement in RG legislation and practices in Macao. Since a number of new integrated resorts have started their operations in Macao, the number of gaming tables has increased drastically (Table 7.2). We hope the Macao government can review the existing gaming legislation to include more efficacious RG measures scrutinizing gaming operators.

In comparison to Macao, Singapore has more comprehensive RG legislations and programs. The National Council on Problem Gambling (NCPG) of Singapore is responsible for providing education and managing problem gambling. Figure 7.6 is a summarized report on RG released on December 31, 2017 (NCPG 2017). The statistics indicated that there were 23,857 of local Singaporeans (including citizens and permanent residents) and 288,917 of foreigners applied for active casino self-exclusions. Ninety-one percent and 86% of those who signed self-exclusion and family exclusion orders, respectively, were Chinese. Ninety-two of those who reported active voluntary casino visit limits were also Chinese. Males aged between 31 and 50 were the highest risk group of problem gambling, followed by those aged between 51 and 64. As an ethnic group, Chinese Singaporean is the most vulnerable ethnicity in gambling disorder.

Table 7.2 Number of gaming tables in Macao in 2010–2017

Year	2010	2011	2012	2013	2014	2015	2016	2017
Number of gaming tables	4791	5.302	5485	5750	5711	5957	6.287	6.419

Source: The Gaming Inspection and Coordination Bureau, 2018

Fig. 7.6 Statistics on active casino exclusions and visit limits in Singapore in 2017. (Source: National Council on Problem Gambling (December 31, 2017). Permission to reprint granted by the authors)

In Singapore, the effectiveness of RG program on reducing gambling disorder has been reported by Subramaniam et al. (2017). The study is a qualitative study (*N* = 25, all aged over 60). Employing Stirling's (2001) six-step thematic network analysis, the participants' text segments were summarized into 27 codes, which were then reduced to 10 basic themes under 2 organizing themes – self-developed strategies to limit gambling-related harm and family interventions to reduce gambling harm. Figure 7.7 illustrates the thematic network derived from the study.

In the study, the participants employed cognitive and behavioral strategies to control their gambling. Such strategies included the perception or understanding of the futility of gambling, setting limits, delayed gratification, maintaining balance, help-seeking, and awareness of disordered gambling in others or in self. The theme "maintaining balance" is unique to Chinese gamblers. In Chinese culture, this is the concept of harmonic balance between *Yin-Yang* (陰陽調和) – the balance between two opposing elements. Applying the *Yin-Yang* concept in gambling, the gamblers participated in gambling activities in a controlled manner.

The idea of controlled gambling or gambling in a responsible manner is consistent with the morals of traditional Chinese culture. Two principles in Chinese philosophy illustrate this notion properly:

(a) "Things will always develop in the opposite direction when they become extreme (物極必反)."

Fig. 7.7 Thematic network representing RG. (Source: Subramaniam et al. (2017). Permission to reprint granted by the authors)

(b) "When the water is crystal clear, there is no fish in it (水至清則無魚)."

These two ideas propose that perfection in anything, including total abstinence in gambling, might not be the optimum state for everyone or the community as a whole. Thus, if a person can control his/her gambling behaviors and as long as the gambling habit does not create any harmful effects on his/her daily life, family and occupation, the community should accept the person's gambling behavior.

Lastly, the model proposes that family intervention is important in gamblers' recovery and rehabilitation. Family can help in seeking exclusion orders for the patients and urging the gamblers to seek proper treatment. Chinese culture, which stresses familial and clan relationships, may have a positive impact on reducing problem gambling in Chinese societies. Being labeled as disordered gamblers is a source of shame and social stigma in these communities (Sobrun-Maharaj et al. 2012). Hence, to protect the reputation of themselves and their families, Chinese gamblers are more likely to control their gambling and seek treatment. Moreover, family members often give their support, mostly financial and emotional, to the gamblers in order to maintain harmony in the families (Fig. 7.8).

Research on RG among Mainland Chinese gamblers is in an infancy stage. At the time of writing, there are little governmental standards and measures of RG in Mainland China. Professor Chen Haiping of Lottery Research Center of China, a Chinese expert in commercial gaming, believed that research on problematic lottery buying lags behind Western countries' (Yan 2017). Responsible lottery gambling (責任彩票) is a viable solution to prevent disordered gambling. Hence, we trust that the Chinese government should take a more active role in promoting RG and subsidizing some non-government institutions in developing programs for the treatment and rehabilitation of gamblers.

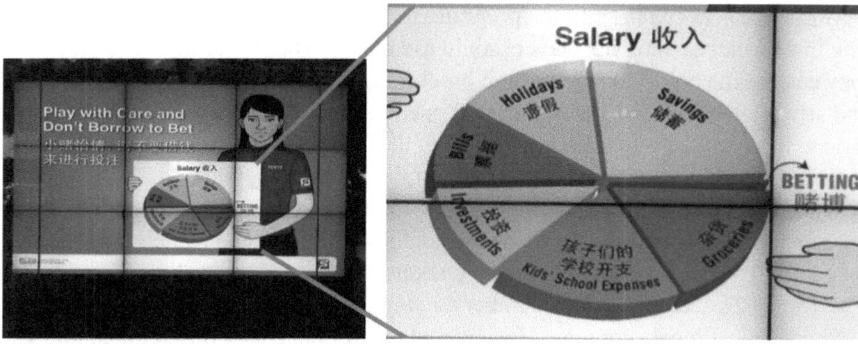

Fig. 7.8 Electronic advertisement of RG at the entrance of Singapore Pools Livewire outlet at Resorts World *Sentosa*, Singapore. (Photo taken by Li Wai Lim on April 3, 2016)

7.4 Casino Resorts in Mainland China: A Possibility?

During Boao Forum for Asia (博鰲亞洲論壇) 2018, President Xi announced the news that a lot of people had longed for – turning Hainan province into a free trade port by supporting tourism in this "China's Hawaii." Foreign news report has speculated that the development of horse racing and sports lotteries are encouraged in Xi's new plan (Bloomberg LP, April 2018).

In light of this view, would the PRC government open legal casinos in Hainan province? If this is done, to what extent would it threaten gaming industry in Mainland China and neighboring countries like Singapore, Cambodia, Laos, and Myanmar? Would the number of disordered gamblers increase drastically in the Southern part of China? Also, would Chinese high-rolling gamblers still consider Macao and other countries as the best gambling venues to "burn" their excessive money? These are the Chinese policymakers need to address before they give their permission and blessing on the development of casinos within Chinese borders.

As we trace the development of gambling in the history of China, one prominent feature is that the Chinese government and authorities have seldom legitimized commercial gambling. The major reason is that gambling is regarded as a social disgrace in Chinese culture. Thus, very few Chinese policymakers would dare to implement a policy that maintains and even promotes a social sin.

However, in the last 30 years, the general attitude toward commercial gambling has drastically changed as more casino resorts have been built in Macao, Malaysia, Singapore, and other parts of Asia. Casino resorts can bring in travelers, entrepreneurs, and investments for local community. Hence, should casinos be built in China? This is the question we attempt to answer in this section.

Sanya (三亞), a southern city in Hainan province (海南省), is a vacation paradise for both local Chinese and foreigners. Its beautiful scenery and tropical climate attract numerous tourists every year. In the early 2010s, Sanya was considered as a potential venue for the development of casino gaming in China (Reuters 2013). A pilot program was initiated in Mangrove Tree Resort World Sanya Bay (三亞灣紅

樹林度假世界木棉酒店). In the program, the hotel offered its guests cashless betting in the hotel casino. The players could use points to bet in the casino. If they win, they can use the points to pay for their hotel charges or to buy luxury goods, jewelry, and artwork in the resort. Later, the hotel operator intended to expand their customer base to local residents in the second stage of the trial program. However, the government outlawed this cashless betting and terminated the program.

The failure of this program might be due to a lack of comprehensive planning on the impact of commercial gaming on the community. Omar and Dallen (2014) interviewed 711 of local residents of Sanya about their opinions on the new proposal. The responses were mixed. A number of respondents supported building a resort casino to boost local economy. However, other respondents worried about the risk of crimes, an increase of disordered gamblers in the community and environmental pollution. At the time of writing, the Chinese government has not yet made a conclusive decision on the establishment of a casino.

Ontologically, commercial gambling rests upon capitalist principles, contrary to the fundamentals of the socialist-communist regime. Such capitalist investment might not be welcomed by many Chinese, especially in a business that might raise problem gambling in the community, increase risks of more crimes and cause changes in environmental structures. However, a number of recent developments in neighboring countries might have changed the mindset of Chinese policymakers. These include:

(a) An increase of casinos in neighboring countries:
Affluent middle-class Chinese players often visit casinos in Macao, Laos, and, more recently, Singapore. Japan has recently passed a gaming law to approve the building of casino in Tokyo. Thus, from an economic perspective, in order to keep the players and their spending within national boundary, it is a wise decision for the Chinese government to allow gaming operators build casinos in China.

(b) The changing attitude toward gambling among Chinese people:
In recent years, there has been a consensus among Chinese people that commercial gaming is a form of socially appropriate leisure activity. Since 2004, with the introduction of Western-styled resort casinos in Macao, there has been a steady increase of visitors from Mainland to Macao (from about 9.5 million in 2004 to about 21.2 million in 2014) (Government of Macao Special Administrative Region Statistics and Census Services 2015). For the majority of these visitors, integrated resort casinos might not be only about gambling – it is a leisure hub that combines gaming with world-class entertainment, luxury shops, and exquisite dining. Thus, for the majority of Chinese visitors, visiting a resort casino is no longer a social vice.

(c) The success of the Singaporean model:
Two resort casinos were built in Singapore in the late 2000s. The casinos have attracted millions of visitors every year, and many of them are from Mainland China. The Singaporean casinos have a good system of responsible gambling and strategies to protect their own citizens from becoming disordered gamblers.

For instance, while foreigners are admitted free in the casinos, local residents have to pay SG100 for admission. Furthermore, the government has sponsored treatment and counseling programs for disordered gamblers. The model of capitalist investment and ventures with suitable governmental supervision and control might be a good inspiration for Chinese gaming policymakers.

7.5 Conclusion

As we anticipate the future of Chinese gambling from a cultural perspective in this chapter, we believe that China is currently opening the door for commercial gaming. In the near future, casino operators might be allowed to build integrated resorts in special administrative regions, where more flexible foreign investment policies are present. A good model of resort casino should also adhere to the highest standards of international gambling policies. The initial stage should be the development of appropriate legislation for the business. Chinese policymakers would need to consider issues like illegal gambling, responsible gaming strategies, the provision of treatment and counseling for disordered gamblers, and, most importantly, the potential increase of crimes in the new resort casinos. As long as commercial gambling is carried out responsibly and morally, we strongly and sincerely believe that it will offer hopes and dreams of a better livelihood, not only for the residents in the jurisdictions where the resort casinos are located but for the people of neighboring provinces in China, a land of diverse cultures and peoples.

References

Blaszczynski, A., Collins, P., Fong, D., Ladouceur, R., Nower, L., Shaffer, H. J., et al. (2011). Responsible gambling: General principles and minimal requirements. *Journal of Gambling Studies, 27*, 565–573. https://doi.org/10.1007/s10899-010-9214-0.

Bloomberg LP. (2018, April 16). "China's Hawaii" gets boost from Xi. So do these business. *Bloomberg Wire Service*. Retrieved from https://search.proquest.com/docview/2025129729?accountid=16210

Chan, C. C. (2014, November). *The psychology of gambling and gambling treatment*. A keynote address at the 2nd Macau Medical Association Forum-MMAF, Macao SAR, China.

Chan, C. C., Li, W. L., & Leung, C. I. (2016). *Problem gambling in Hong Kong and Macao: Etiology, prevalence and treatment*. Singapore: Springer.

Fawthrop, T. (2010, December 24). Laos's Chinese gamble. *The Diplomat*. Retrieved from https://thediplomat.com/2010/12/laoss-chinese-gamble/

Ferris, J., & Wynne, H. (2001). *The Canadian problem gambling index: User's manual*. Toronto: Canadian Centre on Substance Abuse.

Government of Macao Special Administrative Region Statistics and Census Service (2015). Retrieved 20th July, 2018 from http://www.dsec.gov.mo/Home.aspx?lang=en-US

Hing, N. (2010). The evolution of responsible gambling policy and practice: Insights for Asia from Australia. *Asian Journal of Gambling Issues and Public Health, 1*, 19–33.

MacLeod, C. (2015, November 19). $50bn of bets are off as China raids illegal gaming dens. *The Times*, T1. Document T000000020151119ebbj000nb

National Council on Problem Gambling. (2018). Retrieved from https://www.ncpg.org.sg/en/Pages/home.aspx

National Council on Problem Gambling. (2017, December 31). *Update of statistics*. Retrieved February from www.ncpg.org.sg

Omar, M., & Dallen, T. (2014). Eyes on casino gaming in China: Residents' attitudes towards precasino development in Sanya. *UNLV Gaming Research & Review Journal, 18*(1), 85–113.

Pontell, H. N., Fang, Q., & Geis, G. (2014). Economic crime and casinos: China's wager on Macau. *Asian Journal of Criminology, 9*, 1–13.

Reuters. (2013). *Global investors watch how chips fall in China's cashless bar. Reuters*. Retrieved from http://www.reuters.com/article/2013/02/16/china-sanya-casino-idUSL4N0B90QW20130216

Sims, K. (2017). Gambling on the future: Casino enclaves, development, and poverty alleviation in Laos. *Pacific Affairs, 90*(4), 675–699. https://doi.org/10.5509/2017904675.

Sobrun-Maharaj, A., Rossen, F., & Wong, S. K. (2012). *The impact of gambling and problem gambling on Asian families and communities in New Zealand*. Centre for Asian & Ethnic Minority Health Research, UoA. Available online at http://www.health.govt.nz/system/files/documents/pages/impact-gambling-asian-commnities.pdf. Accessed 8 Feb 2018.

Stirling, J. A. (2001). Thematic networks: An analytic tool for qualitative research. *Qualitative Research, 1*, 385–405.

Subramaniam, M., Satghare, P., Vaingankar, J. A., Picco, L., Browning, C. J., Chong, S. A., & Thomas, S. A. (2017). Responsible gambling among older adults: A qualitative exploration. *BMC Psychiatry, 17*, 124. https://doi.org/10.1186/s12888-017-1282-6.

The Gaming Inspection and Coordination Bureau. (2018). Retrieved from http://www.dicj.gov.mo/web/cn/frontpage/index.html

The Hong Kong Jockey Club. (2016). *Combat Illegal Gambling*. Retrieved from http://www.hkjc.com/responsible-gambling/en/anti-illegal/index.aspx

Tian, W. S., & Zheng, L. (2009, October 16). Chongqing dahei tingshen xu (Further details about the Chongqing gang trials). *China Youth Daily*. Retrieved from http://focus.news.163.com/09/1016/10/5LO5IAKD00011SM9.html

Wang, X. D. (2007). The first case of soccer betting in China. *China Sports, 1*, 27–31 (汪曉東. (2007). 中國賭球第一案. 中國體育, *1*, 27–31.)

Wang, P. (2014). Extra-legal protection in China: How guanxi distorts China's legal system and facilitates the rise of unlawful protectors. *British Journal of Criminology, 54*, 809–830.

Wang, P., & Antonopoulos, G. A. (2016). Organized crime and illegal gambling: How do illegal gambling enterprises respond to the challenges posed by their illegality in China? *Australian and New Zealand Journal of Criminology, 49*(2), 258–280. https://doi.org/10.1177/0004865815573874.

Wong, I. L. K., & Chu, C. H. (2017, November). *Illegal Gambling among Hong Kong Chinese Adults*. Poster presented at the National Association for Gambling Studies Inc. 27th Annual Conference 2017, Melbourne, Australia.

Wong, I. L. K., & Tessler, A. (2017, May). An Exploratory Study on Social Impact of Illegal Gambling in Hong Kong. Poster presented at The First Asia-Pacific Conference for Addiction Professionals – Application of the Syndrome Model, Hong Kong.

Xin, K. R., & Pearce, J. L. (1996). Guanxi: Connections as substitutes for formal institutional support. *Academy of Management Journal, 39*, 1641–1658.

Xinhua. (2009, November 5). Chongqing "heidu jiaomu" Xie Caiping fumie ji (The crackdown of Chongqing Godmother Xie Caiping). *Xinhua Net*. Retrieved from http://news.xinhuanet.com/focus/2009-11/05/content_12389432.htm

Yan, P. F. (2017). Advocating responsible lotteries. *Xinmin Weekly*, 28–29. Retrieved from http://xmzk.xinmin.cn (閻鵬飛 (2017). 倡行責任彩票. 新民周刊, 28–29).

Zhao, J. L., & Zhang, S. X. (2009). On net ball gambling in China. *Journal of Physical Education Institute of Shanxi Normal University, 24*(1), 39–41 (趙金嶺, 張淑香. (2009). 我國網絡賭球問題初探. 山西師大體育學院學報, *24*, 1, 39–41).

Epilogue

I Have a Dream

Since my father passed away in January, 2018, I moved back to my parents' place to take care of my ageing mother. Every day is a challenge. The most important task of my day is to make sure she takes the appropriate medicine at the right dosage and at the right time. On top of this, I have to perform my duties and responsibilities as a college lecturer. That means preparing for my daily lectures, grading students' assignments, and working on my research projects and, worse of all, handling the many students' complaints. During the last few months, I know that I have been stressed out. I have little time for myself. I remember I was writing this book on a Saturday afternoon. After several hours of writing and editing, I fell asleep on the sofa in the living room. Possibly in a trance state, I had this dream:

> I was standing in a hotel lobby with a lot of reporters. In front of the camera's flashlights, the announcer, an attractive young TV star, handed me a cheque of 10 million dollars----- I have just won the grand prize of the state lottery, known as the Golden Mark Six, in Hong Kong! I had never won anything significant in my life. I was so happy. I saw people, whom I never knew, hugging and congratulating me on my fortunes. Abruptly, the dream moved to the next scene. That should be on a cruise liner in the Bahamas. There were a lot of young people, mostly attractive women on tight bikinis, dancing along the poolside. The music was loud and I hardly recognized what kind of music they were playing. But one thing that captured my attention ------- the sumptuous moment of joy and happiness that I had long been searching for. Plus, there was an endless flow of good food, beers and, of course, no grading on students' assignments. The sky looked brighter. I also looked a bit taller and younger. Apparently, I didn't have to prepare for my lessons and work hard for a monthly pay cheque anymore. At that moment, I felt like the happiest man alive. But suddenly, the phone rang. I tried to reach out for my mobile phone in my pocket. I thought I should have put my Mark Six winning ticket together with the phone. Shit. I should have dropped everything into the pool. Recklessly, I jumped into the cold pool to search for the winning ticket, only to find that I never learnt how to swim. I thought I was drowning and possibly dying for the gambling money.

C. C. Chan et al., *The Psychology of Chinese Gambling*,
https://doi.org/10.1007/978-981-13-3486-3

But, in a panic, I woke up. The phone still rang. Some salesman named Joe called in to promote a mobile phone plan. After a polite goodbye, I pulled myself together and reflected on the dream. Though I have much reservation on the theoretical foundations of the addictive personality syndrome proposed by Alan Lang (1983), I am more attracted to Kiang Fan's (2010) assertion – gambling in China began as Chinese civilization began. For the majority of ethnic Chinese, being rich is our chief concern in life, and this goal is buried deep in our collective unconscious. And, for a humble worker like myself, gambling is a fast and inexpensive means to achieve personal riches and happiness.

I have to be grateful for finishing this research project. I understand more about Chinese gambling and my own heritage. In the meantime, as I am making some final touches on the manuscripts, I look forward to, rather eagerly and earnestly, the continuation of the audacity of my hopes in the Bahamas dream – tonight.

Kolibri 360 GmbH
Ferdinand-Jühlke-Straße 7
99095 Erfurt, Deutschland
produktsicherheit@kolibri360.de